A People's History of Tennis

'Great news – playing tennis is not inconsistent with radical politics. This is just one of the fascinating facts in this amazing history of our sport.'
– Lord Richard Layard, Emeritus Professor of Economics at the London School of Economics and co-author of *Thrive: The Power of Psychological Therapy*

'This antidote to cream teas and privilege celebrates tennis and its enthusiasts through the sport's hitherto silenced stories. A great read.'
– Kath Woodward, Professor of Sociology, Open University and author of *Social Sciences: The Big Issues*

'We might think of lawn tennis as a sport of the privileged, but this fascinating, beautifully written book reveals that in its 150-year history it has been played with passion by women, lesbians and gays, ethnic minorities and socialists alike.'
– Lucy Bland, Professor of Social and Cultural History, Anglia Ruskin University and author of *Britain's 'Brown Babies': The Stories of Children Born to Black GIs and British Women in the Second World War*

'David Berry's delightfully gossipy book delves into the personal histories of tennis players famous and unknown. He lovingly charts the progress of the game since its beginnings in the Victorian period and explains why so many people, players and spectators, love it.'
– Elizabeth Wilson, author of *Love Game: A History of Tennis, From Victorian Pastime to Global Phenomenon*

'A suffragette plot to burn down Wimbledon, Jewish quotas at your local tennis club, All England Married Couples Championships – you think you know tennis and then along comes this compelling little gem by David Berry, positing a progressive social history of the sport that surprises and delights. Hugely enjoyable and highly informative.'
– David Cohen, Investigations Editor at the London *Evening Standard*

A People's History of Tennis

David Berry

PLUTO  PRESS

First published 2020 by Pluto Press
345 Archway Road, London N6 5AA

www.plutobooks.com

British Library Cataloguing in Publication Data
A catalogue record for this book is available from the British Library

ISBN   978 0 7453 3965 8   Hardback
ISBN   978 1 7868 0632 1   PDF eBook
ISBN   978 1 7868 0634 5   Kindle eBook
ISBN   978 1 7868 0633 8   EPUB eBook

This book is printed on paper suitable for recycling and made from fully
managed and sustained forest sources. Logging, pulping and manufacturing
processes are expected to conform to the environmental standards of the
country of origin.

Typeset by Stanford DTP Services, Northampton, England

Simultaneously printed in the United Kingdom and United States of America

Contents

Introduction

It was Joe Parsons, the night watchman, who spotted them. On the night of 26 February 1913, three women travelled to Wimbledon by train and gathered outside the All England Club's Centre Court in Worple Road at 10.00 pm. They carried five tins of paraffin, five candles wrapped in cotton wool, wood chips, fire-lighters, an electric torch and a sheet of paper with the words 'no peace until women have votes'. Their intention was to destroy the court and set fire to the new stand, but when they were challenged by Parsons they ran away. 'One of them with Joe in hot pursuit fell over in the dark', club secretary, George Hillyard, recalled, 'and Joe, a hefty young fellow just retired from the artillery, fell on top of her and took her in triumph to the pavilion where she was secured pending the arrival of the police. I gave him a sovereign for his smart work.'[1]

The woman, thought to be between 30 and 35 years old, declined to give any explanation. The press called her the 'silent suffragette'. A week later at Wimbledon's police court, she was found guilty of an attempted felony and sentenced to two months imprisonment. That seemed to be the end of the matter, except there were one or two details that remained puzzling.

Parsons had been appointed just the previous day. There had been no need for a night watchman before. It all seemed a little fortuitous. Was Hillyard tipped off about an attack? Did he have information he chose not to share with the police? And why did the woman not say anything in court? Suffragettes generally used their moments before the magistrates to speak out for their cause. She remained silent. Was she protecting someone, someone with inside knowledge?

George Hillyard, the son of a police officer, swerved round these irritating niggles. The All England Club Committee was so relieved Wimbledon escaped damage they considered the matter closed. When Hillyard retired a decade later, however, he still felt he had some explaining to do. In *Forty Years of First-Class Tennis*, published in 1924, he pointed out that he 'never did the suffragettes any harm. For all they knew I might have been a male suffragette.'[2] It was true his wife Blanche, six times Wimbledon Women's champion, was sympathetic to their cause, but Hillyard thought it extremely unlikely she would do anything to hurt the sport she loved, although with Blanche you could never be absolutely sure.

The attack on Wimbledon that February night in 1913 was one of the first actions of the suffragettes' new firebombing campaign to try and force parliament to grant women the vote. Sport was singled out as a target and cricket pavilions, boathouses, golf clubs and football stands across the country were set alight. On June 8, Emily Davison died in hospital four days after she had tried to throw a robe in suffragette colours over the king's horse as it galloped past her in the Derby. Horse racing, golf, football and cricket were seen by the suffragettes' organisation, the Women's Social and Political Union, as legitimate targets because they were public activities run by and for men. Lawn tennis was more complicated.

The sport was certainly *controlled* by men. There would be no women on the ruling committees of the All England Club or the Lawn Tennis Association until the 1950s. But since tennis had been introduced as a garden party pastime into the country houses of late Victorian Britain, it had been played as avidly by women as men. If the suffragettes continued to include tennis among their sporting targets, they risked alienating many of their supporters. Margaret Marshall, the wife of William Marshall, the runner-up at the first Wimbledon Championships in 1877, was an ardent suffragette and served as secretary of the Suffrage Society in Haslemere in 1909.[3] Frederick Pethick-Lawrence, one of the keenest of the early tennis players, spent nine months in prison in 1912 for his active support of the suffragette cause. His wife, Emmeline, had been treasurer of the Women's Social and Political Union a few years before. Perhaps after the Wimbledon raid, someone like Emmeline, Frederick or Margaret had pointed out the connections between tennis and suffrage. Perhaps it was Blanche Hillyard herself. There is no record of the suffragette leadership ever discussing tennis but Wimbledon was never troubled again.[4]

The thwarted raid in 1913 is one indication that the common perception of lawn tennis as a sport of the establishment is too simplistic. The dominant view of the game today, in Britain and abroad, is that tennis has always had a blue tint, a respectable conservatism that is most on display during the Wimbledon Championships every summer, when the pavilions and lawns exude the leafy charms of the prosperous shires and wealthy English suburbs. While it is true that lawn tennis is a game with roots in the suburb rather than the inner city, not everything that has emerged from suburbia has been antagonistic to progressive politics and not all the people who have come from there have been opposed to social change.

Blanche Hillyard, a tall, severe-looking woman who rarely gave much away, grew up in suburban Ealing in the 1870s, the daughter of a wealthy industrialist. She had a privileged existence all her life but this did not stop her campaigning for women's tennis when it was under attack from men. She stood up not just for her game but for women's sport. Blanche was no radical, but it is not too wide of the mark to describe her as one of Britain's first sporting feminists.

This book is about Blanche and other tennis champions like Lottie Dod, Leif Rovsing, Alice Marble, Arthur Ashe, Billie Jean King and Venus Williams who have seen lawn tennis not just as an enjoyable sport but as a site of struggle for freedom, fairness and equality. It is also about people who never won any cups or trophies. Some are public figures like Frederick Pethick-Lawrence, who would go on to serve in two Labour governments but always found time for tennis. Most of the people featured here, though, are not well known but enjoyed tennis as an absorbing recreation or followed the game as fans. Some of them loved playing the game so much they would turn up on court every week of the year whether the sun was shining, the wind howling or temperatures below zero. I know this kind of love. I suffer from it myself.

I first played the game in the 1960s when I was 12, a working-class boy from a council estate in Bracknell, Berkshire, whose parents never imagined tennis was meant for people like them. The mother of one of the boys on my street was a Labour Party councillor and she campaigned to build tennis courts in each of the neighbourhoods of our new town. In my neighbourhood, Priestwood, all the boys played football and the girls hockey and so, in the summer of 1966, my friends and I discovered three new tennis courts deserted and at our disposal. We played through the holidays and, unlike the other sports we shared together where I was mediocre, it turned out that I was good at tennis or at least better than they were. That was 50 years ago. Today I play three times a week, hips, back and knees permitting, in a tennis club in north London with members who have a diversity of political views but most closer to the Left than the Right.

Until I started delving into the history of tennis a dozen years ago for a television documentary that never made it to air, I thought my club was an exception. It turns out that lawn tennis has always attracted individuals who were mavericks in their thinking and oppositional in their behaviour. This book makes the case that tennis is a more progressive sport than its public perception suggests, and that the discriminations that have undoubtedly been present over the last 150 years have also produced a politics of resistance which has led to change not only in tennis but in society as well. Underneath its establishment image, tennis is a surprisingly radical game.

It would be wrong, though, to deny there have been times and places when the reality of playing tennis has left much to be desired, where certain kinds of people have been excluded, where the politics of the sport has been reactionary. While emphasising the progressive side of tennis, I have tried not to ignore the times when tennis has been anything but. Like other popular histories, I have been reliant on the work of academic historians and sociologists who have trod this ground before me, often reaching different conclusions. In the Notes I have tried to acknowledge the specific times when I am dependent on their insights or research, but for the sake of readability I have kept these to a minimum. The Bibliography lists all the books I am indebted to.

Lawn tennis was first played in London in 1874 and quickly became a popular sport all over the British Isles. Within a few years, it had spread to continental Europe, the USA and much of the old British Empire. By the first decades of the twentieth century, it was being played in most parts of the world. These days it is only surpassed by football and hockey as the sport with the most global reach among players and fans. It is not possible in a short book to tell a people's history of tennis that covers even the main half a dozen countries where tennis has developed its strongest roots, let alone places like China and Japan where the sport is likely to grow in the twenty-first century. Most of the stories I include in this book are from Britain but I have tried at specific points to widen the lens and acknowledge where tennis has developed differently elsewhere, particularly if it has taken on a more radical hue. Fortunately, there is one annual event, the Wimbledon Championships in south-west London every July, that brings the different forces shaping tennis across the world into focus. When I write about the elite game, I concentrate on Wimbledon and mostly ignore the three other Grand Slam tournaments in Melbourne, New York and Paris. I have also paid little attention to tennis at the Olympic Games or in the Davis and Federation Cups. There are one or two tennis champions who never shone at Wimbledon but were outstanding in these competitions but only one or two.

When writing about tennis champions, I have focussed on the stars because a true people's history cannot fail to see tennis as an entertainment as well as a game, a spectacle as much as a sport. Stars are the link between players and spectators. The Left in Britain and elsewhere has often been inclined to dismiss the watching of sport as an undesirable indulgence of meek passivity and tribal behaviour.[5] But tennis needed its spectators. It only became a world sport because it attracted millions of people who found the top players 'beautiful, inspiring and embodying achievement in a totally unambiguous way'.[6] Tennis fans have their stories to tell and I have tried to capture some of these as well.

I use the word 'stories' because this is not an academic book but a work of narrative non-fiction written by a journalist. I have kept context to a minimum and I do not attempt to apply the ideas of Marx or Foucault to tennis or spend time considering the history of the sport through the theoretical lens of Pierre Bourdieu or Norbert Elias, or at least not consciously. I have tried instead to see tennis playing not just as a social and historical fact but also as a 'form of theatre which enacts moral reflection', and an 'aesthetic activity which has beauty and value in itself'.[7] And I agree with Richard Holt that the first requirement of the historian is to try and construct an argument which acquires a 'cumulative plausibility'.[8]

Most readers will be familiar with the basic form of tennis, its rules and scoring systems, and I haven't dwelt on these. There are plenty of other histories of the game that do. I also haven't spent much time describing the actual experience on court: what it feels like to hit a beautiful shot or win a tough match. Tennis is difficult to learn but even more difficult to write about and I felt there was little I could add to the lyrical accounts of play by such masters as David Foster Wallace, John McPhee and most recently Rowan Ricardo Phillips. None of them, though, write about Blanche Hillyard or her husband George.

The Hillyards played tennis on their honeymoon in the late 1880s and never stopped playing for the rest of their lives. They represented Britain at the 1908 Olympics and toured Europe, often travelling to tournaments in the red Mercedes-Benz of their friend Toupie Lowther with Toupie, the first openly lesbian woman in sport, at the wheel. In the first two decades of the twentieth century, Blanche and George also welcomed players from abroad to their house in Leicestershire, including May Sutton and Norman Brookes, the first Wimbledon champions from outside the British Isles. Together, the Hillyards won the All England Married Couples Championships three times from 1910 to 1912, and carried on playing in the competition occasionally until it was cancelled in 1923 because of acrimony between husbands and wives. George and Blanche were not beyond arguing themselves. George asked Blanche to write the chapter on women's tennis for his book but Blanche, detecting tokenism, refused. Like her contemporary, Virginia Woolf, she was always able to challenge her impetuous husband because she had money of her own.

I admire the Hillyards and was pleased to discover that the attempted firebombing of Wimbledon in February 1913 was one suffragette action that was not successful. Even though Blanche's playing standard inevitably went down as she aged she continued to enter tournaments knowing she would lose to people she would have demolished in her prime. Not many champions risk such humiliation, but Blanche loved playing tennis and simply didn't care.

George was a man who took 'deep pleasure in friendship' and whose friends were convinced he would have been as formidable a Wimbledon champion as his wife if 'he were to play more and think less'.[9] I know exactly what they mean. A few years before the suffragette attack on Wimbledon, the sports writer Percy Vaile justified his own contribution to the avalanche of books on lawn tennis by pointing out that it was not always the best players that produce the best books. I know exactly what he means too.

The chronology of this book may be a little confusing, at least initially. The book starts with the first public exhibition of lawn tennis in London in May 1874 and ends with the Wimbledon Championships of July 2019, but it doesn't follow a straight line through this 150 years of lawn tennis history. It darts backwards and forwards to connect themes that emerge.

The first two chapters look at the early lawn tennis players and I have split their stories up along gender lines. The men's stories are told in Chapter 1 ('Mavericks') and the women's in Chapter 2 ('Feminists'). The next two chapters take the story up to 1920 by focussing on the two aspects of tennis which ensured its survival both as a popular game (Chapter 3, 'Members') and as an enjoyable mass entertainment (Chapter 4, 'Stars'). Chapters

5–9 look at the golden age of tennis from 1920 to the late 1960s through the eyes of grass-roots players (Chapter 5, 'Players' and Chapter 6, 'Socialists'); people who made a living out of tennis (Chapter 7, 'Entrepreneurs'); elite players who became television stars (Chapter 8, 'Performers') and tennis club stalwarts (Chapter 9, 'Enthusiasts'). The next two chapters range across the whole time period of the book by looking at two groups who have often been excluded from the tennis court: black people (Chapter 10, 'Immigrants') and Jews (Chapter 11, 'Outsiders'). Chapter 12 ('Trailblazers'), the longest chapter in the book, surveys the pivotal role that LGBTQ (lesbian, gay, bisexual, transgender, queer) people have played in tennis. The final two substantive chapters take the story from the start of open tennis in 1968 to the present day through the experiences of the top players and their spectators (Chapter 13, 'Professionals'), and tennis playing in clubs and public parks (Chapter 14, 'Amateurs'). The concluding chapter pulls together the central argument of the book that tennis is a truly radical sport.

As I have said, all this darting back and forth may seem a little confusing, but the book is designed to be read as an enjoyable narrative from the Introduction to the Conclusion and hopefully any puzzlement will disappear as the links between chapters become apparent. I have also included a Timeline at the end of the book which I hope will help.

David Berry,
London, January 2020.

1

Mavericks

The first game of lawn tennis, at least in public, was played on Wednesday 6 May 1874, not in Wimbledon but in Knightsbridge in the land between Lennox Gardens Mews, Hans Place and Cadogan Square. Today it is one of the most expensive slabs of real estate in the world, but then it was a cricket ground surrounded by tall trees and owned by the Prince's Club, one of Victorian London's most popular sporting clubs. To mark the start of the cricket season a demonstration of the new game of 'lawn tennis' was arranged. It was organised by its inventor, Walter Wingfield, a country gentleman originally from North Wales who had recently retired from the army with the rank of major.

There had been much interest in Major Wingfield's game since he had begun promoting it two months earlier. On the Monday before its Prince's Club debut, the *Morning Post* urged readers to go along and catch this 'clever adaptation of tennis to the exigencies of an ordinary lawn' which would 'undoubtedly become a national pastime'.[1] The paper's enthusiasm may well have been influenced by the adverts Wingfield placed in their columns, but it was shared by other publications of the time as their editors looked for something that might replace croquet and rinking, two popular pastimes of the previous decade which had unaccountably fallen out of fashion.

On the morning of the demonstration, Wingfield ensured that a court 60 feet long and 30 feet wide was marked out in the shape of an hourglass on one corner of the cricket ground. A net was erected five feet high in the middle of the court and everything was ready for a game of doubles.[2] Wingfield was joined on court by his close friend Clement Scott, theatre critic of the *Daily Telegraph*, Captain Alfred Thompson and a cricket player called Lubbock. What they wore is not recorded but it is likely to have been the clothes of the Victorian sportsman: plus-fours, long-sleeved T-shirt and cricketing cap. In front of an audience of *Morning Post* subscribers, amused bystanders and sceptical cricketers, the match began.

Wingfield's 'lawn tennis' turned out to be a deceptively simple game. All the players were required to do was to hit a soft rubber ball with a wooden racket backwards and forwards over the net making sure the ball stayed in court. As anyone who has ever played tennis can testify, however, this is by no means as easy as it sounds. One can imagine the frustration of the four players that morning as they slowly realised this new pastime was a little more difficult than they had thought. Many of their balls would have hit the net or sailed out to the jeers of the watching cricketers who were convinced the game would never catch on.

The cricketers were wrong. Within a year, lawn tennis had spread all over Britain and within a couple of years across the world as it evolved into the sport we know today as simply 'tennis'. It is an extraordinary story and it is worth getting to know more about its inventor, Walter Wingfield. But first it is useful to note that lawn tennis is a relatively recent addition to the racket sports family. There are other games that are much older.

Tennis historians have traced similar ball games back to medieval tournaments and one or two have speculated (with no evidence) that tennis in some form or another could have been played in ancient Rome or Egypt. But lawn tennis's most recognisable antecedent is the game we now call *real* or *royal* or *court* tennis which originated in French monasteries in the thirteenth century. This was played indoors on a stone floor and quickly became a favoured pastime of the European aristocracy. At the peak of its popularity in the sixteenth century, Paris alone had 250 courts, including one at the Louvre and another at Versailles, the latter of which was occupied in the revolution of 1879 by the Third Estate as a symbolic protest at the elitist nature of this sport. The most famous real tennis court in Britain was built in 1519 in Hampton Court Palace for Henry VIII, a keen player, at least in his younger days. It is still in use today by some of the few thousand enthusi-asts in Britain, France and the United States who keep this version of tennis alive.

In early nineteenth-century Britain, a variant of real tennis migrated outdoors and became known as *field* or *long* or *open* tennis depending on which part of the country it was being played. One version in the 1830s had six people on each side and a court 160 yards long, six times longer than today's tennis court. These games never amounted to anything more than passing fads despite initial concerns that they threatened 'to bowl out cricket' (at that time the most popular sport in the world).[3] So in 1874 nobody expected Wingfield's new invention to be anything more than a craze which would last a season or two. There were, after all, several other racket games also vying for attention around this time such as *five-ten*, which combined real tennis with fives, and *Hildegarde*, which combined real tennis with rounders and cricket. These games flared brightly for a while and then quickly faded. Lawn tennis survived to become one of the three most watched sports in the world today and one of the six most played. The interesting question is why.

One simple answer is that it was a more satisfying game than any of its rivals. It would have done well wherever and whenever it was introduced. All it was waiting for were a couple of technical innovations. In 1827 in the village of Thrupp, Gloucestershire, Edwin Budding developed the world's first lawn mower. In 1844, in the city of Philadelphia, Charles Goodyear discovered the process of vulcanisation which allowed a ball to be made out of waterproof rubber and filled with air, although rubber balls did not become commercially available for another couple of decades. When a cut lawn and a soft rubber ball were eventually put together, lawn tennis became inevitable and, because it was such a satisfying game to play, inevitably popular. But popularity can wane as fashions change and popular satisfaction is no guarantee something will survive.

We need a little context, so it is useful to remember that tennis was not the only major sport to emerge during this time.

The modern forms of football, golf, hockey and cricket were all developed too. Games became popular in late nineteenth-century Britain because the country had been the first to industrialise and so develop a working day that was organised and regulated with time off for leisure, at least for some. New jobs towards the end of the century like clerical and shop work were less tiring, and better transport enabled people to travel more easily to a game. Most importantly, there was money around, again at least for some. By 1870, the *average* standard of living in England was the highest in the world. Even though Britain remained, in Disraeli's phrase, a 'country of two nations', the distance between rich and poor was narrowing as the wages of skilled workers began to rise. For those who did have money, there were ample opportunities for leisure.

Old recreations were plundered and new ones discovered as Britain experienced a 'great sports craze'.[4] The country's wealth, empire and dominant position in trade ensured that any game popular in Britain would spread quickly to Europe, North America and the colonies. Team sports like cricket and football became public events which appealed to everyone as participants or spectators, but individual games like tennis and golf found a niche too because they provided a private space for an insurgent middle class of bankers, merchants, clerics, factory owners and professionals to socialise with an aristocracy intent on holding on to at least some of their political power. Lawn tennis, according to the sociologist Robert Lake, enabled 'middle-class aspiration' to meet 'upper-class status insecurity' within a framework of 'appropriate gentlemanly conduct and budding female emancipation'.[5] In other words, it came at exactly the right time. All it needed was a Major Wingfield.

Walter Wingfield was born into a comfortable family in rural North Wales in 1833, although this congenial upbringing was soon shattered by the death of his mother when he was two years old and then his father, a British army major, when he was 13. Family connections allowed Walter to sign up with the Dragoon Guards at 17 and he eventually rose to the rank of captain. Wingfield served in India and was present in 1860 at the capture of Peking, returning home with a Pekinese dog called Joss. A year later, he retired from the army to become a country gentleman on land inherited from his father. The fields and mountains of North Wales proved no match for the attractions of the Orient, and Wingfield soon quit the countryside to rejoin the army before retiring again a few years later, this time with the title of major. He remained a ceremonial Royal Body Guard for most of his life.

In the late spring of 1873, we find him living in a Georgian terraced house in Belgrave Road in Pimlico, not yet 40 years old, with a wife, Alice, four children and a household of servants to support. Pimlico at the time was 'genteel, sacred to professional men ... a cut above Chelsea which is only commercial'.[6] It was the place to be for someone who needed to make money while not appearing to be trade. Wingfield had excellent contacts and decided to reinvent himself as an entrepreneur.

In the next three decades he would devise a range of upmarket products and services with varying degrees of ingenuity. There would be a butterfly bicycle, a smoking mixture and a French cookery school, all a little ahead of their time. Wingfield's relatively brief venture into lawn tennis was his most successful enterprise by far, although how he stumbled across the game is by no means clear. He does not appear to have witnessed any of the other half-dozen attempts around this time to find a new outdoor pastime with bat and ball. He seems to have discovered tennis entirely on his own.

Sometime in late 1873, Wingfield assembled a portable set to play a game he called 'lawn tennis'. In a chocolate-coloured box, he arranged a net, four wooden bats made by the sports equipment manufacturer Jefferies & Mallings, a bag of India rubber balls imported from Germany and assorted poles, pegs and netting to mark out a court which could be done, according to Wingfield, 'in five minutes'. Then almost as an afterthought he threw in a book about how to play this new game which contained six simple rules. Wingfield's nets, rackets, balls and poles have all long gone and his hourglass court would soon be replaced by the rectangle we know today. But you can still read his rules and marvel at how close it is to how tennis has been played ever since.[7]

In his book, Major Wingfield claimed that lawn tennis had been tested at several country houses across Britain and been found to be so 'full of interest and so great a success that it has been decided to bring it before the Public'.[8] There is little independent evidence, however, that any such testing took place apart, perhaps, from one visit to his cousin on the Earnshill estate in Somerset in the summer of 1873 where he seems to have come up with the idea. Later that year, Wingfield did attend a spectacular pre-Christmas gathering in Nantclywd, Denbighshire given by his friend, Major Thomas Naylor-Leyland, for 200 guests, but these few days away in North Wales were dominated by amateur dramatics not by trying out lawn tennis, even if this had been possible in deep midwinter. Naylor-Leyland's event was useful though because it gave Wingfield a story. Like marketing people ever since, the major recognised the power of narrative. He realised he would be able to charge a premium if he associated his 'lawn tennis' with the leisure activities of the English country house. He dedicated his new tennis sets to 'The Party Assembled at Nantclywd in December 1873'. It worked even better than he imagined.

After advertising in *Army and Navy Gazette* on 7 March 1874 and, over the next few weeks, in *London Court Journal*, *Morning Post* and *Land and Water*, the first 1,000 tennis sets sold at the not inconsiderable price of five guineas, the equivalent today of £350. A third of them were bought by the aristocracy and, in subsequent editions, Wingfield listed the eleven princes and 54 earls who had purchased a set and were satisfied with the result.[9] Perhaps unsurprisingly, he left out any reference to customers who were less pleased, like the correspondent to *The Field* who protested about the 'absurdly high price for this tennis set, all very roughly made'.[10] Wingfield took little notice. He preferred to quote his friends at the *Morning Post* ('a source of amusement to a large and fashionable concourse of ladies and gentlemen') and the *Sporting Gazette* ('I hear from Paris that people are all raving about it') which testified to his tennis sets' appeal here and overseas, at least to the well-heeled.[11]

The sets were indeed a triumph. The only mistake Wingfield made was in the name. In a futile attempt to try and stop others stealing his idea, he started calling his new game *sphairistikè*. Unfortunately few customers knew how to pronounce this word or indeed what it meant (it was garbled Ancient Greek for 'belonging to the ball').[12] The game soon became known by Wingfield's original choice, 'lawn tennis', although it owed as much to rackets as it did to real tennis. But then rackets, a sport originally developed in debtors' prisons in the eighteenth century, did not have the same cachet as real tennis, the sport of kings.

In a few short years in the mid-1870s, Wingfield's game became a desirable summer activity for the leisured upper middle class, not just in Britain but in France, Canada, China, America and Germany where the first tennis was played in the spa town of Bad Homburg as early as 1874. Lawn tennis reached Brazil and India the next year and had a strong appeal in the British colonies of the southern hemisphere where the climate favoured outdoor play. Tennis was being played regularly in Melbourne by 1878 and the first mention of the game in South Africa was in 1875 when Sir Garnet Wolseley, a colonial administrator in Natal, 'tried to play lawn tennis on very bad stony ground with wretched balls'.[13] As the sports writer and historian, Julian Marshall, noted at the time, 'never has a game sprung so rapidly into favour. It is now played in all quarters of the world and with steadily increasing zeal.'[14]

Wingfield's connections with the army undoubtedly helped these early foreign sales, but just as important were the testimonials the sets were receiving in London, the empire's hub. There, the game had been picked up by society magazines and played by celebrities including Oscar Wilde. Queen Victoria's second son, Alfred, Duke of Edinburgh, purchased a set and laid down a court in the grounds of Buckingham Palace. Many of these fashionable folk would soon tire of lawn tennis and seek out new excitements. Wilde moved on to golf. But these initial endorsements by stars and royalty attracted the people who would sustain the game –

aspiring men from the new middle classes who would make lawn tennis their own.

In order for a sport to flourish, it needs not only an elite who compete at the highest level but also a solid base of players who turn out week after week and make it part of their lives. Without them, all you have is spectacle. One reason why tennis was able to prosper in the late nineteenth century was that it quickly discovered its first constituency, gentlemen from the professions. At the end of the century, there were some 20,000 lawyers and 19,000 doctors in England alone, not to mention thousands of architects, accountants, engineers and surveyors. Many had established practices and were able to take time off for recreation and pleasure. They had been forced to endure team sports at public school, and as they settled into partnerships and prosperous lives, they wanted a game that was more individual, a sport that was competitive but less physically demanding than rugby or cricket. Lawn tennis was ideal. It combined moderate exercise with the Victorian equivalent of networking. A correspondent to *The Field* in early 1875, who had played lawn tennis in Suffolk and North Wales the previous summer, thought the new game 'well-suited for middle aged gentlemen'.[15] One middle-aged gentleman who was one of the earliest lawn tennis players was Tom 'Harry' Gem, a lawyer from Birmingham.

Harry Gem was a short, eccentric man with an enthusiastic manner and piercing gaze. He was born in 1819, the son of a solicitor whose practice he inherited when he was 35 years old. Gem would go on to become clerk to the Birmingham Magistrates, but more important for him were his extra-curricular activities of which there were many. In his twenties he set up a cricket club. In his thirties, he founded the Birmingham Union Club where business and professional men could meet to discuss politics and culture. In the summer of 1859, he became secretary of a committee to set up a Birmingham branch of the Volunteer Rifles in which he would subsequently serve, reaching the rank of major. That summer too, 15 years before Wingfield's invention was introduced to the world, Harry Gem played lawn tennis.

That at least is the claim of a blue plaque sponsored by Birmingham Civic Society and unveiled in 1982 by the Lawn Tennis Association on the wall of a detached house in the affluent inner-city suburb of Edgbaston. On the back lawn of this house, the plaque proclaims, the game of lawn tennis was first played in 1865 by Juan Bautista 'Augurio' Perera, a Spanish merchant based in Birmingham who lived in the house at the time, and his friend Major Harry Gem, who lived in Moseley, just down the road.

It is a lovely story, and it is a pity it turns out not to be true. The tale can be traced back to a letter Gem sent to *The Field* in November 1874 in which he claimed that he and Perera first played Wingfield's new game 15 years before.[16] Harry Gem was trustworthy all his life and there is no reason to believe he wasn't telling the truth, at least as he perceived it. But meticulous research in the last few years by tennis historians Robert Everitt and Richard Hillway shows convincingly that Gem was mistaken. Gem and Perera, both keen indoor rackets players, were not experimenting with lawn tennis at all but with a version of outdoor rackets played with a solid and not a rubber ball.[17]

Whichever game it was, it cannot have made a strong impression. After this experiment, Gem and Perera seem to have lost interest and only came back to playing outdoors in the summer of 1874 a few months after Wingfield's tennis sets became widely available. By then they had both moved to Leamington Spa in Warwickshire, and sometime that summer they set up a 'lawn tennis club', the first one dedicated only to the game although the game they actually played seems to have been a mixture of Wingfield's lawn tennis and their own outdoor rackets. The club was situated at the back of the town's Manor House Hotel and its initial members were two young hospital doctors, Frederick Haynes and Arthur Tomkins, as Harry Gem recalled in verse:

Let all our deeds be written on the lasting roll of fame,
How Homer bet the shilling and Tomkins won the game,
How Haynes' youthful vigour placed him high upon the list,
And baffled all who hadn't got the great Perera twist.

When he wrote this, Gem was in his fifties and Perera only a few years younger. The two medics, Haynes and Tomkins, were not yet 30. But as the millions of people who have played tennis since can testify, the cleverness of middle age can often prove quite capable of foiling the athleticism of youth. The 'Perera twist' – the spin Augurio put on the ball – was able to confound Haynes' 'youthful vigour' and give them all something to talk about over a glass or two of claret-cup at the end:

> Farewell the turf, the bounding ball and nets are in the box,
> The rackets on the shelf are laid to wait next season's knocks;
> Then let us now pass round the wine, a brimming bumper fill,
> And drink the great Pelota game, Lawn Tennis if you will.[18]

The passion Harry Gem quickly developed for his new pastime, which he and Perera also called pelota after a Spanish ball game, was not unusual among tennis enthusiasts then or now. Tennis is a sport that inspires deep affection among its devotees if not thankfully a great deal of poetry. No profession in Victorian Britain was more appreciative of this than the clergy. There were 24,000 of them in late nineteenth-century Britain and many not only took up the game but introduced it to their local church. A tennis club in Ilkley, West Yorkshire, was formed in 1880 by the Reverend Ottley. The winner of their first tournament was a solicitor called Fletcher who Ottley described as the 'best type of English Christian gentleman'. In Kirktonhill in the West of Scotland in the late 1890s, the Reverend Stephen reported that his club 'was well supported by the congregation and as tennis is on the boom in the town, the new club has secured a firm footing'.[19] The first bishop of Birmingham, Charles Gore, was known for his Christian socialism and his love of tennis. His older brother, Spencer, was the first Wimbledon champion in 1877. It was hardly surprising that *The Field* proclaimed lawn tennis 'a game for vicars'.

The vicars who took up tennis in the last decades of the nineteenth century gave tennis a softer character than other sports. There was little of the *braggadocio* heard in the scrum or nineteenth hole. Lawn tennis was an activity that seemed unembarrassed about its links with the Christian faith, as one early instructional manual proclaimed: 'Tennis should be played ... with a bright warm sun overhead. There should be a cool shadow of a tree, strawberries and cream, an iced claret mug and a few spectators who do not want to play but are lovers of the game. If these conditions are present, an afternoon spent at lawn tennis is a highly Christian and beneficent pastime.'[20]

The words are those of Robert Osborn, the first philosopher of the game. He was born in 1835 to a British military family in Agra in India. Like his father, he joined the Indian army and reached the rank of lieutenant-colonel. In his spare time, he studied Eastern religions and wrote two sympathetic books about Islam which were among the first books in English to try and understand the religion and its culture. In 1879 Osborn retired from the army and settled in Britain to devote himself to religion, tennis and the links between the two.

In *Lawn Tennis, Its Players and How to Play*, published in 1881, Osborn argued that tennis was a 'moral discipline much superior to a Sunday sermon' which produces a 'benevolence towards the human race' and encourages 'that great Christian virtue, hope'. In tennis, the lieutenant-colonel argues, success is still possible until the very last ball. He advised players 'not to try too much' and to cultivate good temper which is as 'indispensable for the enjoyment of lawn tennis as warm sunny weather and a smooth shaven lawn'.[21] These were all sentiments shared with Walter Wingfield who had urged his customers to 'hit the ball softly' a few years before. If the new players of the game had followed this advice lawn tennis would have died out long ago. Tennis became an international sport because it was taken up by rackets and real tennis players who were used to hitting a hard ball with pace and aggression and saw no reason why a game with a soft ball should be played any differently. All it needed was skill and technique. All it needed was a Herbert Lawford.

Lawford, a stockbroker from London, was one of the first lawn tennis players to start stroking his racket over the ball to produce a shot which became known as 'top spin'. The effect was miraculous. Top spin dipped the ball in mid-flight to ensure it did not go out. It then accelerated the ball so it zoomed past an opponent. With this powerful new weapon, lawn tennis shook off the derisory name of 'pat-ball' given to it by cricketers and become a contest that favoured the brave.

The aggressive play developed by Lawford and his friends was appreciated by spectators at the lawn tennis tournaments that started appearing across the British Isles towards the end of the 1870s. The most popular one was organised by the All England Club. The club had been set up in 1868 to play championship croquet in Wimbledon, a fast-expanding village only nine miles from London where the price of land was cheap. The fashion for croquet, however, soon peaked, and by the mid-1870s the club needed to attract new members and replenish funds. In 1875, it converted a couple of its croquet lawns into tennis courts and in 1877 decided to hold a national lawn tennis tournament.

Entries were invited for a 'Gentlemen's Singles' to be held at the club's grounds in Worple Road which were connected to Wimbledon station by a footpath. The tournament would run for ten days in July, although there would be a two-day break in the middle to allow club members to go to the annual Eton vs Harrow cricket match at Lords. Spectators would be charged sixpence a day plus an extra sixpence for a programme. The entry fee for competitors was one guinea with the winner receiving twelve guineas and a silver cup worth 25 guineas. The referee and organiser would be Henry Jones, the All England Club member who came up with the idea in the first place.

In later years, Jones cut an eccentric figure. Often regarded as arrogant and odd, he would parade around Wimbledon in white flannel trousers with a white helmet and a white umbrella. By then, he sported a long black beard, smoked Turkish cigarettes and had views on everything which he dispatched with brusqueness and, occasionally, malice. But for much of his life Henry Jones was an innovator. He had been born in London in 1831, the son of a surgeon when surgery was on the cusp of becoming a respectable profession. He qualified in medicine and practised in Soho Square but what he really wanted to be was a sportswriter.

He started writing about the card games he had learned from his father, especially whist, the precursor of bridge. He then branched out to cover billiards and croquet and switched to lawn tennis as the game was spreading across Britain. Jones was an enthusiastic but critical fan and his acerbic comments in *The Field*, written under the pen name of 'Cavendish', made his reputation as the world's first tennis writer. What irritated him most was that there was no consistency across the country in the rules the new tennis players were following.

Some played according to the original rules of Major Wingfield, some to those suggested by competitors like 'garden tennis' or 'outdoor tennis' which had entered the market after Wingfield's early success. Some made up their own rules or followed those published in *The Field* by Harry Gem of Leamington. If lawn tennis was ever going to become a national sport, standardisation was required. In 1875, the Marylebone Cricket Club (MCC) devised a new set of rules based on those of Wingfield. Their adoption of his hourglass court, however, did not find favour with other clubs like Harry Gem's in Leamington and the Prince's Club in Knightsbridge which both favoured the rectangle. Henry Jones was determined that his Wimbledon tournament in July 1877 would attract the best players from the new clubs and he decided to adjust the rules once more.

A few weeks before the tournament at the All England Club was due to start, Jones met up with sport historian Julian Marshall and real tennis player John Heathcote and they devised a way of playing lawn tennis that has remained virtually unchanged ever since. They amended the MCC rules, replacing Wingfield's hourglass court with the rectangle, lowering the net and changing the scoring system from the one used in rackets to the one in real tennis. These amendments produced matches that were more exhilarating and dramatic than any lawn tennis games that had been seen before, even if some of the terms that were borrowed from real tennis like 'deuce' and 'love' were a trifle obscure.

The first Wimbledon Championships began on 9 July 1877 with 22 entrants including a barrister, an architect, two vicars and the mayor of Norwich. It attracted 200 spectators, men dressed in top hats with silver canes and women in a 'vast array of flowers, bows, frills, extravagant hats, narrow-waisted floor length gowns and elegant multicover parasols'.[22] The winner was a local man, Spencer Gore, a 27-year-old surveyor whose long reach and ability to volley helped him gain an easy victory against William Marshall, an architect from Surrey. The following year, Gore attempted to retain his title but this time his athleticism was no match for Frank Hadow, a big-game hunter who ran a coffee plantation in Ceylon and who returned there after the tournament never to be seen at Wimbledon again. In 1879, the wealthy playboy Vere St Leger Goold lost easily to John Thorneycroft Hartley, the only vicar ever to win a Wimbledon title. Goold would eventually end up in prison on Devil's Island off the coast of South America serving a life sentence for murdering his French wife. Hartley became canon of York Cathedral but not before defending his title the next year in one of the most thrilling matches lawn tennis had ever seen. His opponent was Herbert Lawford.

They both wore the handlebar moustaches fashionable at the time but there the similarities ended. Lawford was dressed in a striped jersey, white pants with stockings and a pork pie cap. Hartley was educated at Harrow and all in white. Lawford was muscular and powerful; Hartley was slow about court but adept at keeping the ball in play. On the grass of Worple Road on that hot July afternoon in front of 1,300 people the cunning of the country parson ensnared the master of top spin to produce a match which bridged the gap between sport and entertainment. Lawn tennis had already become a national game. Now it became a game that would change the nature of sport.

Until tennis, sport had emphasised physical prowess and controlled aggression played by men in a team. The exemplar was cricket which celebrated leadership, self-sacrifice and loyalty. It was loved by the 'new man' of early Victorian Britain because it chimed with his punishing work ethic and commitment to family. It was also adored by the majority of these men's sons and grandsons who connected cricket with the type of camaraderie and 'stiff upper lip' praised in the adventure stories of Robert Louis Stevenson and Arthur Conan-Doyle.

Lawn tennis was different. It was played 'as much with the head as the hand' and it encouraged playfulness and an enjoyment of performance.[23] It was appreciated by the minority of middle-class men in late Victorian Britain who were intellectual and aesthetic, were sympathetic to the campaign for suffrage and identified with the novels of Thomas Hardy and George Gissing. These men were mavericks. They saw conventional forms of masculinity as a 'cruel constraint' and they wanted a new way of being male that did not shirk from expressing feelings or sensibilities.[24] There was another difference as well.

In this story of the origins of lawn tennis there has been something missing, or rather some people. There they are on the cover of Walter Wingfield's tennis sets playing in crinolines alongside men with moustaches. One of Wingfield's key selling points for his new game was that it could (and indeed should) be played 'by both sexes'. The radical distinction between men who played tennis and those who played other sports was that male tennis players enjoyed sharing their sport with women.

2

Feminists

In July 1877, the American novelist Henry James visited the county of Warwickshire, the 'grassy centre and core of the English world'. Walking in the lanes near Kenilworth Castle, he came across the village of Berkswell, only a few miles from industrial Coventry but seemingly from an older, agrarian time. James stopped for a while at the local rectory, an 'ancient, gabled building of pale red brick, white stone facings and clambering vines'. It was the 'model of a quiet, spacious English home', but what he admired most was the rectory's garden or rather the activity taking place in it. In an article, published a few months later in the New York literary magazine, *The Galaxy*, he praised 'the cushiony lawn [that] stretched away to the edge of a brook and affording a number of very amiable people an opportunity for playing lawn-tennis'.[1]

Only three years after Walter Wingfield had advertised his tennis sets in London magazines, lawn tennis had become a popular part of the summer for the leisured classes, not just across Britain but overseas as well. Among the first foreign purchasers of Wingfield's sets were three Americans, one based in a fort in the territory of Arizona, another from Staten Island, New York, and another from Nahant, Massachusetts. The game quickly spread along the east and west coasts, inland to Chicago and south to New Orleans. In his article in 1877, then, James felt no need to explain 'lawn-tennis' to his American readers since many would know about it already. 'There were half a dozen games going forward at once', James continued, 'and at each of them a great many "nice girls," as they say in England, were distinguishing themselves'. These 'nice girls' clearly made a strong impression on the unmarried novelist. They 'kept the ball going and gave me a chance to admire their flexibility of figure and their freedom of action. When they came back to the house, after the games, flushed a little and a little dishevelled, they might have passed for the attendant nymphs of Diana.'

Henry James does not identify any of these dishevelled nymphs of Diana for *Galaxy* readers, which was a pity because seven years later in July 1884, one of them, Maud Watson, would keep the ball going so well she became Wimbledon's first Women's Singles champion.[2] At the All England Club that July afternoon, Maud defeated her older sister Lilian in a fierce final which went to three sets. James, flush from the success of his latest novel, *Portrait of a Lady*, does not seem to have made it to Wimbledon that day to see his 'nymphs of Diana' play, but 400 spectators did and each paid 10s 6d to watch Maud and Lilian Watson become the first female tennis stars. They were not, though, the first women to pick up tennis rackets.

In 1427, Lady Margot from Hainault was a regular player at the tennis court in the Louvre in Paris where she beat most of her male opponents. Other women followed her over the next centuries including, in 1760, a Madame Masson who had a 'vigorous wrist' and was able to 'cut the ball well' and a Madame Bunuel in France who was then 60 years old and 'frequently played with the Prince de Condé'.[3] The game these women played, though, was not lawn but real tennis played indoors with a hard ball on a stone floor.

By the start of the nineteenth century, respectable women in Britain had retreated from real tennis and other sports to take on the role of 'perfect wife' in the new Victorian family. While their domestic duties did not exclude them from exercise, strenuous effort in public was now considered inappropriate and the only sports regarded as fully acceptable for women were horse riding and archery since they required little obvious physical movement. In the 1850s, these sports were joined by croquet, a new game introduced into Britain from Ireland. Croquet clubs sprung up across the country in the next decade and the croquet lawn became the fashionable location for upper-middle-class women and men to be seen together as the role of these women began to change from 'perfect wife' at home to 'perfect lady' who accompanied her husband on social occasions.[4] Many of the women turned out to be better at the sport than men. In Berkswell, it was not the Reverend Henry Watson who was the croquet champion but his wife Emily.

By the start of the 1870s, however, the fascination with croquet was coming to an end.[5] For a while, it seemed that badminton might take its place but that game was too easily disrupted by wind. The more solid lawn tennis had no such problem and on country house and vicarage lawns throughout Britain in the summers of the mid and late 1870s, tennis nets replaced croquet hoops and rubber balls took the place of shuttlecocks. It was a small step for women to shift from croquet to tennis. It turned out to be a giant leap for womankind.

In Berkswell Rectory, the Watsons started playing tennis in the garden sometime around 1875. They were encouraged by male students staying there for maths tuition with the Reverend Henry Watson who once taught the subject at Harrow. Tennis would have come as a welcome diversion for the young men after advanced algebra or geometry with the rector, especially if it gave them a chance to be introduced to his 18-year-old daughter, Lilian. Her 13-year-old sister, Maud, fell in love not with any student but with the new game. She would spend hours practising on her own against the wall in the garden. Soon she was good enough to beat Lilian. Soon she was good enough to beat anyone.

Why did young women like the Watson sisters take up this new summer pastime with such passionate enthusiasm? One reason was the sport was aimed at them. When Walter Wingfield marketed his game in the spring of 1874, he saw the equal participation of women as essential for lawn tennis's success. In *The Major's Game of Lawn Tennis* he made sure there were illustrations showing women playing as well as men. He subsequently included advertisements for 'ladies bats' and gave his female customers a discount of a guinea a set. One customer who called herself a 'Tennisonian' wrote in to praise him as having the 'good sense to see that games are not to be despised because women can join in them and occasionally distinguish themselves'.[6] This inclusion of women by Major Wingfield ensured that tennis had a very different beginning from other Victorian sports which started out as male-only activities and allowed women in only decades later. With tennis, women were there from the start and so were able to have a crucial influence on its culture, etiquette and style. All this, though, did not come in isolation.

Wingfield's tennis sets came onto the market at a time when there was a shifting set of standards for what the daughters of the upper and upper middle class were permitted to do. Emancipation for women was on the political agenda. The 1860s saw the start of a women's movement, and the feminist cause was supported by the popular philosopher and MP John Stuart Mill, who argued in the second reform bill of 1866 for the right of women to vote. Day schools for girls like Cheltenham Ladies' College and North London Collegiate opened, and they were modelled on the boys' public schools, especially their attachment to games. A political campaign to ensure higher education for women resulted in the founding of Bedford College in London in 1849 and, twenty years later, Girton College in Cambridge, the first female residential college. After they completed their education, many women started looking for employment opportunities outside the home in professions such as journalism, teaching and nursing.

The definitions, then, of what women could and could not do had begun to change as some of the cultural and economic spaces that had been all male opened up. Once more, lawn tennis came at exactly the right time. It had no defining masculine codes, it was played with a soft ball that relied as much on guile as on strength and it fitted in well to the roster of sports and pastimes the girls' schools and colleges were keen to offer potential students. Lawn tennis offered an opportunity in an acceptable social setting for young women to develop more physical freedom than croquet and archery allowed. There was another benefit as well. Tennis allowed them to display their talents as 'cultured ladies' while also providing a marriage market in a 'seemingly innocent and acceptable way'.[7]

As with any marriage market, though, there was little that was truly innocent about this one. Older girls like Lilian and their mothers or aunts who acted as chaperones were aware of the sexual tensions that swirled around the first tennis parties. What nobody noticed was how the imagination of their younger sisters was being captured by the sport itself. It is difficult to overestimate the excitement that the game evoked in eleven-, twelve- and thirteen-year-old Mauds, Charlottes, Blanches and Dotheas as their parents queued up to buy Wingfield's tennis sets. Their mothers saw the game as a new social fad, their older sisters as a possible way to meet a husband. But for the younger girls, tennis itself was the passion, the one sport they could play alongside their brothers. The energy that had been swallowed up in previous generations by needlework, novels and the pianoforte – and gymnastics if you were lucky – was unleashed and, once set free, would not be deterred.

In the early summer of 1881, Maud and Lilian Watson decided that if their tennis was going to improve, they needed to enter the tournaments that were sprouting up around the country. It must have taken considerable courage for the two young women to leave the safety of Berkswell Rectory and compete in competitions far from home. But they may well have been encouraged by an editorial in the *Daily Telegraph* in May 1881. 'Lawn Tennis', the newspaper noted with approval, 'is exactly seven years old. That which can now be fairly called a national pastime has withstood the test of temper, taste and criticism. Ladies are not banished in this case but have proved themselves in many instances no mean antagonists for the stronger sex.'[8]

The first recorded ladies' tennis championships took place at the Fitzwilliam Club in Dublin in 1879. By the time the *Daily Telegraph* gave its approval two years later, there was a fledgling circuit of sorts with open competitions for women as well as men in Bath, Exmouth, Cheltenham and in Edgbaston 20 miles from the Watsons' home. The sisters entered the 1881 Edgbaston tournament which was held in the middle of May. Maud, then 16 years old with dark curly hair and intense, expressive eyes, won. All her practice against the rectory wall had produced a game 'with no apparent weaknesses', 'excellent judgment' and 'cool concentration'.[9] For her next 55 matches Maud was undefeated, culminating in that first Wimbledon ladies final against Lilian three years later in 1884. She wasn't, though, the only female player that attracted the early tennis crowds.

The Watson sisters joined a group of elite women tennis players who travelled from tournament to tournament to be tested (but rarely beaten) by local women. Lillian and Maud Watson, Charlotte 'Chattie' Cooper, May 'Toupie' Lowther and Blanche Hillyard (their names alone conjure up a different age) inspired a generation of young women to take up tennis and make the sport their own. The facilities provided for women at most of these early tennis tournaments were often rudimentary. 'Ladies are catered for very badly', wrote Dorothea 'Dolly' Douglas, 'I am sure if men had to experience the changing room accommodation afforded for our use there would not be many of them competing.'[10]

Changing rooms aside, though, these women loved their tennis experience. They travelled by rail with their mothers or aunts: by the turn of the century, every significant town and city in Britain was connected by train and fares were inexpensive, particularly to the new seaside resorts which competed with each other for visitors by putting on lawn tennis competitions. 'My mother', wrote Charlotte Cooper, 'turned a deaf ear to anyone who advised her not to allow my sister and myself to travel about'. Cooper, known for her happy demeanour and enjoyment of the game, entered the Fitzwilliam in Dublin and the Northern in Manchester most years in the 1890s. She also played in Newcastle and the seaside tournaments, and ended the summer with a 'wind-up of the season at Brighton and Eastbourne. Most enjoyable.' When asked to give advice to other women players, she said they must develop 'pluck'. 'Ladies make these tournaments much more attractive!', she exhorted, 'the chief qualities you need are judgement and pluck'.[11]

Toupie Lowther agreed. 'Ladies unlike men do not break down in matches. Is it that they have more pluck?' Lowther never won Wimbledon partly because of her temperament – which ironically could break down in a tense match – and partly because of the many other activities to which she devoted her life. She took a degree in science from the Sorbonne and was an expert fencer. Stephen, the central character in Radclyffe Hall's masterpiece of lesbian literature, *The Well of Loneliness*, published in 1928, is modelled partly on her.

Charlotte Cooper and Blanche Hillyard, as well as bringing up children, played championship tennis well into their forties. In 1907, when she was 37, Cooper became the oldest woman to win Wimbledon, a record that still stands today. Hillyard was a semi-finalist in 1912 when she was 49 and always saw women's tennis on a par with men's. It was 'the one game in which a girl can to some extent hold her own', and she was sure that if 'more ladies would take it up and play regularly they would be far more healthy and strong'.[12] Just as male tennis players were redefining masculinity in sport, so these tennis-playing women performed femininity in ways very different from their mothers. They played like gentlemen but behaved like ladies. They were the first sporting feminists.

One of the ways this feminism was expressed was challenging acceptable forms of female dress. When women first started playing tennis they wore the social uniform of mid-Victorian Britain. Their arms and legs were fully covered and their bodies held in by whalebone corsets. Tennis aprons, petticoats and ankle-high, black leather boots completed an outfit more suited to discouraging desire than encouraging movement around court.

In 1881 Walter Wingfield proposed shorter skirts for women after playing a game against a female friend who was 'younger and quicker' than he was. 'How then did I win? I was dressed for lawn tennis and she was not.'[13] By this time, though, his influence on the game he invented had passed and in the next two decades women played in the restricted garb captured by the Irish painter John Lavery. His *Tennis Party* and *A Rally*, both from 1885, show female players desperately trying to stretch down for tennis balls but being held back by white voluminous dresses. The men, dressed more appropriately in slim cricketers' outfits, look on with amusement.

As Lavery's paintings demonstrated, the older women who started playing tennis as a substitute for croquet were handicapped by wearing clothes not designed for physical exertion. Younger players inspired by the Rational Dress Society, founded in London in 1881, discovered ways around the Victorian dress rules. Maud Watson recalled that the ladies she played against wore 'long skirts and coloured dresses, veils and high heels'. She and her sister Lilian were the 'first to wear light wool skirts with a little bustle as it was the style'.[14] Her skirt was still down to her ankles and she still had to show an hourglass waist on court (corsets were worn well into the 1920s) but on her feet were not boots but India rubber shoes and on her head was not a bonnet but a jaunty lightweight sailor hat to keep out the sun.

Maud Watson could enjoy this freedom because she started playing tennis when she was an adolescent and her original tennis dress resembled school uniform. Another adolescent in the mid-1880s also found ways around the restricted dress codes. 'As the skirt must be endured', she later wrote, 'it is important to have it made somewhat short, cut half an inch or an inch shorter at the back than the front. It will then appear uniform in length and will not trip you up when you run backwards in volleying.'[15] The words are those of Charlotte 'Lottie' Dod who turned out to be an even more formidable player than Maud Watson. Many consider her to have been the greatest British sportswoman of all time.

Like the Watsons, Dod grew up in a village on the edge of an industrial city. Her father, Joseph, made his fortune as a cotton merchant in Liverpool and the family moved out to Bebington which was then in rural Cheshire but is now swallowed up by Birkenhead. They lived in Edgeworth House, a substantial Victorian villa. On the back lawn, Joseph Dod marked out two of the first tennis courts in the north-west. In the summer holidays, his teenage sons played tennis with their friends, and nine-year-old Lottie and her older sister Anne were occasionally allowed to join in. Soon the girls were good. Soon they started beating their brothers.

In 1883 the Dod sisters entered the Northern Championships held that year in Manchester. Annie was 16, Lottie was 11. They did not win but the younger girl was entranced by the 19-year-old Maud Watson who did, and Watson became her role model.

Two years later, when she was 13, Dod almost beat Watson in the 1885 Northern final. The press called her 'the little wonder'. Two years after that, at Wimbledon in 1887, she triumphed to become Ladies Champion. She was just 15 years old, the youngest champion ever, male or female. A century later, she still is.

From the time of this first Wimbledon victory until she gave up tennis at 21 to pursue other challenges, Lottie Dod dominated the game. She lost only five matches in her entire tennis career. She would go on to represent England at hockey, become a British Ladies Champion in golf, win a silver medal for archery at the 1908 Olympics, and toboggan down the Cresta Run. But it is for her tennis she is most remembered today. While Maud Watson was known for her consistency and temperament, Dod was feared because of her aggression. She hit every shot with venom and smashed and volleyed as hard as any man. She looked a little terrifying too. One tennis commentator of the time noted her 'close cropped hair, her unusual height and strength, and determined smile'. Another commentator praised her 'great quality of anticipating her opponents reply. She hits her forehand stroke with the pace of a man's.'[16] Wherever she played, Dod was news. She was the first player to attract her own fan club, young girls who followed her from tournament to tournament. Many of these girls went back to their tennis clubs and copied Dod's forthright manner and loose, flexible dress as well as her strokes. They brought about a quiet revolution. The trouble was that it was not quite quiet enough.

As women like Watson and Dod proved they could hold their own on court, some prominent male players tried to marginalise the women's game. This had first been tried in the mid-1870s. Just a few weeks after Major Wingfield advertised his lawn tennis sets in March 1874 as a new game for men *and* women, doubts started creeping in. One man wrote to *The Field* claiming that the new tennis rackets are 'too heavy for their small wrists'.[17] Another wondered whether 'any lady can or ever will be able to play the game as it is very hard work for a man'.[18] The debate spread to the letter pages of *The Times* where a correspondent warned, 'anyone playing in partnership with a lady needs to be ready for certain eventuali-ties. A lady will be invariably nonplussed by the drop shot.'[19]

These bad-tempered clamourings could be dismissed as tittle-tattle if they had not been taken up by other men who had power in the new game. The first real setback for women came at the All England Club. After the success of the Men's Singles at Wimbledon in 1877 and 1878, a Mr Hora on the club committee proposed a ladies event as well. Apart from Henry Jones, he received no support. The minutes of the committee meeting record that it was 'not desirable to have a ladies tennis cup under any circumstances'. What they suggested instead was that women should use a smaller court, lighter racket and a lighter ball which would be allowed to bounce twice. If this suggestion had been taken up, men's and women's tennis would have separated. The men's game would have continued to develop as a public sport, with the resources, money and power that entailed, while the new softer women's game would have remained a private pastime. There were one or two things, though, that the male proponents of an easier game for women had not properly considered.

The most obvious one was that it would destroy the game of mixed doubles which men and women played together. From the very first tennis parties organised in the summer of 1874 on country house lawns, mixed doubles had been a defining feature of the new pastime. Many of the men who had played in all-male sports like cricket and rackets discovered they liked playing with women. One early Wimbledon champion commented that 'a game in which two gentlemen are partnered by two good ladies is almost as enjoyable and almost as difficult to play well as a men's singles'.[20] It was almost as profitable too, since mixed doubles competitions were popular at the first tennis tournaments with spectators as well as competitors. So were the matches between women.

In 1884, over 6,000 people watched the women's final at the Fitzwilliam Club in Dublin. *Pastime* noted that those 'dear old gentlemen who so firmly believe in the superiority of men and the inability of women to participate in any so-called masculine pastime have received a huge shock at Dublin. The most interesting topic of conversation was the ladies' championship.'[21]

The 'dear old gentlemen' *Pastime* had in mind were the men from the All England Club at Wimbledon. The club might not like the idea of a ladies' championship but it could not fail to notice that tournaments that catered for men *and* women were the most popular. For a club like the All England, always aware of the need to cover its costs, this was a windfall that could not be ignored. When a rival club, London Athletic, announced it was going ahead with the first British women's tennis championship in the summer of 1884, the All England Club Committee changed its mind. Seven years after it had held the first open tennis tournament for men in 1877, Wimbledon introduced a Ladies' Singles with a first prize of a silver flower-basket valued at 20 guineas.

A battle for women's tennis was won but the war was by no means over. As the historian of women's sport, Kathleen McCrone, has argued, the first generation of ordinary female players were no great threat to the male ego because they hit the ball softly and were restricted in their movements. But as women players became better and their dress more flexible, more was at stake.[22] A correspondent to *Pastime* in 1885 reported that it is now 'several summers since ladies appeared at a club we know of and successfully defeated all the crack players including one who fancied himself for the championship. He then said ladies shouldn't play because they did not look pretty and were ungraceful just like a cow. The reason why some men object is because they are smarting from defeat.'[23] This was not an uncommon occurrence. Some of the first women players were better than many men and this was difficult for men to deal with. One male player decided he did not like it at all.

Herbert Chipp was a tall, forbidding man with a moustache almost as long as his tennis racket. He had an unorthodox playing style – he was one of the first players to use a double-handed backhand – but managed to reach the semi-finals of Wimbledon in 1884 when he was defeated by Herbert Lawford. That defeat, the closest Chipp came to winning a major championship, seems to have left him permanently disgruntled and he focussed his displeasure on the women's game which he felt was holding men's tennis back. In 1886, he publicly derided that year's Wimbledon champion, Blanche Hillyard, because she volleyed only 'when she found the ball on her racket' with a service, he carried on with malicious delight, which 'possesses no great virtue' and a smash which was 'absolutely deficient'.[24]

Chipp's views found sympathy with some of his regular tennis partners at the Hyde Park Tennis Club, one of the first indoor clubs built on top of a disused skating rink. One complained that women players 'need to make up their mind to run about'.[25] Another said that they play 'for the sake of costume. They are troubled with fears lest they should be growing too red in the face.'[26] The problem for these male separatists was that their barbs clearly did not apply to one player who ran around court as well as they did. All the disparaging remarks about women's tennis keeping men's tennis back were clearly not true of Lottie Dod who wasn't worried about her appearance, moved as fast as any man and hit the ball just as hard.

In August 1888, the seaside town of Exmouth advertised a 'battle of the sexes' charity match. Representing the men was Dod's regular mixed doubles partner, Ernest Renshaw, a tall, dapper 27 year old who went on to win Wimbledon the following year. Representing the women was Dod herself, ten years younger, four inches shorter with jet black hair. They played in front of a capacity crowd who cheered every shot. Renshaw gave Dod two points each game but then he didn't have to wear the restrictive dress that even the rebellious Dod had to put up with. He won but only just. 'Our woman champion', *Pastime* reported, 'played so well that Renshaw had to run about as much as against a first rate player of his own sex'.[27]

As powerful female players like Dod took centre stage, the arguments for separating out the women's and the men's game started to shift. Separation was now important not for men but for women. Playing tennis regularly might lead to strained muscles, blows to the eye and exhaustion. Tennis was seen by some doctors as acceptable exercise for women only if it was done in moderation and did not endanger their ability to reproduce. In 1894 the *British Medical Journal* recommended that women avoid 'violent physical exertion' on the tennis court because it might be damaging for future motherhood.[28] There was no evidence that running around vigorously on court had any effect on the ability to reproduce, but the arguments about the damage women could do to themselves and their unborn children were not about this but about what the female body was allowed to experience.

In late Victorian Britain, this body was a focus for the battle of power between men and women. Women who wanted to play tennis had to contest the stereotype of the 'frail middle-class lady' which was used to uphold Victorian patriarchy. It was not only women's frailty on the tennis court that was of concern but also their moral development. Chipp classified the young female tennis players of the 1880s as 'joining in pursuits' which have been once regarded as 'unalloyed heathenism'.[29]

His words had weight. In January 1888, Chipp had been appointed secretary of the new Lawn Tennis Association and he refused to do anything to help the female game. Women tennis players would be given no encouragement or resources and had to fend for themselves. One woman fought back.

In the late 1880s, Lottie Dod was asked by the Heathcote brothers to write a chapter on women's tennis in their popular anthology, *Tennis, Lawn Tennis, Rackets and Fives*, which would stay in print for several editions well into the next decade. Dod used the opportunity to lay down a direct challenge to Chipp and his supporters. She argued that the reason tennis was successful was because it was the first sport where men and women played together. Male players stopped any tendency for the women to pat the ball back, and women demonstrated they could cope with the weight of the racket since the game did not depend on strength alone. Dod then delivered her *coup de grâce*. Reviewing the attempts a decade before to introduce an easier game for women, she argued that there was still a danger men's and women's tennis could be 'entirely separated with different grounds, balls and laws'.

This would be disastrous for the women's game – and also for the men's. The men who wanted to treat women's tennis differently were 'invested with the prerogative of an irresponsible despot'.[30]

It was a crucial blow, not least for Chipp, who did not appreciate the implication that he might be an 'irresponsible despot'. Nobody could dispute Dod's authority, a young woman who was admired both by women and men for her game. In 1898, the Lawn Tennis Association finally agreed to assume responsibility for women's tennis as Chipp conceded that women would remain central to the sport. Although the 'athleticism of the fin-de-siècle women', he wrote in his memoirs, 'would appear sometimes too pronounced, still it cannot be denied that on the whole the changes which have been brought about must ultimately prove beneficial to the race at large, at all events physically'. He couldn't, however, resist a final barb. 'Whether the benefit will be as great morally is a question which only time can settle.'[31]

Whatever Chipp's caveats, it was a remarkable victory. Without the courage of Dod and many of the early female champions to stand up to attempts to marginalise their game, women's tennis might well have been sidelined. Their strength in dealing with powerful men came partly from their upbringing. The first female players were a 'privileged group of affluent white middle-class women' who were not radical by nature but became radical in practice because they mounted a 'resistance to the prevailing idea that their primary roles were … wives and mothers'.[32] At the heart of this resistance was the remarkable Lottie Dod, and she had another source of inner power as well.

Dod lived a life that was not dependent on men. She never married and never had children. Instead her time, like Toupie Lowther's, was given over to sport and to the many voluntary projects to which she was committed. During the First World War, Dod worked for the Red Cross and was subsequently awarded a gold medal for nursing. In the Spanish Civil War, she was a volunteer for the Republicans and then assisted in a girls' club in east London before moving to Hampshire where she died in 1960 listening to the coverage of Wimbledon on a radio next to her bed.

Lottie Dod saw the game of lawn tennis not simply as a challenging pastime for women as well as men, but as a liberating force which gave opportunities for women to free themselves from the constraints of Victorian femininity. With Blanche Hillyard, Toupie Lowther, Charlotte Cooper, Dorothea Lambert Chambers and Maud Watson she helped shift the definitions of legitimate female physical activity, which was significant not just for sport but for suffrage and freedom.

3

Members

At the start of January 1892, the Reverend Arthur Sloman was 41 years old. The son of a surgeon from Surrey, he had won a scholarship to study classics at Oxford. He then taught at Westminster School before moving, in the spring of 1886, to the Wirral peninsula to take over as headmaster of Birkenhead, a boy's public school which had fallen on troubled times. Sloman was the fourth head in two years but his 'scholarship and charming manner', not to mention his Irish wife Bessie, had steadied the school and this new year he could take a little time for himself.[1] Although he was a keen cricketer and mountaineer – he was a member of the Alpine Club – Sloman could not afford to take the days away from school that mountains or indeed cricket matches required. Instead, he decided to take up lawn tennis, a new game that was being talked about in rectories and vicarages around the country, which would occupy only an afternoon or two a week and which he could share with Bessie. The trouble was there wasn't anywhere local to play.

Undeterred, the Reverend Sloman, a striking man with wavy hair and a clipped moustache, did what most nineteenth-century gentlemen of boundless energy but limited means did when they had a new project. He called a public meeting. It took place a few weeks later on the evening of 26 January 1892, across the River Mersey in Liverpool. The venue was Peters Buildings in Rumford Street, a short stroll from George's Dock.

This dock, Liverpool's smallest, would soon be replaced by Pier Head, now a UNESCO World Heritage Site. The space that was once Peters Buildings is today a parking lot. In the 1890s, though, this part of the city was the centre of Liverpool's thriving cotton trade. Imported cotton came through the docks on its way to the Lancashire mills and was traded at the old cotton exchange in

Chapel Street. Rumford Street was just a few minutes' walk away, and at Number 11 were the offices of Hubert Braddyll, one of the most successful cotton brokers in the city. Braddyll lived with his family not far from Sloman and Birkenhead School in the village of Oxton, and he provided the meeting room where this proposed new tennis venture could be properly discussed. There is no record of the kind of people who attended that Tuesday evening in early 1892, but it seems likely they were members of Birkenhead's increasingly prosperous middle class who commuted each day by rail through the new Mersey Tunnel to Liverpool for work. There were already a couple of tennis clubs in the city but nothing across the river. Lawn tennis in Birkenhead would have to start from scratch.

The meeting elected a committee of ten people with Arthur Sloman as chairman. They met a month later. Suitable land was identified near Birkenhead School just off the Shrewsbury Road, but the new club would need funds to rent it from the Earl of Shrewsbury and to build four grass courts and a wooden pavilion estimated to cost £65. To raise the money, membership was offered to 15 men and 18 ladies, including the Reverend Sloman's wife Bessie. Six months later, the Shrewsbury Road Lawn Tennis Club was ready for play. Tennis had come to Birkenhead.

The Slomans only benefitted from the club for a few years. Birkenhead School failed to attract new pupils, and in 1897 Arthur Sloman resigned and moved with Bessie to Huntingdon-shire where he eventually became vicar of Godmanchester.[2] The tennis club survived his departure, and 130 years on is still there, although it has been renamed Birkenhead Lawn Tennis Club. Today, it has six hard courts (three with floodlights), a kitchen, a bar and a clubhouse made of materials a little sturdier than wood. It remains run by committee and owned by its members, now 100 men and 150 women, although it is no longer surrounded by fields and footpaths but by streets and semis. For 130 years Birkenhead Lawn Tennis Club has provided an opportunity for the people on the Wirral to play tennis, but it has done more than that. At the end of the nineteenth century, this club and dozens like it that were founded around the same time kept the new sport of lawn tennis alive.

The previous decade, tennis could not have been more popular. In seaside resorts and spa towns in the 1880s, tennis courts were a key attraction alongside bathing machines and indoor gardens. Tennis tournaments were held all around the British Isles and entries were not restricted to top players. There were competitions for juniors (Framlingham offered a Boys' Singles in 1886) and older players (Eastbourne advertised a Veterans' Singles in 1888). For people who were knocked out in the first round there were consolation events, and weaker players could enter the 'handicap' where they were given 15 or 30 points every game. If it was a little unclear at the end who deserved the silverware, tournament organisers could always consult *Lawn Tennis Tournaments, the True Method of Assigning Prizes*, a short booklet published in 1883 by the Oxford vicar and mathematician, Charles Dodgson, better known as Lewis Carroll.

By the start of the 1890s, however, Reverend Dodgson had tired of tennis (and indeed of Alice) and shifted his attention to billiards and stamp collecting. His defection was one indication that the fashion for the game was coming to an end. The tennis parties captured so vividly on canvas by the painter John Lavery a few years earlier became remembrances of summers gone. Attendances at Wimbledon declined and, in 1896, the Ladies' Singles received only seven entrants. About this time too there was renewed interest in archery and croquet, and the invention of the safety bicycle opened up cycling as a new pursuit that was particularly popular with independent young women. In *Sports of the World*, published in 1903 and edited by Frederick Aflalo, a fellow of the Royal Geographical Society, it was noted that lawn tennis had been 'dropped as an adjunct to fashionable parties' sometime in the previous decade. Aflalo gave tennis the same space in the book as whippet racing, elk shooting and hunting for kangaroos.[3] Lawn tennis looked set to become, like real tennis, a minority pastime for aficionados.

Away from fashionable London society, however, tennis had developed surprisingly strong roots. Archery and croquet clubs found that their members were interested in playing tennis as well. The first two tennis clubs in Liverpool, like many across the country, were originally formed to play archery. Cycling tended to encourage lawn tennis rather than replace it. 'Retford tennis players would think nothing of cycling as far as Grantham for a match', tennis historian Andy Lusis discovered, 'there was no reason why the two pastimes could not be combined'.[4] In Nottingham, Liverpool, Birmingham, Newcastle and many other provincial towns and cities across the British Isles, tennis by the 1890s had become embedded in local culture. Its setting – and saviour – was the members-owned, voluntarily run tennis club.

Clubs were formed as far apart as Sittingbourne in Kent (1875), Aberaeron in Cardigan Bay (1881), Framlingham in Norfolk (1883), Sparkhill in Birmingham (1888), Cullercoats in Tyneside (1893) and Pit Farm in Guildford (1897). By 1900, there were 300 tennis clubs affiliated to the Lawn Tennis Association and probably as many again where play was more informal. By the First World War there were 1,000. Like Birkenhead, each had its own idiosyncratic beginnings.

A club in Aughton in Lancashire was founded by a local antique trader, John Livesey, on a large meadow near his home. Another in Hale in Cheshire was established with money borrowed from Adam Fletcher, a Manchester builder. In Chesham, the vicar started a tennis club by allowing the use of a court in the old rectory. In Blundellsands, up the coast from Liverpool, the local archery club raised £65 from members to invest in four grass tennis courts and a clubhouse. Some of these clubs were in villages, some in market towns and some were in the new suburbs.

The first great expansion of British suburbia took place in the last decades of the nineteenth century as new estates spread out from towns and cities along roads and railway lines. The homes that were built here, in tree-lined avenues with large back gardens, attracted derision from architects at the time, but for the people who bought them an individually designed house was less important than a cosy home, efficient public transport and facilities for recreation. For this new kind of living, tennis was ideal. In June 1886, the *Shrewsbury Journal* noted the 'constant appearance of young men and maidens in the suburbs armed with a racket'.[5] Lawn tennis, the pastime that had originally triumphed because it offered an alliance between the Victorian upper and upper middle classes, flourished in Edwardian times because it fulfilled the desires of the 'new comfortable' who yearned for a semi-rural life.[6] These people were under the radar of the fashionable London magazines and their lives went largely unrecorded. As the upper-class hero of John Buchan's popular 1904 novel, *The Thirty-Nine Steps*, put it, 'what fellows like me don't understand is the great, comfortable, satisfied middle class world, the folk that live in villas and suburbs'.[7]

These middle-class folk took up lawn tennis because they had more leisure time and more disposable income than ever before. Lawn tennis cost £10 a year at the turn of the century, about the same as piano lessons. Joining a tennis club 'involved little or no expenses beyond one guinea entrance fee and between 1–2 guineas annual sub'.[8] The game also provided less tangible benefits. The suburban tennis club with its plush lawns hidden behind rhododendron bushes allowed its members to forget the increasingly timetabled urban world. It provided easy exercise with congenial companions who might become firm friends.

The attractions of tennis were recognised by builders nationwide who ensured that tennis courts were included in new estates. When Telford Park, one of the first experiments in suburbia, was built in the fields of the old parish of Streatham, south London, in the late 1870s, tennis was a central feature. The first houses were completed in 1878 and tennis courts laid down in 1880. A tennis club was formed and it developed a wide range of social activities that went far beyond sport. The lure of an instant community organised around a tennis club became a unique selling point for the British suburbs built before the First World War. Another attraction was that these clubs were open to men and women.

In the nineteenth century, sports clubs were generally restricted to men, whether there were pub-based angling clubs, village cricket teams or rackets clubs in town. These clubs helped promote business, professional or, in the case of fishing, trade union links. But at the turn of the century public space was no longer entirely occupied by men. In the Edwardian office there were female typists and clerks, and women worked alongside men in department stores, elementary schools, hospitals and telegraph offices. In the workplace this interchange between men and women was regulated by strict hierarchies, but in leisure this was more difficult. Power was diffuse and needed to be negotiated. Tennis clubs at the turn of the century provided an early model of how men and women could learn to share social space together, although it was a sharing not without tension.

In 1906 there were complaints from men at the East Gloucestershire Tennis Club that women took up too much space in the pavilion. About the same time in Chesham, women were asked to abstain from using courts on Sunday mornings. In Jesmond Tennis Club in Newcastle in April 1905, the all-male committee resolved not to allow any more women to become members 'until the proportion of gentlemen to ladies be as three to two'.[9] In Dyvours, a club in Edinburgh, women were only allowed to play during four prescribed hours of the day. None of these attempts by men to limit women's participation worked because there were other forces at play.

The men and women who took up lawn tennis in the first decades of the sport discovered they needed each other, not simply to play mixed doubles – popular as that game was – but for their identity as sportspeople. At a time when tennis was still regarded by some sportsmen as close to homosexuality, the presence of women helped male players assert their manliness even if it was in chivalrous mode. And at a time when there were doubts about whether women should take strenuous exercise, the presence of men pushed female players into embracing tennis as a tough physical challenge and not just a gentle pastime. There were attempts during this time to set up separate men's and women's tennis clubs, particularly on the east coast of America, but these did not last. When either men or women were absent from a tennis club, something seemed wrong. Being a mixed sport was part of tennis's DNA. In the years before the First World War, a decade or two before women won the vote, the lawn tennis club became one of the first social institutions where men shared at least some of their power with women.

The new female power was initially informal. With one or two notable exceptions, women did not become tennis club officials until the 1920s, and for some clubs long after that. In Woodford Wells in Essex, women could vote at the annual club meeting in 1905, but it was still 'many years' before they were allowed on the general committee. Jesmond in Newcastle was at this time 'known for its ladies', but it was not until 1956 that they were invited to join the club's managing committee. But even where women had no formal power, they often owned much of the club's social capital, and not just in Britain.

In Ojai Tennis Club in California, founded in 1888, the serving of afternoon tea quickly became the 'Ojai's most enduring social event and in many ways it defined the atmosphere'. The club's Tea Tent was 'sacred ground' and run over the years by the 'cream of the valley's ladies'.[10] In the Seattle tennis club founded two years later in 1890, the manager was 'Alice Rollins who wore long black skirts and kept her hair in a bun. The board of the Tennis Club thought they ran the place but they really didn't. Mrs Rollins did. She was fearsome.'[11] These formidable women in tennis clubs across the world used their power over social events to control much of the conduct of the club and deal with its most destructive element: unwanted passion.

The relatively easy mixing of non-related men and women at tennis clubs before the First World War was full of opportunity but fraught with danger. There were no chaperones so conventions developed instead. A common one was that men were not allowed to ask women to play but had to wait for an invitation. Some clubs like Woodford Wells in Essex went further and insisted that couples who wanted to play mixed doubles must be husband and wife, brother and sister or engaged – which must be 'bona fide not ad hoc'. In the popular novels of the time, the tennis club become a key location for romantic interest, intrigue and rivalry.

In *Love Among the Chickens* by P.G. Wodehouse, first published in 1906, a young male writer falls in love with a woman at the tennis club but she is smitten with another, a dashing naval lieutenant. 'His service was bottled lightning. His returns behaved like jumping crackers ... I felt a worm and no man. Phyllis would probably judge my entire character from this exhibition. A man she would reflect, who could be so feeble and miserable a failure at tennis, could not be good for much in any department of life.'[12]

Tennis as a testing ground for the judgement of a potential partner in Edwardian Britain was also a theme of *Room with a View* by E.M. Forster, published two years later in 1908. Lucy Honeychurch, a young woman trying to live an independent life, tells Cecil Vyse, a sophisticated man about town, that their engagement is finished because Cecil won't join in with tennis. "'Things must come to a breaking point some time and it happened to be today. If you want to know quite a little thing decided me to speak to you when you wouldn't play tennis with Freddy". "I never do play tennis", said Cecil painfully bewildered, "I never could play". "You play well enough to make up a four".'[13]

It wasn't just young men who had to prove themselves on court. In *The Crowded Street* by Winifred Holtby, published in 1924 but set before the First World War, 20-year-old Muriel Hammond joined her local tennis club in Yorkshire and was entranced by bachelor Godfrey Neale. When they were partnered together in a mixed double, Muriel was determined to impress. 'She played with serious care. The air shimmered with dancing gold. Never before shone grass so green. Never were balls so white. Never was the joy of swift movement so exhilarating.'[14] Unfortunately, it did her no good. Muriel was not the wife the women in the club intended for the dashing but dim Godfrey and they ensured she was not his doubles partner again.

This policing of desire, where only certain kinds of partnerships were allowed and others forbidden, must have been maddening to the young Muriels and Godfreys, but it ensured that mixed tennis clubs in the decades before the First World War flourished and survived. Through words, gestures and gossip, older female club members discouraged some pairings but promoted others. Weddings became a common occurrence. At the Priory Club in Edgbaston in 1893, Charles Wood met a Miss Warden whom he married and played mixed doubles with for the next 40 years. 'The game of lawn tennis', he remembered fondly in 1946, ' has added greatly to the health and happiness of our married life.'[15] In 1907 the president of Bromley Tennis Club proposed to a new woman member and their marriage was the first of 15 at the club that can be traced back to initial meetings on their courts.

Once couples were married though, other problems emerged. The tennis court could become an irresistible arena for the tensions of a long-term commitment and few couples could pass over the temptation. So another convention developed that it was desirable for members to play mixed doubles with someone other than their spouse. This led tennis clubs in the first two decades of the century to pioneer a new relationship between the sexes that had rarely been seen in public before: friendship. The early tennis clubs' radical contribution to sport and society was to start developing a social practice where adult men and women who were not related could be friends. It came, though, at a price. People wanted to be friends with others like themselves and that meant keeping those who were different out.

In some tennis clubs, this exclusion was explicit. Sittingbourne boasted in 1884 that to 'keep the society select all new members are elected by ballot after being proposed and seconded by a member of the committee'.[16] When somebody was proposed to become a member of the club, however, there was another obstacle to overcome. At the secret ballot, 'blackballing' was allowed which ensured any applicant considered undesirable by any member could be kept out. Other clubs did not bother with elaborate rituals to exclude people. In 1897 Ormskirk tennis club refused admission to a 'Kirkby Lad' who gave his occupation as a 'common labourer'. Kirktonhill tennis club in the West of Scotland maintained it was 'open to all' but in practice it was open only to people who would fit in. Tennis clubs before the First World War in Britain and abroad may have developed a rough equality between men and women not seen before outside church or voluntary work, but it was an equality between middle-class men and middle-class women. For working-class people the gates of most tennis clubs before the First World War, and in some for decades after, remained firmly closed.

4

Stars

One day in the middle of July 1900, two brothers from London keep an appointment at a fashionable photographic studio in Paris. In front of an oil-painted landscape lit by the rays of an evening sun, they pose for the camera in long white shirts, black socks and perfectly pressed white trousers. Both young men have fine features no longer hidden by the moustaches that had been fashionable for Victorian gentlemen only a few years before. Reginald Doherty stretches out languidly on the studio floor while his younger brother Laurie, like Reggie tall and thin, sits up behind looking only a little less bored with the proceedings. They ooze a sense of effortless superiority as they stare into the distance with neatly waved dark-brown hair parted seductively down the middle. It is a ravishing look, a photographic pin-up for the new Edwardian age that will be ushered in when Queen Victoria dies in six months' time. The Dohertys' fame, though, comes not from the popular entertainments of theatre or music hall but from sport, the sport of lawn tennis.

The visit to the studio had been arranged to mark Laurie's victory in the Men's Singles at the 2nd Olympic Games held in Paris in the summer of 1900. Lawn tennis had been included in the games at the insistence of the organiser, Baron Pierre de Coubertin, a tennis fan. The tennis competition took place at his club, the Cercle de Sports, on the Île de Puteaux in the middle of the River Seine in the second week of July. In the men's final, powerful volleys and what one commentator of the time described as a 'perfect smash' enabled Laurie Doherty to brush aside the other finalist, a 33-year-old Irishman called Harold Mahony. Mahony had been Wimbledon champion a few years before but was now known on the tournament circuit more for his romantic entanglements than his speed about court. It is doubtful though if anyone could have stopped the 25-year-old Doherty that week. He was playing exceptionally well. The only competitor who might have beaten him was his brother Reggie, three years older and the current Wimbledon champion. But when the brothers met in the semi-final, Reggie refused to play his younger brother in 'such a minor tournament' and withdrew.

Reginald Doherty may well have come to regret this act of brotherly hubris because his health deteriorated after the Olympics and he never won a major singles title again, while Laurie went on to win Wimbledon five times. The moment in the photographic studio in July 1900 captures the two men at the point when the younger brother is poised to take over from his older sibling. When the photograph was published in the brothers' autobiography three years later, it marked not just the ascendancy of Laurie Doherty to stardom but also the shift that had taken place in lawn tennis from a parochial pastime played in the British Isles to a popular sport contested on the international stage.

At the Paris Olympics that summer of 1900, there were more French tennis players than British, a sign that the sport had become firmly established on that side of the Channel. Lawn tennis was played there shortly after it made its debut in Britain. The sales ledgers for Major Wingfield tennis sets for the 1874/5 financial year show that several were bought by customers living in France. In 1877 the Decimal Club was founded in Paris by ten British residents of the city and it was followed by tennis clubs in Dinard, Le Havre and resorts in the south. Perhaps because of its resemblance to *jeu du paume*, a popular indoor game in France similar to real tennis, the French quickly became enchanted with this new form of tennis played outdoors on a lawn. What they were not so keen on was the actual lawn.

On the Côte d'Azur, where tennis flourished in the late 1870s and 1880s, grass courts wilted under the rays of the Mediterranean sun, so a new surface made out of crushed brick, ceramic or stone was tried. This became known as 'red clay' and it stood up well to high temperatures while handling a tennis ball as dependably as grass, although the rallies were longer since clay took pace off the ball. The tennis at the Paris Olympics in 1900 was played on red clay courts and the French players were expected to do well against the British who had learned their tennis on the faster surface of grass. That would have been the case, if it hadn't been for the Riviera.

Since the late eighteenth century, the Riviera had established a reputation as the winter destination of choice for the English aristocracy who went there for health and recreation. The arrival of the railway in Nice in the 1860s opened up the coast to other kinds of visitors. If the south of France had not yet become, in Somerset Maugham's words, a 'sunny place for shady people',[1] in the last two decades of the nineteenth century it attracted the European *demi* as well as *beau monde*. The warm temperatures, sparkling sun, turquoise sea and umbrella pine trees enchanted American entrepreneurs, German princes and Parisian *rentiers*; painters like Henri Matisse and philosophers like Friedrich Nietzsche, who wrote his 1886 masterpiece, *Beyond Good and Evil*, amid the greenery and waterfalls of the Parc de Chateaux in Nice.

Into this melange strolled the first lawn tennis players from Britain as they looked for somewhere to practice in the winter months when the grass courts at home were submerged under water or frost. One day in the autumn of 1883 a young man from Cheltenham stepped out of the Gare de Cannes, a small, elegant building with a rooftop spanning both tracks of the railway line, one track going east to Nice, the other west to Marseille. William Renshaw was 23 years old. A few months before, he had won the Men's Singles at Wimbledon for the third time, the last two years against his twin Ernest. He knew he could always beat Ernest, but now that the net was lower – in 1883 it was reduced to its present height, three feet six inches at the posts, three feet at the centre – the topspin of the London stockbroker Herbert Lawford would become more of a problem. Renshaw could see that his usual winter practice with Herbert Chipp and Robert Osborn at the indoor courts of the Hyde Park Club would no longer be sufficient preparation. He needed to go south, where tennis could be played outdoors all year around. The upmarket 'English' tourist town of Cannes, with its reputation for games, seemed the perfect place to start. The first lawn tennis court in the town had been laid out at the home of a British landowner in late 1874.

Winding his way down from Cannes station through the acacia and mimosa trees that dotted the newly constructed *Croisette*, Renshaw headed for the Hotel Beau-Site. The Beau-Site had recently been advertised in *Bradshaw's* continental travel guide as offering 'an unequalled view of the Sea' in the 'finest part of the town' with 'extensive Croquet Ground and Lawn Tennis'.[2] The ad was placed by the hotel's new owner, Georges Gougoltz, a Swiss entrepreneur with a somewhat careless attitude to money which would eventually lead him to bankruptcy and then, in 1902, to three bullets in the head which the local police passed off as suicide. In the early 1880s, however, he was very much alive and determined to turn the Beau-Site into the most attractive hotel in town whatever the cost. He redesigned the hotel's gardens and constructed half a dozen striking red clay courts surrounded by terraces of orange and eucalyptus trees. They were the first hard courts on the Riviera, perhaps the first in the world. Certainly at that time they were the best.

That Riviera winter of 1883 and all subsequent winters that decade when his twin Ernest joined him, William Renshaw perfected his game. The brothers had learned lawn tennis at school in Cheltenham where they excelled at sport. After serving in the Royal Lancashire Militia, they looked around for something to do. Their father, Charles, a successful industrial magnate, had died leaving them enough money never to have to work and lawn tennis seemed as suitable a way as any to pass the time. Ernest was the quicker, more gifted player but William took the ball earlier, struck it harder and was cooler under pressure. In the south of France, days were spent by the twins on the Beau-Site's tennis courts hitting balls backwards and forwards much like modern practice by professionals today. Like today's star players too, their practice enticed spectators. Tennis, reported the *New York Times*, was the 'centre of attraction in the winter months' and the Renshaw brothers can be 'seen at all times hard at work'.[3]

The brothers kept no diary of their time in Cannes but in the evenings it seems likely they relaxed at the casino or at one of the many parties given by the town's wealthy visitors. 'At the tennis one meets everyone', Agatha Christie's creation, Hercule Poirot, would later proclaim.[4] The two handsome young men would have been as much in demand as dancing partners at night as well as demonstrators of lawn tennis during the day.

Ernest was the better dancer but it was William who profited most from their Riviera sojourns. He went on to win Wimbledon another three times, beating the 'grim, determined' Lawford each time in contests which Herbert Chipp later remembered as the 'high-water mark of lawn tennis'.[5] Ernest reached the Wimbledon final four times but won only once in 1888 when William couldn't play. Together with Lottie Dod and Blanche Hillyard, the two female champions with whom they played mixed doubles, the Renshaw twins transformed tournament tennis from a game played as an amusing hobby to one that was a full-time sport. William and Ernest introduced shots like the smash and the lob and turned the overhead serve from a simple way of starting a game into a weapon feared by all. Their elegant, aggressive game was buttressed by impeccable sportsmanship. This combination of exciting shots, youthful good looks and unblemished manners attracted a new audience to tennis who were not players themselves but spectators who would willingly pay for the Renshaws to entertain them.

We know little about these early spectators, the first tennis fans. The memoirs about tennis are written by champions not by those who watched them. Many of the Victorian upper middle-class men who organised sport in the late nineteenth century looked down on the experience of watching as 'mindless fanaticism, obstinate and arbitrary ... little different from mobs that had baited bulls'.[6] This was simply snobbery since many football and cricket fans came from skilled working-class backgrounds while in tennis the most enthusiastic spectators were often young women. It was also inaccurate. Watching sport was far from mindless. Following a tennis game required an appreciation of how different individuals played and how shot selection was as important as fluent hitting of the ball. These first tennis spectators, like the first football and cricket fans, were participating in a shared experience which was stimulating, relaxing and fun. If tennis as a spectator sport was not at the time in the same league as cricket (in 1892, 100,000 people watched Nottingham play Surrey in an ordinary three-day county cricket game) or football (in the 1890s, the new professional league attracted two million people every season) it did well enough. In the late 1880s, the Wimbledon fortnight drew over 20,000 people. They were crucial to the development of the game.

If spectators hadn't flocked to watch the first tennis tournaments, the sport would have ended up like its contemporary, badminton, adored by the millions of people who play (more people in the world today play badminton than tennis) but ignored by everyone else. Tennis became a world sport to rival football and cricket because it reached out to a wider public who loved seeing their idols perform on an outdoor stage, and there were no idols in the first decades of lawn tennis who performed better than William and Ernest Renshaw.

Each year the twins played Wimbledon attendances went up in what became known as the 'Renshaw rush'. This spread out from the All England Club to other tennis tournaments held in cities and holiday resorts first around Britain and Ireland and then on the continent. Cities like Manchester and Baden Baden, Nice and Scheveningen competed for the top players by offering generous appearance fees and considerable prize money. Wimbledon, however, remained at the pinnacle of the game, not only because of its historic role as the first major tennis tournament but also because of the care taken by the All England Club to ensure that every summer its Championships were a unique experience featuring guaranteed stars like the Renshaws. In 1890, however, the twins retired and there were no players charismatic enough to step into their spotlight. For a decade spectators stayed away until they were lured back by two men, also brothers but not twins, who had star appeal etched into their every shot.

Reggie and Laurie Doherty were born in Beulah Road, Wimbledon, just across the railway line from the All England Club in Worple Road. There is no record of them ever watching the Renshaws play but on a warm Saturday in the middle of July 1885, when Laurie Doherty was 10 and Reginald 13, 3,000 people passed through Wimbledon station to see William Renshaw win his fifth singles title and the crowds would have been impossible to miss. Perhaps seeing them ignited the desire in Laurie and Reggie to play tennis at championship level. It was a desire that lasted all their lives and started in their mid-teens.

In 1887, Reginald won a tournament in Wales when he was 15. Three years later in 1890, when he was the same age, Laurie won the National Under 16 Boys' Championships held that year in Scarborough. The Doherty brothers were undoubtedly blessed with a natural ability to hit a ball but, like the Renshaw twins, they recognised the danger of relying on talent alone. They both worked hard at developing a solid technique. The elegant ease on court in summer tournaments, which became a Doherty trademark, came from months of dedicated winter practice, honing their shots so that they seemed to flow 'naturally' off their rackets. Much of this practice took place, like the Renshaws' a decade before, on the red clay courts of the Riviera, but not this time in Cannes. The serious players had by then moved up the coast to Nice. In Nice at the turn of the century, Reginald and Laurie Doherty perfected the 'English style' of play: not appearing to try too hard, always behaving with flawless courtesy, and caring more about playing the game than winning the trophy. It was, of course, a charade.

The Doherty brothers cared very much about trophies and the rewards that came with victory. Unlike the Renshaws, they had no private income. Their father was a printer successful enough to pay for their education at Westminster School and Cambridge University but not willing or able to subsidise them after that. They had to find jobs in the City until they were able to make money from tennis to support themselves. Their leisured existence on the Côte d'Azur, where they became known as 'princes of the Riviera', was sustained by giving lessons to the wintering rich and negotiating fees and 'expenses' at the tournaments they played up and down the Mediterranean coast.

In London, too, the brothers took every opportunity to cash in on their fame. The 'Doherty Lawn Tennis Racket', manufactured by Slazenger, was available for two decades. It was just one example of how the brothers turned their name into a brand. In 1903, they published a best-selling manual about the game, *R.F. & H.L. Doherty on Lawn Tennis*, and they would make themselves available anytime for interviews and photo sessions with popular newspapers like the *Daily Mail*, launched in 1896 and developing a reputation for its stories about the stars. In the first decade of the twentieth century, there were few stars who worked harder than the Dohertys at seeming to be so effortless at everything they did.

The brothers were a major factor in returning Wimbledon to popularity and profitability. In 1904, the All England Club made a profit of £1,400. In the years before the First World War, the Championships became a vivid illustration of the British Empire at its most powerful and flamboyant. Every July the old ground at Worple Road was decked out with flowers and ribbons. Women in neat dresses, huge feathered hats and gaily decorated parasols strolled along the terraces before taking tea on the lawn which was served by white-aproned waitresses. Royalty was often present. Queen Victoria was known to have tried tennis at Balmoral, but she never went to Wimbledon. Now, in 1910, her grandson, King George V, became patron of the club and would often turn up to watch the finals while his son, the Prince of Wales, was present for most of the fortnight. This vivid spectacle every July became a key event for upper-class society but would never have happened without the Dohertys, two middle-class boys from the suburbs. When Laurie Doherty died in 1919, *The Times* mourned him as a 'loss to the lawn tennis community, but it is more than that ... he played an English game in the spirit in which Englishmen think games should be played'.[7]

It was a moving tribute to a mere tennis player, but what it failed to mention is that by the time this obituary was published, most lawn tennis champions no longer played the game in an English spirit for one very obvious reason. They weren't English. In 1905, May Sutton, a nerveless 18 year old from California, became the first player from outside the British Isles to win a Wimbledon singles title. Two years later she won again, and 1907 also saw the Men's Singles go to a player from outside Britain for the first time, Norman Brooks from Australia. It was the beginning of the end of British domination at Wimbledon, at least in singles. Since 1919, foreigners have commandeered this 'English' game. In the last 100 years, the Wimbledon Women's Singles has been won by 40 different players from countries as diverse as Brazil, Russia and Romania. Only five have come from Britain and none since Virginia Wade in 1977. Of the 52 players who won the Men's Singles in this time, only two – Fred Perry and Andy Murray – were British. The other 50 have been spread across the globe from Serbia to Australia, Switzerland to the United States. This foreign takeover of lawn tennis, at least in the most popular game of singles, was virtually complete by 1920. It has made little difference to attendances at Wimbledon or to the enjoyment of spectators.

Conventional histories of tennis emphasise the conservatism of Wimbledon and its obsession with class, status and tradition. These certainly became a noteworthy feature during this time, but so did something else which is only mentioned in passing if it is mentioned at all. While fans from other sports identify with place, tennis fans at Wimbledon connect with character. The spectators at the annual Championships, most of whom have been British, have consistently shown a refreshing ability to embrace a new champion whatever their nationality, and this started in these years around the First World War. Whether a champion becomes a star and a favourite of the Wimbledon crowd over the years has depended more on personality than place of birth. In 1910, Wimbledon embraced Antony Wilding from New Zealand when he won the first of his four singles titles at the expense of his British challenger, Arthur Gore. Other champions the Wimbledon crowd have loved included Maria Bueno, the first champion from South America in the late 1950s, the stateless Jaroslav Drobny who was at his best a few years earlier, the fiercely nationalistic Goran Ivanisevic from Croatia who was one of the most popular Wimbledon champions in 2001 and, in 1919, a startling young woman from France.

It was the first Championships for six years. Wimbledon had closed down for the First World War and Europe had been through five years of slaughter with millions of young men dead including Wilding, the best player of his generation. When the gates at the old ground in Worple Road opened on June 23, people had queued all night. The desire to forget about the war was strong and what better distraction than to spend a couple of weeks watching a feast of sporting skill where all that mattered was getting a ball over a net. If Wilding was sadly no longer around, there were whispers of a new star whose play was reputedly more thrilling than any in the history of the women's game. Suzanne Lenglen did not disappoint. Even though she was barely out of her teens, she took to the Wimbledon stage like a princess surrounded by an entourage of admirers. Her origins, though, were humble enough.

She was born in 1899, a child of the provincial bourgeoisie in Compiegne, a small urban *department* north of Paris. Her parents owned a carriage company, which was not immensely profitable but had enabled them to buy a small holiday home in the south of France. On one of their Mediterranean visits, Suzanne's father Charles noticed the popularity of lawn tennis and how its star English players like the Doherty brothers enjoyed a privileged place in Riviera society. Charles Lenglen decided this charmed life was a better prospect for his only child than the carriage business. Although Suzanne's mother, Anais, was a strong presence and well known for her acid comments, it was Charles who made his daughter the most famous woman in the world.

When Suzanne was barely in her teens, Papa Lenglen developed a training regime which bordered on abuse. On the dusty red clay courts of the south of France, when the English players had retired for tea, he worked Suzanne hard and his criticisms were severe. He ordered her to hit ball after ball after ball with pinpoint precision. He made her skip and jump around court as if she were a dancer. Above all he taught her to regard any error in a match as unforgivable, a point given away. It was a harsh regime, but Suzanne and her mother had no complaints. It turned Suzanne Lenglen into a champion.

At her Wimbledon debut in 1919 she thrilled the crowd not simply by her play – she won her way through to the women's final with ease – but by her style. On court, she wore a short mid-calf skirt designed by Parisian couturier Jean Patou. Around her shoulders was a fashionable cardigan in red or orange which she changed every match. Around her head she wrapped a bandeau of shaded silk chiffon, a look she borrowed from the ballet. In 1913, the impresario Sergei Diaghilev had staged *Jeux* in Paris with music from Claude Debussy. It featured three dancers, one male and two female, searching for a lost tennis ball. Six years later, when Suzanne Lenglen made her debut at Wimbledon, she looked like something out of *Jeux* except her ball was never lost. She danced around her early opponents with athletic jumps and it was impossible to take your eyes off her. In between points, Lenglen repaired her make-up, blew kisses to her fans and sucked sugar cubes soaked with brandy. When she finished a match, victorious as usual, she wrapped herself up in white ermine fur and received admirers in the bath. Her detractors called her the 'French Hussey' but her fans could not care less. One of them, Rudyard Kipling, remarked that she 'positively clawed the balls out of the sky' while another, the tennis designer Teddy Tinling, recalled that Suzanne was 'not a beautiful woman' – she had a long jaw and strong face – but she was 'a beautiful athlete'. Women, Tinling added, 'worshipped Suzanne for daring to enact their secret dreams'.[8]

That summer of 1919, it seemed inevitable that Suzanne Lenglen would win the Women's Singles at Wimbledon and that it would be the first of many. Her opponent in the final was Dorothea Lambert Chambers, a once-formidable British player who had won Wimbledon seven times, although the last was before the First World War and she was now 40 years old.

Suzanne was just 20. They met on a cloudless day in July and the contrast between them was stark.

Lenglen was surrounded by crowds. Lambert Chambers was alone with her wooden racket. Lenglen's dress was startlingly brief, a simple frock with short sleeves, white stockings and no foundation garments which anticipated the relaxation in women's dress the next decade would bring. Lambert Chambers wore a weighty, ankle length Edwardian skirt, mannish blazer, shirt fastened at the neck and steel-boned corset and seemed buried in the past. Her square, plain face was covered with an eye shield while Lenglen's fashionably bobbed hair blew freely in the breeze. As the two women warmed up, it became clear to the 8,000 people who had crammed into Centre Court that this would be a tussle between the steady but penetrating ground shots of the Englishwoman, a vicar's daughter from Ealing, and the rapier volleys and all-court balletic game of the girl from Compiegne. So it turned out. Every point was fiercely contested in a final that was remembered for many years.

In the first set the score fluctuated backwards and forwards until the Frenchwoman won 10–8. In the second, Lambert Chambers' 'long sweeping strokes' pushed Lenglen back to the baseline where she was less effective. Lambert Chambers won 6–4, the first set Lenglen had lost for several years. At this point both players requested a short interval. Lenglen asked for brandy. Lambert Chambers was tempted to retire. 'I felt I had had enough exercise for one day', she later recalled, 'and there was another set to be played'.[9]

In her book, *Lawn Tennis for Ladies*, published almost ten years before, Dorothea Lambert Chambers maintained that female players in a match should not worry about looking pretty but be content to show 'signs of excitement', 'muscles strained' and 'face set'. Now she did not disguise how excited she was nor how exhausted she felt. In her book too, she had also claimed that lawn tennis required 'scientific application, finesse, skill and delicacy of touch all of which women are just as capable of exercising as men'.[10] And exercise them now she did.

In the final set she went 6–5 up and had two match points, but then nervous exhaustion set in. Lenglen was also feeling the strain. She came up to the net after one of her short returns which, according to Lambert Chambers, she would 'never normally do'. Lambert Chambers lobbed her but her stroke was not quite deep enough. Lenglen put her racket up more out of hope than anything else. Lambert Chambers remembers precisely what happened next. The ball 'touched the tip of the wood and hit the top of the net falling on my side. She told me afterwards she never saw the ball and if ever there was a lucky shot it was that one.'[11]

Luck stayed with Lenglen that afternoon. She survived a second match point and went on to win her first Wimbledon title 9–7. At 46 games it was one of the longest women's finals ever. The enraptured King George V sent down a message saying he would like to congratulate them both in the Royal Box but they were too wiped out. Suzanne's feet were bleeding and Dorothea's corset stained in blood. Instead of taking tea with royalty, the two women went back to the women's locker room together, washed, changed and became the best of friends.

Suzanne's success in 1919 cemented her fame. In the next six years she never lost at Wimbledon, and only once elsewhere, as she rewrote the rules for women's tennis. She played aggressively in mixed doubles and her comprehensive repertoire and stubborn self-reliance epitomised the independent and ambitious 'new woman' of the 1920s. Lenglen's captivating public manner made her a star, and her antics off court were followed by the press as avidly as any Hollywood actress. She became a global celebrity, the first sportswoman to be referred to by just her first name. Her box office appeal also gave the All England Club the confidence to move in 1922 from Worple Road near Wimbledon station to much larger premises in Church Road a mile and a half past Wimbledon village, where it has been ever since.

Lambert Chambers spent a few winters playing on the Riviera and then retired from competitive tennis, raised a family and became a professional coach, one of the first in Britain. Her old-fashioned feminism, forthright manner and modest dress stopped her from becoming a star even with all the titles she won. *Lawn Tennis for Ladies*, though, has never been out of print partly because it ranged far wider than sport. 'Woman,' she wrote, 'is a second edition of man if you like and like most second editions an improvement.'[12]

Suzanne Lenglen's stardom proved more problematic for her and for female tennis players ever since. While many of the women who flocked to see her regarded her as a role model, many of the men came to see glimpses of her bare thighs. There was nothing new in tennis about women's bodies being on parade. It was there from the 1880s, which was one reason why some Victorian husbands tried to restrain their wives from taking up the game. What Lenglen did was push this gaze up another level. The price of her fame was not simply that she shared her performances on court with her fans. She shared her identity as well. The focus she brought to her female body in the 1920s meant that women players subsequently had to meet higher standards of dress and deportment on the tennis court than men as their physical appearance faced much greater scrutiny.

Lenglen remained under public scrutiny all her life, particularly when she turned professional,[13] but for the last decade she found the demands of stardom too difficult to cope with. She never married and died in 1938 of anaemia at only 39 years old, still struggling to come to terms with the man who dominated her life, her father Charles. She was not the only one of these early tennis stars to die young. The Doherty brothers died at 38 and 43. In a bizarre coincidence, so did the Renshaw twins at exactly the same ages. None of them ever married. William Renshaw died of epileptic convulsions, Laurie Doherty of anaemia, Reginald Doherty of heart failure – all natural causes, but I wonder about the role the stress of being a star played. It does seem odd that they all died around 40 years old, and that this wasn't true of other tennis champions from their time who never became celebrities. Dorothea Lambert Chambers lived till she was 81. Herbert Lawford died when he was 82, the Reverend John Hartley when he was 86. Charlotte Cooper lived till she was 96. But in those early days of sporting stardom there were no agents to protect the players, no psychologists to soothe them, no previous stars to pass on their wisdom. If there had been, perhaps at least Ernest Renshaw would have lived longer. He died from ingesting carbolic acid at just 38 years old.

5

Players

In the early 1920s, George Newnes, an enterprising publisher based in London, spotted the potential of a lovable rogue called William Brown. William was the hero of several stories that had appeared in *Home Notes* magazine which detailed the boy's amusing escapades with a gang of friends known as 'The Outlaws'. The publishers thought there might be a wider audience if these stories were collected in a book, and their instinct proved correct. *Just William*, published in 1922, was a bestseller. The adventures of an eleven-year-old rebel in a village not far from suburban Bromley seemed to chime with adults as well as children and came as a welcome relief from vivid memories of the First World War.

Another popular distraction from reminders of war in 1920s Britain was sport, particularly the new sport of lawn tennis, which soon started popping up in William's world. In *William Again*, published in 1923, Robert and Ethel, William's grown-up brother and sister, had 'joined a tennis club and were out all day'. 'Or what they call tennis', William moaned to his mother, aggrieved at being excluded once more from adult fun and suspecting something else was going on than a mere game.[1]

William's creator was a young unmarried schoolteacher called Richmal Crompton, who taught classics at Bromley High School. The year she wrote *William Again*, she lost the use of a leg from polio and so was unable to join a tennis club, an increasingly popular activity in the 1920s for young, single women. In her stories, the game of lawn tennis does not come out well. William's sister, Ethel, has taken up tennis solely to find a husband and William's tennis-obsessed older brother, Robert, is portrayed as a social climber whose main ambitions are to own a swanky sports car and become secretary of his local tennis club.

Around the same time as the *Just William* stories were being conceived, a young man called Arthur Bell really did take over as secretary of Richmal Crompton's local tennis club, Bromley Wendover. The previous secretary, Percy Gardner, a clerk with Martins Bank, was killed at the Battle of Bellancourt in France in May 1917 and Bromley Wendover Lawn Tennis Club had been reduced to 16 members. Within 18 months, Bell helped push its membership back up to 56, but he was not entirely satisfied with how the club was developing. In his report for 1920 he appealed to the more aspiring members 'to mix in with everyone' and not form 'cliques'.[2] He clearly didn't want people in his club like the fictional Robert Brown.

Orthodox histories of lawn tennis portray the 1920s and 1930s as a time that cemented the sport's reputation in Britain and elsewhere as an activity for the entitled or aspirational. In the popular culture of these decades, if it wasn't a character like Robert Brown using a tennis club to impress, then it was a sallow young man dressed in a striped blazer coming through conservatory doors and asking, 'tennis anyone?', as indeed Humphrey Bogart did in his very first appearance on stage on Broadway in 1933. There is some truth in these tropes, although they do not represent the whole picture. Tennis between the wars was used as a tool for social advancement, and many tennis clubs in Britain if not across the world did develop a reputation for being 'stuck-up'.[3] But these narratives ignore other aspects of the sport at this time which were more egalitarian, even progressive. Arthur Bell in Bromley wasn't alone in wanting his more snobbish tennis club members to welcome everyone in. It was a wish reflected not just in Britain but in other parts of the world.

When Suzanne Lenglen won her first Wimbledon in 1919, seven different countries were represented in the Men's or Women's Singles. By the time she died in 1938, that number had risen to 38 including players from Argentina, India, China, Indonesia, Mexico and South Africa. When the International Lawn Tennis Federation moved to London the following year, it had 59 member nations. Lawn tennis had spread far beyond its initial outposts in European holiday resorts and the white communities of the old British Empire to become a truly global sport. In the mid-1920s you could find the game played on the carefully manicured grass of exclusive clubs from Boston to Bombay; the soft red clay of suburban tennis clubs from Rome to Rio; the hard cement, asphalt or tarmacadam favoured by local authorities in municipal parks from Sheffield to San Francisco; the wooden boards that covered disused skating rinks in Liverpool and London. The two decades between the wars saw an expansion in tennis as a popular sport that had not been seen before or since. This was particularly true in the United States.

In the early 1880s, the novelist Edith Wharton was engaged to Henry Stevens, the son of a wealthy businessman and one of the first American tennis players. Much of her carousing with Stevens at this time is captured in fictional form in her most acclaimed book, *The Age of Innocence*, which includes a powerful image of the moment when tennis surfaced in American society. 'The Newport Archery Club always held its August meeting at the Beauforts. The sport, which had hitherto known no rival but croquet, was beginning to be discarded in favour of lawn-tennis but the latter game was still considered too rough and inelegant for social occasions.'[4]

Any concerns about roughness and inelegance in early 1880s America were quickly brushed aside as tennis spread throughout the United States, initially through the new country clubs that had blossomed on the outskirts of cities and in the heart of opulent suburbs. Lawn tennis, the summer pastime originally played in country house Britain, fitted easily into country club America where old money met new wealth. While golf usually remained the clubs' strongest sporting attraction, some clubs like Germantown in Philadelphia, Tuxedo in New York and Longwood in Massachusetts specialised in tennis, and several of their best players proved good enough to enter Wimbledon. In 1900, the Americans beat the British in the first Davis Cup. By 1930, America had become the pre-eminent tennis nation, a position it kept for 70 years. The reasons were not difficult to find.

In the first three decades of the twentieth century, the United States developed the largest economy the world had ever seen with a people who were fitter and better fed than anywhere else. Like work and religion, Americans took their sport seriously and tennis chimed well with the heroic individualism at the heart of the stories Americans told themselves. If anybody could be president, anyone could win Wimbledon. All they had to do was put the work in. So American tennis developed a style of play different from the nonchalant elegance perfected by British champions like the Doherty brothers. 'Americans force the play', *Lawn Tennis and Cricket* had observed as early as 1904, while the British let their 'opponent beat himself up by his errors'.[5] What was noticeable at the time was the scientific seriousness in which Americans approached tennis, their emphasis on expert coaching and their insistence on finding the correct grip for every shot. British players continued to place their trust in self-reliance, pluck and using whichever grip felt right. There was another difference as well. While some top American players like Bill Tilden and Helen Wills came from comfortable backgrounds and learned to play at country clubs, others were from poorer families and learned their tennis in a public park.

Park tennis in America was pioneered in California where public courts date back to the 1880s. By 1901, the sport had become so popular in San Francisco that the city opened its own municipal tennis centre in Golden Gate Park, just a stroll from the park's famous windmills, carousels and Japanese tea garden. The centre had eight clay courts for adults and two for children and people could play there for just a few cents. One young man who did so was Maurice McLoughlin, who reached the final of Wimbledon in 1913. One young woman was Eleanor Tennant, who became America's first female tennis coach. Tennant's many prodigies would later include Wimbledon champions Bobby Riggs and Maureen Connolly, but the first player she propelled to stardom was Alice Marble who she saw play as a teenager in Golden Gate Park.

These days Marble's reputation is sealed as the glamorous blond in shorts who won Wimbledon in 1939 and then had a colourful life as a singer, actress, reporter and spy. When Tennant took her on, she was a volatile schoolgirl from a backwoods family who had moved from the country to San Francisco to find work. The young Alice wanted to play baseball but Tennant persuaded her to focus on tennis and turned her into a champion by teaching her the discipline to harness her naturally powerful strokes. Under Tennant's direction, Marble started following her serve into the net, learned to volley and smash as hard as a man and dressed in a clean-cut male style that exuded both beauty and power. Marble's talent, courage and attitude changed women's tennis, but without the public courts in Golden Gate Park and the perspicacity of Eleanor Tennant who, like several other people, was more than half in love with her, Alice Marble would have never taken up the game and one of the most colourful characters in the history of lawn tennis would have been lost.

In the first decades of the twentieth century, most cities across the United States copied San Francisco's model and built public courts where anybody could play (although in the south they were not available to black people). In 1923, the National Public Parks Tennis Association organised its first tournament for men followed a few years later by one for women. By the end of the 1920s, four million people played regularly in a public park, a sign that tennis in America had spread beyond its upper-middle-class beginnings to become a more inclusive sport, at least if you were white.

The first public courts in Britain date back to the 1880s: in Cannon Hill park, a vast open space just a mile south of Birmingham city centre, lawn tennis courts were marked out in 1883. By the turn of the century, most British cities and many towns offered tennis as one of the more popular attractions of their new municipal parks. The great expansion in public tennis in Britain, though, came with the Workmen's Act of 1905 which allowed local authorities to improve parks by hiring the unemployed. In the next three decades, thousands of public courts were constructed from Bristol to Birkenhead, St Helens to Scarborough. As soon as the courts were built, they were in use, such was the demand for the game.

In 1924 the tennis writer A.J. Aitken published *Lawn Tennis for Public Court Players* which was aimed at the '500,000 men and girls who play in the parks and on public courts'.[6] Aitken noted with 'great enthusiasm' that courts were being laid down everywhere. 'My study overlooks one of the largest fields of public lawn tennis courts in Great Britain. Play here begins at half past six in the morning so people can get a set in before work at 8.' The thirst for the game identified in Aitken's book – the only book I have discovered specifically aimed at park tennis players – was apparent all over the country in the 1920s. In Sheffield, public park tennis competitions attracted hundreds of entries. In Edinburgh, where a court cost two pence an hour, bookings had to be made well in advance. Tennis was played so passionately on the public courts in Manchester that the *Manchester Evening News* warned in 1925 of 'tennis intemperance'.[7] The park players there paid little heed. Their games of tennis were as competitive as in any private club.

In Birmingham in the 1920s there were as many people playing in the parks as there were in tennis clubs, as local tennis historian Ronald Lerry recalls: 'It was no uncommon sight to see players queuing up in Small Heath Park for a game. There was no advance booking and so no alternative but to wait patiently in a line. The booking system did not always work that well because the official in charge would occasionally adopt a "biblical method" – the first shall be last and the last shall be first.'[8] To deal with such autocratic behaviour, the Birmingham Parks Tennis Association was formed in 1923 to represent regular players. Like a dozen other similar associations nationwide, it organised its own leagues, arranged matches with other cities and put on a tournament every year with a Challenge Trophy sponsored by a local newspaper for the best player. One of the tasks of the Association's energetic treasurer, David Ayres, was to press Birmingham Council to convert some of the city's 360 grass courts to a hard surface which could be played on all year round. Birmingham council was reluctant to invest any more money in tennis, so in the spring of 1924 the canny Ayres, a friendly but persistent presence on court and off, arranged a match with Manchester, Birmingham's great rival for the title of Britain's second city. As Ayres anticipated, the northern city won easily because their public parks had 300 hard courts to Birmingham's 45, which enabled their players to practice all winter. Birmingham Council took note and found the money.

Another venture Ayres arranged was a friendly match with Edgbaston Priory, the most prestigious private tennis club in the city. 'Edgbaston Priory won comfortably,' Ronald Lerry reported, 'but the parks' players put up a creditable show. Thus the door to a wider world of lawn tennis was opened.' But, despite the Birmingham parks teams often having players like Ayres of 'considerable maturity', the number that actually passed through this door was 'small'.[9]

On one level, the reason was straightforward. The gulf in playing standards between a regular park player and an average tennis club member was wide. This was usually due, as A.J. Aitken pointed out, to technique. Park players often start 'hitting the ball naturally' but in tennis the 'best shots aren't the natural ways to hit the ball'. Instead you have to develop 'learned strokes'.[10] To learn these strokes, however, requires coaching. At the time Aitken published his book, in 1924, there were no more than a couple of dozen professional coaches in Britain and they were based not on the cold benches of a public park but in the warm clubhouses of the richer tennis clubs.

On another level, though, this technical explanation does not delve deep enough. There were many uninspiring players in even the most upmarket tennis clubs, as well as many park players like David Ayres himself who were close to county standard. The more fundamental reason why British tennis clubs never opened their gates to talented park players between the wars was class. Public park tennis in the first decades of the twentieth century attracted a wide variety of people, not perhaps the poorest or the unemployed – rackets and balls were still relatively expensive – but certainly men and women from the skilled working classes – bus drivers, postmen, hospital workers and miners. One study of sport in Liverpool noted that, in 1930, 100,000 players used the city's public tennis courts, many of them from working-class backgrounds, women as well as men. Another study in the same city showed that tennis the previous decade had been the fastest growing sport in the city.[11] This growing popularity among working people received no encouragement from private tennis clubs.

Most of the larger British tennis clubs between the wars had little interest in recruiting good players from the working class because they were preoccupied instead with a different class tension, that between the upper and the lower middle classes, between professional people and people who relied for their living on commerce and trade.

Sometime in 1905, a young London builder called Ernest Jarvis cycled out to Hertfordshire from his home in Enfield. He had heard there was land for sale in the small town of Harpenden, 33 miles from London. The main railway line from London to the north routed through the Harpenden valley and Jarvis could see that the place, less than an hour by train to London, was ready for expansion. He bought a parcel of land and started building houses for people who worked in the City of London and were looking for a home in suburbia. Jarvis liked Harpenden and in 1910 decided to settle in the town himself, building a rather larger house for his family than the usual Jarvis home. He applied to join Harpenden Lawn Tennis Club but was turned down. Even though he was running what was already one of the most energetic businesses in the area, Jarvis was not acceptable to the club because he was 'trade'.

After the First World War he tried again, this time with his younger brother Frank. Frank Jarvis was as mad about tennis as his brother but a good deal better. A dashing left-hander, he had played for Oxford University, reached the fourth round at Wimbledon and participated in a private match with the Duke of York, later King George VI. With such talent and connections on offer, it proved difficult for Harpenden Lawn Tennis Club to resist the Jarvis brothers despite their occupations as 'mere' builders. Even so there was debate in the club about whether they would really 'fit in' and whether they could have Frank without Ernest. They decided they would take a chance on both and within a few years the Jarvis brothers were helping run the club. Frank's skill on court and Ernest's 'wicked sense of humour' removed any lingering prejudice club members had against trade. It also changed the club's style for ever.[12]

Many British tennis clubs went through a similar transformation in the decades between the wars and this was their great achievement. They provided a place for the various sections of the British middle classes to come together at play. Previously golf clubs had absorbed the energies of the commercial middle class but now tennis took over. Only 239 golf clubs were founded between 1919 and 1939, fewer than in the 1890s. Tennis clubs in Britain more than doubled in this time reaching a peak of 3,220 in 1937, and these were only the clubs affiliated to the Lawn Tennis Association. There were probably twice as many that were too small or too poor to afford the annual association subscription. Nottinghamshire, for example, had 500 clubs between the wars with an average size of between 50 and 100 members. Even the smallest of villages in the county had a tennis club, as did most churches with the 'vicar or minister often providing the land for the court'.[13] If you were middle class in Britain in the 1930s you joined a tennis club. It wasn't simply that tennis at this time expressed middle-class identity. It forged it.

This new class identity that tennis clubs in Britain offered between the wars was particularly attractive to the lower middle class who could afford the moderately priced houses builders like Ernest Jarvis were putting up on the edges of towns and cities. Three million homes were built in the suburbs between 1919 and 1939, and if these houses – as George Orwell memorably described in his 1938 novel, *Coming Up for Air* – all had the same 'stucco front, creosoted gate, privet hedge, green front door' with names like 'The Laurels', 'The Hawthorns', 'The Myrtles' and 'Belle Vue', they were at least pleasant places to live.[14] They also tended to be close to a tennis club, which held out the allure of something precious and priceless: social advancement.

The opportunities for social climbing came not so much from the actual tennis a club offered but from the wide variety of events it organised, which included dances, picnics and dinners. In March 1935, Waverley tennis club in Edinburgh celebrated 50 years of lawn tennis with a dinner dance and bridge. Finals' day at the Telford Park Tennis Club in Streatham, south London 'resumed its pre-war elegance of dress, band, club entertainers and Chinese lanterns' in the 1920s.[15] The difference now in clubs like Waverley and Telford Park was that people in commerce or trade were as welcome as the professions. One new member in Streatham was a 24 year old called Dennis Wheatley who worked in his family's wine business. During the time he was at Telford Park Lawn Tennis Club, Wheatley started writing popular novels that specialised in Satanism, but there are, unfortunately, no references to tennis clubs in *The Devil Rides Out* or in any of his other occult novels, or at least none I could find.

Telford Park was at the more select end of the tennis club spectrum. Even here, though, the people who were the backbone of the club tended to be lower rather than upper middle class. Apart from symbolic positions of leadership like 'president' and 'chairman', which were usually filled by local notaries, tennis clubs at this time were kept going by the energy and commitment of the schoolteacher, the bank clerk, the insurance official and their spouses. The culture of the British tennis club changed from one derived from the manners of the upper and professional middle class to one inspired by the etiquette of the white-collar worker. For many of these members of the new middle class, the tennis club became their life, especially for women who dominated club tennis in the 1920s when it was difficult for some clubs to find new male members.

In 1929, Elaine Lewis joined Aberaeron tennis club on the west coast of Wales after going away to college and then returning to her home town. 'Tennis was my game. I had two rackets to play with. One was a Slazenger which had been brought home for me as a present by my sea-faring father. It was special because it had my name printed on it.'[16] Soon she was spending every evening playing tennis. 'The boys were expected to mow the court and cut the tall grass around to save our losing balls in it. We started at 4.30pm and played if possible until we couldn't see a ball.'[17] In the 1930s, Elaine usually turned out for the club's first team in a long white tennis dress which came down to her ankles. Unlike Waverley and Telford Park tennis clubs, Aberaeron did not have the money for dinner-dances or Chinese lanterns. 'Match day was a great occasion. Tea had to be prepared and a fire was lit at the back of the pavilion to boil a large tin kettle.' Food was provided by players and to have 'egg and tomato sandwiches was a real treat. Biscuits were far too expensive to buy.'

The scrimping and saving Elaine Lewis witnessed in mid-Wales was common in many tennis clubs all over Britain during the recession of the early 1930s when dinner-dances were replaced by penny hops. There were a few wealthy tennis clubs which seemed unaffected by the economic downturn and kept their elegant restaurants, champagne bars and tea served by waiters on the lawn, but these clubs were a minority, perhaps only a few dozen in the major cities in Britain and throughout the world. Most tennis clubs at this time were seriously strapped for cash. The facilities at Surbiton Tennis Club, one of the most famous in the country with its annual Surrey Championships attracting players from all over the world, remained rudimentary. 'The club pavilion consisted of two small rooms and a sort of room in between with a counter running along the front which came in handy at teatime. Hot water and baths were seldom met with in pavilions those days. The club colours, chocolate with a thin red stripe, were not beautiful except to the eye of the Hon Secretary Elmhurst O. Dunn who invented them.'[18] When Dunn died, there was no money to repaint. In 1930, the club was in severe financial difficulties and faced closure which it only managed to avoid by calling a special meeting and begging its members to bail it out.

In Stockport, the conditions at another renowned tennis club, Bramhall Lane, remained equally primitive. Members came in 'via a wide field gate' approached by walking on a path across the fields. For refreshment, tea was served in the shed, the water carried in milk cans from a nearby member's house and then boiled up on a primus stove. In Suffolk, 'stuck-up' Felixstowe Tennis Club experienced the early 1930s as 'worrying years'. Subscriptions could not 'cover expenses as the effects of the economic depression were being felt in Felixstowe as in other parts of the world'.[19]

Many British tennis clubs were in a similar position in the years before the Second World War and the obvious solution would have been to expand membership by recruiting the best players in their local park. But that would mean allowing into the club not just people who worked in the wine trade like Dennis Wheatley, or ran successful building companies like Ernest Jarvis, but gas fitters, railway workers, engineers and craftsmen. These people, in turn, would change the nature of the club as they would bring with them their own traditions, cultures and politics. There was a danger, more imagined than real, that much of the pleasure of a tennis club – the cliquey familiarity of being around similar souls – would vanish and the friendship networks painstakingly established over years of dances and doubles would be diluted and perhaps disappear. This was too much to bear, but it was a moment when both the image and the reality of club tennis in Britain could have shifted forever, a moment that was missed.

The exclusion of working-class people from many private tennis clubs was (and to some extent still is) a blight on tennis in Britain and in other countries across the world, although it is fair to point out that this is true not just of tennis clubs but other sports with a predominately middle-class clientele like golf, badminton and bowls. In tennis it never seems to have been a deliberate policy. It certainly would have been frowned upon by Lottie Dod, Blanche Hillyard, Robert Osborn, Harry Gem, Henry Jones and many of the feminists and mavericks who first championed the game in the 1870s and 1880s. It was also true, as the sociologist Joyce Kay points out, that there were many smaller tennis clubs in between the wars in Britain that happily admitted anyone who wanted to play, whatever their background.[20] In the larger and more prestigious clubs, however, during this time tennis became an identifying marker of being middle class.

One way to keep out people who were not middle class was to ensure that the cost of joining a club was 'large enough to exclude most working class incomes.'[21] Another was through geography. Many clubs were often hidden away in the suburbs behind hedges and lime trees where 'the shelter afforded was not so much from the sun as from the intrusive gaze of the common herd.'[22] If working people did make the effort to travel there and find a club, they often found the atmosphere and ethos intimidating. People talked differently, as Gwendolen Freeman, a female insurance collector in Birmingham in the 1930s, discovered when she visited houses in the poorer areas of the city. She wasn't accepted because she spoke 'lawn tennis' and so was not to be trusted.[23] In the years between the wars, to be a member of many British tennis clubs you had to do more than just play lawn tennis, you had to be able to speak it too.

Instead of recruiting people who didn't speak 'lawn tennis', tennis clubs during this time relied on existing members to keep afloat, often by encouraging them to bring their children even though it would mean the adults surrendering court time. The other way to ensure survival was to cut costs. Saving money became a major pre-occupation and fund raising an essential strategy to ensure bills were paid. At Hazlewood Lawn Tennis Club in north London, money-making schemes included a matchbox label competition, a gymkhana and a pin-ball machine in the clubhouse. In Aberaeron, club members bought lemonade from the local shops which they then 'diluted and sold at a profit' as well as currant buns which were 'cut in half and sold for half a penny each.'[24] At Birkenhead Lawn Tennis Club, the recession of 1931 led to Mr Derrigan, the groundsman, 'put on a three-day week from November 1'. Derrigan resumed full-time work from April 1932, but the following October his 'wages were reduced to £2 per week it having been ruled by the Ministry of Labour that he was ineligible for Unemployment Benefit.'[25] Groundsmen were often the only paid employees of a tennis club. Everything else was done by members.

The value of 'making do' was upheld in the club by women who started assuming positions of formal power during this time. Tennis before the Second World War in Britain was the sport, according to social historian Ross McKibbin, which 'most approached gender equality'.[26] But this equality only extended to middle-class women, as the private tennis clubs ensured that membership remained for people like them. The people who weren't – black people, Jewish people, the working class – had to find their own ways of playing tennis if they wanted to play at a higher level than the local park could provide. Many didn't bother and that was tennis' greatest loss. But some did.

6

Socialists

The Woodcote Road in Reading is one of those busy arterial roads that radiate out from provincial towns across the south of England. It twists its way up through the prosperous suburb of Caversham Heights leaving the Thames far below before heading off to Wall-ingford and Oxford. Eighty years ago, this was a desirable address but, over the last decade or two, the endless traffic choking up the hill has turned it into a drab thoroughfare and not somewhere you would associate with pleasure, camaraderie and games. Yet here, on the weekend of 10 and 11 September 1932, the finals of a remarkable tennis tournament took place. Fifty socialists from all across Britain gathered in the back garden of a Victorian villa called 'Nuthurst' off the Woodcote Road for the culmination of the National Workers' Tennis Championships, soon to become better known as 'Workers' Wimbledon'.

Today, there is no trace of Nuthurst or its tennis courts. Workers' Wimbledon has disappeared too, forgotten by most tennis his-torians and meriting only an inaccurate line or two by the rest. Yet for 20 years, the tournament was followed avidly by national newspapers as well as the radical press. Its finals were watched by celebrities and politicians, many of whom proclaimed it as the true home of amateur tennis since, by this time, Wimbledon itself had become dominated by players who were professional in all but name. The tournament's greatest contribution, though, was the type of player it attracted. In the 150 years lawn tennis has been played in the British Isles, Workers' Wimbledon was the most powerful argument that tennis could be enjoyed as much by the working as the middle classes. Its origins, however, can be traced back to one middle-class man who had no interest in tennis whatsoever.

In the mid-1920s, Herbert Morrison, the son of a policeman from Stockwell, south London, was at the start of his political career. He would go on to become deputy prime minister in the Labour Party government of 1945–51 and be responsible for the 1951 Festival of Britain, but he made his political reputation 25 years before with another form of cultural politics. He was one of a new breed of local politicians who were trying to extend socialism into everyday life. As a leading London councillor, he was impressed by the Social Democratic Party in Germany who saw the socialist project as much wider than capturing parliamentary power. Morrison encouraged local labour parties in London to copy the German initiative and organise speaker classes, choral unions, radical libraries and socialist sports clubs. It was the first time a Labour Party leader in Britain had taken sport seriously, and there was a very good reason to do so.

In 1923, the British Workers' Sports Federation had been formed by trades union officials, Labour Party sympathisers and members of the Clarion Cycling Clubs. The intention was to bring together all the local sports initiatives that were run by and for working people. In the absence of any national Labour Party interest, however, the new Federation quickly came under the influence of the Communist Party who saw sport as an opportunity to recruit young people. Herbert Morrison, an avid football fan, was determined to win sport back to Labour. In Hackney, he encouraged his local Labour Party to set up a Sports Club and soon there was one in nearby Tottenham too. By the end of the 1920s, there were twelve Labour Party Sports Clubs in London and the idea had spread outside the capital. Most clubs concentrated on cricket and soccer but some were more eclectic. One member of the Labour Party in Ealing recalled a cycling club and a dramatic society in the 1930s with a 'very high level of involvement. In those days it was almost an alternative way of life.'[1] Tennis was also featured but Ealing Labour Party Sports Club was not the first Labour club to take up the game. That accolade belongs 40 miles away, in Reading.

In the spring of 1927, two public park tennis players, George Deacon and Ivy Noyes, were looking for somewhere more competitive to play. They both lived in the suburb of Caversham, George in a terraced house in Oakley Road, and Ivy in an equally modest house in St John's Road. On Caversham's public tennis courts, then situated in Christchurch Meadows down by the river, the 22-year-old Ivy was able to beat everyone while the older and more awkward George made up for his lack of ability with a startling enthusiasm for the game. It was time to extend their horizons and join a tennis club.

Reading, at the time a prosperous manufacturing town of some 80,000 people, supported half a dozen tennis clubs all keen to attract new members as long as they were the right sort. Ivy worked as a clerk and George ran his own small business. Before the First World War they might have had trouble, but by the 1920s tennis clubs in Britain had opened their doors to the lower middle class and Ivy and George would have been welcomed as members. The problem was that this relaxation in social criteria for potential members did not extend to working-class people, at least in most clubs. Ivy and George were active members of the Reading Labour Party and they realised that many of their party comrades interested in taking up tennis would not be accepted by any tennis club in town because their collars were not white but blue.

So Ivy Noyes and George Deacon decided to set up their own club under the auspices of the Reading Labour Party Sports Association. It would be a tennis club where all their friends in the local party, one of the largest in the country with members who were railwaymen, gas and post office workers, craftsmen and employees at the giant Huntley & Palmers biscuit factory, could play. In the summer of 1927, they rented part of the Old Athletic Ground in Caversham, collected 40 pounds to roll out four grass courts and then put up nets and posts. The Reading Labour Party Tennis Club was born, the first socialist tennis club in Britain.

Unlike most other tennis clubs, its captain was not a solicitor or a retired major but a tall post office union official called Rowland Bishop who would electrify the 1931 Labour Party conference with a speech demanding more nationalisation. Bishop helped the new tennis club arrange matches against other clubs and hold tournaments that were open to all. In the spring of 1932, the *Reading Citizen* reported that the club was 'full with 90 members'. That was something well worth celebrating and George and Ivy had an idea what this celebration might be.

In June, they put an advert in the *New Clarion* for a tennis tournament which would take place over the weekend of 10 and 11 September 1932, with the finals held in the 'magnificently situated courts' of Nuthurst on the Woodcote Road. Invitations were extended to members of the dozen other Labour Party tennis clubs that had been set up by this time, including ones in Slough, Bristol, Swindon, Oxford, York, Liverpool and Manchester. Unattached players who were members of a trade union, the Labour League of Youth or the local co-op were also encouraged to come along. The entrance fee was two shillings and accommodation was available on the Saturday night for half a crown. There would be a social and a consolation event for those who were knocked out in the first round. Play would start at 10.00 am sharp although there would be a 'special dispensation' for people who had to work on Saturday morning. They would be allowed to play in the afternoon.

With all the planning involved, it would have been gratifying if the sun had shone brightly that weekend. It didn't. Wind and rain dominated play and only 36 people finished their matches. Lionel Winyard, a postal worker from Southend, won the men's singles. Peggy Wheatstone caused an upset in the women's by beating Ivy Noyes in the final on the Sunday afternoon, although this could be because Ivy was still recovering from her main task for the weekend, organising the social. This took place on the Saturday night in the Boston Hall at the back of the New Thought Centre on Oxford Road in the centre of town. Players, supporters and friends all paid a shilling to drink and dance in the company of Frederick Roberts, minister of pensions in the Labour governments of the 1920s, who entertained the appreciative audience with stories about the perfidy of Ramsay Macdonald and a dozen tunes on his fiddle. Despite the lousy weather the tournament was judged a success and George Elvin, the losing finalist in the men's singles, saw its potential.

Like many tennis players of the era, Elvin does not look like someone who enjoyed sport. Photographs show an earnest young man in his late twenties with small, round glasses and slick black hair parted at the side. He was the kind of person who might well stand for parliament as indeed he did a few years later for Weston-super-Mare under the slogan 'Vote for Elvin and provide scholarships not battleships'. In conservative Somerset, this kind of pacifist talk did not go down well. He came last. Instead of becoming a Labour MP, George Elvin copied his father, Herbert, and worked all his life as a trade union official. If he never reached the heights of his dad, who served as president of the Trades Union Congress (TUC) in 1938, Elvin did end up as one of the longest serving trade union leaders of his generation. He was general secretary of the Association of Cine Technicians for 35 years. In his spare time, from his home in Willesden, north-west London, he ran the workers' sports movement.

Two years before the tournament in Reading, at a meeting in July 1930 at Transport House, the Labour Party and the Trade Union Congress set up the National Workers' Sports Association. The idea behind the association was to 'encourage, promote and control amateur sports and recreation among working class organisations'. 'Control' was the key word here. Despite all the local Labour Party sports associations that had sprung up over the last few years, the influence of the Communist Party on the British Workers' Sports Federation remained strong, particularly at national level. The Labour Party and the TUC needed the new association to wrestle working-class sport away from the Communist Party and it was crucial to find someone to run it whom they could trust. Herbert Elvin's sports-mad son, George, seemed just the man. He became the association's first secretary, an honorary position he would keep for the next three decades.

The association – soon, and rather confusingly, renamed the British Workers' Sports Association – would survive until the start of the 1960s, but its heyday was its first decade. In a couple of years, it attracted 5,000 members, many transferring from the British Workers' Sports Federation which was soon wound up. The new association was organised into 145 separate clubs, some based in trade unions, others in cooperative societies, but most attached to local Labour Party branches. Eighteen different sports were offered including soccer, cricket and cycling. Elvin himself enjoyed cricket and athletics, and in his younger days he was a very able footballer, but tennis was his true passion. He saw an annual tennis tournament as the ideal opportunity to encourage people from working-class and trade union backgrounds to take up the game. It also had the added attraction of being a sport frowned upon by the Communist Party as 'bourgeois' and so would give the new British Workers' Sports Association a distinct identity from its old communist rival.

With a marketing flair unusual for socialists at that time – the *Daily Herald* would later describe him as a 'young man for whom progress is never fast enough'[2] – Elvin helped George Deacon and Ivy Noyes organise a second, more ambitious tournament the following year. In glorious sunshine on the weekend of 15 and 16 June 1933, over a hundred contestants turned up in Reading for another two days of workers' tennis. They included engine drivers, miners, clerks, postmen, secretaries, pattern-makers, engineers and an old Etonian, Frederick Pethick-Lawrence, who was now an MP and would later became secretary for India in the 1945 Labour government. The entrance fee for the tournament was two shillings and the matches were completed, as the *New Clarion* reported, 'with never a complaint', not even from Pethick-Lawrence who was knocked out in the first round. The official name of the tournament was ignored. Players and supporters simply referred to it as 'Workers' Wimbledon'. 'How it originated', Elvin reflected afterwards, 'nobody seems sure, but it is a good name and we are sticking to it.' For more than 20 years they did.

The following summer, the competition was held in Reading for the third time, with trophies presented by Walter Citrine, general secretary of the TUC, who remarked that he was 'very impressed by the way unsuccessful competitors congratulated their opponents'. 'A further pleasing feature', he continued, is that 'several competitors enter each year knowing full well they have little chance.' [3] By the time the fourth tournament was held, in Brockwell Park in south London in the summer of 1935, Workers' Wimbledon had become the centrepiece of an alternative tennis culture in Britain which encompassed Labour Party tennis clubs, miners', postal workers' and railwaymen's tennis leagues and public park tennis associations. Together they challenged the ethos of the private middle-class tennis club, with its codes of exclusion, and they championed an approach to the game that had different values from most tournament tennis at that time. Competition and rivalry could coexist on court with courtesy, friendliness and cooperation. Your opponent was also your comrade.

At the 1936 Workers' Wimbledon, held once more in Brockwell Park, the talk soon strayed from correct socialist etiquette on court to the conduct of a brilliant tennis player from a trade union family who showed little interest in socialism or manners. Fred Perry was far too good to play at Workers' Wimbledon. A few weeks before, he had won the Men's Singles at that year's Wimbledon Championships for the third time. Perry certainly did not regard his opponents as his comrades, often commentating sarcastically when they hit a winning shot that they were 'very clevah'. Victory for Perry was far more important than taking part. It is not difficult to see where these attitudes came from.

When the young Fred first turned up as a 15-year-old grammar schoolboy to play at the national schools championship at Queen's in the mid-1920s, a competition dominated by public schools, an official asked him what school he represented. When he said Ealing County, he was told there was 'no room for you here'. When he thrashed the Australian Jack Crawford to win his first Wimbledon title in 1934, he overheard an All England Club official say to Crawford that 'this was one day when the best man didn't win'. [4] Even after he had captained Britain to success in the Davis Cup in 1936, he was still not regarded by the Lawn Tennis Association as 'one of us', and he wasn't for what Perry considered were fairly obvious reasons: 'I was from the North Country rather than old school tie country.'⁵ This was true, but it was more complicated than that.

Perry was born in Stockport in 1909. His father, Sam, was an active trade unionist and his grandfather worked in a cotton mill. If the family had stayed among the northern working class, it is doubtful whether the young Fred would have taken up tennis at all let alone become a champion. There was no Labour Party tennis club in Stockport when he was growing up, yet alone any Workers' Wimbledon. But by the time Fred was nine, Sam Perry had risen through organised labour's ranks and been appointed national secretary of the Cooperative Party. The family moved to Ealing, a West London suburb with a long tennis tradition dating back to Dorothea Lambert Chambers and Blanche Hillyard. With the support of his father, Sam, who saw lawn tennis as a vehicle for his son's social advancement, Fred Perry switched to tennis after considerable success at table tennis: he had been world champion in 1929. He joined a couple of local tennis clubs, Chiswick Park and Herga, both long vanished, where his talent was immediately recognised.

In the early 1930s, as Fred was winning titles, his father was winning friends in the Houses of Parliament where he had been returned as a Labour MP. Sam Perry became close to several famous parliamentarians who loved tennis including the conservative Stanley Baldwin and the liberal Lloyd George, both of whom took an active interest in young Fred's progress. But even with his father's contacts, Fred Perry was never fully accepted into the inner sanctum of British tennis. His love of money did not endear him to Wimbledon officials who steadfastly upheld the amateur game. His absolute determination to win was alien to the Lawn Tennis Association's view that it was more important to play well than to triumph badly, but it was his character that set him apart. Dan Maskell, the All England Club coach (and later BBC tennis commentator), himself of working-class origin, said that Perry at this time had a chip on his shoulder and could be stubborn and truculent. Jack Kramer, the American champion who was the son of a blue-collar railroad worker, called him 'selfish and egotistical. The worst best tennis player in the world.'

It was true that Perry was not charming in the way that his contemporary, the elegant aristocrat Gottfried von Cramm, clearly was. But in the top tennis world of the 1930s, perhaps that was the only way a young man from a working-class background could survive. Von Cramm had a grace that came from privilege. Perry could not afford to be gracious. He had to keep his guard up or reward for victory might be taken away from him. It was not that Perry was conscious of this but it was there in the deep structure of his character formed from generations of working-class struggle. This made Perry acutely aware of sleights or dismissals, real or imaginary, so he hit back first. It is unsurprising that a few months after he won his third Wimbledon victory, Perry left the class-ridden world of British amateur tennis to go to America and become a professional.

Perry's likely defection to the professional camp dominated the sports pages in the summer of 1936 and it dominated conversation in the cafes and pubs in Herne Hill in south London to where the participants in the fifth Workers' Wimbledon adjourned after their matches in Brockwell Park. Entrants that year came not just from Britain but from Belgium, France, Holland and Austria, from where the hard-hitting Fritz Jellinick brought fraternal greetings. In 1936, his club in Vienna, the Workers' Tennis Club, had over 3,000 members. A couple of years later, in 1938, it would be shut down by the Nazis. In Brockwell Park, Jellinick was not good enough to reach any of the finals but he was liked by everyone and he encouraged the keener players that weekend to consider going to the Third Workers' Summer Olympiad in Antwerp which was taking place the following year.

The 100 members of the British Workers' Sports Association team that eventually travelled to Antwerp in the last week of July 1937 included ten tennis players. Britain was one of 15 countries that took part in the Olympiad and 20 sports were contested including basketball, water polo, gymnastics and chess. Tennis was the most successful event for the British, with railwayman Fred

Curl narrowly losing to Pedro Messip from Spain in the men's final. Curl picked up the medals for both of them as Messip was wanted 'back at the battlefront' to fight for the Republicans in the Spanish Civil War.[6] The women's singles at Antwerp was a triumph for 15-year-old Joan Holman, the daughter of Percy Holman who would later become Labour MP for Bethnal Green. Joan won easily and gained a second gold medal for Britain in the doubles when she was partnered by Ivy Noyes. It was the first time Ivy had been abroad and she kept a diary.

After twelve hours of travel they arrived in Antwerp, Ivy noted, 'very tired and hungry'. 'On our first few days, we had to practice so no sightseeing, but we did manage to get away with some of the other teams for a day to Brussels where we saw country dancing and we all met in the centre of town to sing the Internationale.'[7] The following day was the Olympiad's opening parade. Ivy enjoyed the Czech team's 'demonstration of physical culture wearing navy shorts, white blouses, red ties and red caps'. Then came the Norwegians who were dressed in 'tunics of amber and brown which were symbols of music and art' and a young team from Belgium 'giving a pageant demonstrating working class life'. After her successful doubles triumph on the Sunday, Ivy joined the rest of the British team for the closing ceremony in a stadium packed with 73,000 people. 'We wound up with a torch-light procession through the streets of Antwerp singing "no passeran: they shall not pass".'[8]

There was nothing like this at Workers' Wimbledon, but the two years before the outbreak of the Second World War saw the tournament at its best. In 1938 it moved to Southsea and the matches were played on the grass courts at Canoe Lake which overlooked the sea. The tournament, according to the *Portsmouth Evening News*, attracted over a hundred entrants and was a 'great success'.[9] In the men's final, a dockland engineer called Blackman beat a boilerman called Breeze. The women's singles was won with consummate ease by Joan Holman. George Elvin noted her 'flawless backhand and ability to hit low skimming shots straight down the line'. Joan had done well that summer in the Girls' Singles at the

Wimbledon Championships and Elvin confidently predicted that she would 'snatch the Wimbledon limelight within a few years'. She may have done if war and marriage to a Polish count had not intervened.

In 1939, Workers' Wimbledon returned to Canoe Lake and the local paper noted approvingly that the 'competitors were ordinary working people and quite a number of them never had a minute's coaching in their lives. Their tennis has been snatched after hours, hurriedly, but the result is surprisingly good.'[10] A few years before, George Elvin had indulged in a little prophesy: 'I am ambitious enough to look forward to the day when our major tennis tournament, Workers' Wimbledon, will command more popular interest than any other.'[11] Sadly this turned out not to be true. The 1939 tournament was Workers' Wimbledon's peak.

The tournament was revived after the Second World War but the energy had gone. To try and rekindle interest, George Deacon procured an invitation from the All England Lawn Tennis Club and arranged for the 1947 Workers' Wimbledon to be held at Wimbledon itself. These were the days of a campaigning Labour government in Britain and the club liked to keep in with whoever was in power. Sir Louis Greig, the president of the All England Club, presented trophies to the winners who included the RAF champion Howard Walton from Birmingham. But by then the tournament had become a side attraction for the leading players rather than a serious competition. Walton's main tennis was elsewhere. He'd already played for Britain in the Davis Cup and would go on to appear three times at Wimbledon itself, once stretching the champion Frank Sedgman in three closely fought sets.

In 1951, the twelfth Workers' Wimbledon was also held at the All England Club, at least for the first day. The programme carried a stirring welcome from the new national tennis secretary, Lionel Winyard, who had won the men's singles title at that first tournament in Reading 20 years before. 'I don't suppose you ever expected to play at Wimbledon. Quite frankly neither did we. Workers' Wimbledon is getting bigger and stronger every year.'[12] This was wishful thinking. The 1951 tournament was less a serious competition and more a reunion for old friends like Winyard, George Elvin and Frederick Pethick-Lawrence. Pethick-Lawrence had been elevated to the peerage in 1945 so he could serve in Atlee's government but he didn't give up his regular tennis game, which he played most lunchtimes on Lincoln's Inn Fields. He regarded himself as a 'rabbit' on court compared with 'proper players' and nobody at Workers' Wimbledon disagreed, but he was liked by everyone despite an accent still rooted in Eton and Cambridge.[13]

Present too was Ivy Noyes from Reading. She was pleased to meet up with her close friend George Deacon again who now lived in New Malden. Deacon was the organiser and referee that weekend and he was seen throughout the competition dressed in a boater and green blazer wandering wistfully around the All England Club's grounds much like Henry Jones had done almost 70 years before. The tournament received none of the attention from the press it had done only a dozen years before and took place not on the grass of Wimbledon's Centre Court but on the hard courts out the back.

The world had changed, and Labour Party members had lost interest not just in Workers' Wimbledon but in workers' sport. The combination of socialist politics and sporting endeavour, which the Labour Party tennis clubs represented so well in the 1930s, now seemed out of place in 1950s Britain which looked more to American enterprise than European collective action. At the same time, many private tennis clubs in Britain started accepting talented players from working-class backgrounds as long as they knew – or could be taught – how to behave. These clubs received grants from the Lawn Tennis Association to upgrade their courts and build proper clubhouses. The socialist tennis clubs received no money as they were deemed 'political'. A gap opened up and only the most dedicated socialist tennis player after the Second World War would chose to play at a Labour Party Tennis Club rather than a private tennis club, and sometimes not even then.

George Elvin did his best to keep morale and interest alive. Workers' Wimbledon was 'one of the movement's great successes', he wrote in a booklet in 1951 which celebrated 21 years of workers' sport, but by then it was too late. The twelfth Workers' Wimbledon in 1951 was the last. The socialist tennis clubs petered out. Their nets were pulled up and their grounds handed back to local authorities as the Labour Party retreated from organising sport for its members. In 1960, the British Workers' Sports Association was wound up too. George Elvin died in 1978. The tragedy is that all his work for working-class sport disappeared too.

Workers' Wimbledon could be seen as merely a sideshow to the real politics of British socialism in those crucial decades between the wars. Certainly the workers' tennis culture in Britain lacked the centrality of workers' sport in Europe. There were no shouts of 'no passeran' after the matches in Brockwell Park but rather gentle murmurs of 'well done'. This dismissive view, though, underestimates the power of soft politics in bringing about change. At its best, the tournament provided an image of how sport could be organised in a spirit of radical cooperation rather than competitive individualism, and it reminded the rest of the British Left that people joined a political party not simply to go on marches or organise meetings but also to forge friendships and have fun. Certainly that was true for the two people who dreamed it all up.

There is a photograph of 20 members of Reading Labour Party Tennis Club in the *New Clarion* in 1932 and there they both are, George Deacon and Ivy Noyes, standing close together at one end, Ivy with a racket in hand, George in long white peg-topped cricket trousers, their legs brushing against each other. Tennis clubs in the 1930s were often places of romance so it is not entirely fanciful to imagine that the shy smile Ivy is giving the camera captures a sign of her affection for George. Perhaps the real reason for George's sudden move away from Reading to New Malden was that his friendship with Ivy was becoming a little too noticeable. Both were married to other people who did not share their passion for the game.

Ivy Noyes stayed in Caversham all her life. In 1946, she went to play tennis again in Europe, a tournament in Switzerland called 'Peace through Sport', and she kept another diary. 'At the grand parade in Basle', she observed, 'we were cheered all along the route. A bystander would call out "hello England". At the top of the parade, there were hundreds of girls and boys with hoops, a sight so impressive that it made me wish that others could see what a wonderful sports movement this is and what fine specimens of manhood and womanhood it produces.' The competition moved on to Zurich and Ivy recorded that they were looked after by members of the local workers' tennis club. 'I cannot describe the generosity of these people. Nothing was too much trouble. Whenever we tried to thank them, they said it was nothing compared with what we had done in the war.' On their last evening at the city's town hall, the British team were presented with bouquets of flowers. It was an emotional occasion lit up by a glorious evening sun, as Ivy recalled: 'They didn't want us to leave and they all expressed great hopes we would send a much larger contingent next year.' There is no record of this happening or of Ivy ever going abroad again.

There is very little record of Workers' Wimbledon too beyond a couple of post-war programmes kept in the basement of the Kenneth Richie Library at the All England Club in Wimbledon. All other signs of the tournament have vanished apart from one odd remnant. On Oxford Road, Reading, at the back of the building that was once the New Thought Centre but is now a shop selling hearing aids, the Boston Hall is still there, more a shack than anything else. A few years ago, I went to look for the place where Ivy Noyes organised the social for the first Workers' Wimbledon in 1932 and discovered that it was occupied by the Living Spring Tabernacle, a 'friendly and informal church of all ages and nationalities'. I wanted to go in and at least imagine I could hear Frederick Roberts play the fiddle as he denounced Ramsay McDonald but it wasn't possible. The doors were heavily padlocked.

7

Entrepreneurs

On 9 October 1926, the new Madison Square Garden in New York, built just twelve months before to stage concerts and circuses, hosted a very different kind of event. That Saturday night 13,000 people, many in evening dress, turned up at the arena on 8th Avenue to watch an exhibition of professional tennis. The menu for the evening started with the American Vincent Richards, until recently the number one male player in the world but now banished from official tennis which remained resolutely amateur. He played the Frenchman Paul Ferret and won in two close sets, but their match was merely an aperitif. After a short interval, the lights dimmed, the orchestra played *La Marseillaise* and the crowd burst into spontaneous applause as the spotlight picked out two women walking towards the court. One was former American champion Mary Kendall Browne, winner of three US Opens but now at 35 a little past her best. The other was her opponent, Suzanne Lenglen, the best female tennis player in the world perhaps the best the world had ever seen. This was her first match as a professional.

Lenglen had been in town all week giving interviews to the press, being seen at baseball matches and Broadway shows and promoting perfume and lingerie on the radio. All New York wanted to see her play. In the audience that night were Governor Al Smith and Mayor Jimmy Walker, and they were hoping to see this imperious Frenchwoman taught a tennis lesson by their plucky American. But once the hullabaloo died down and the match started, it was not the thrilling contest the spectators desired. In just under 40 minutes, Lenglen brushed Browne aside in a display of shot making which the *New York Times* reported as 'one of the most masterly exhibitions of court general-ship that has been seen in this country'.[1] One person watching in the wings, however, was pleased enough with the one-sided contest that night: Charles Pyle, the man who arranged and financed it all.

Pyle, a tall, avuncular man with an eye always on the main chance, was the son of a Methodist minister from Illinois. In a colourful career, he owned theatres, represented American football players, exhibited at Chicago's World Fair and organised the first coast-to-coast walking race. Some of his ventures made money but others were not successful, and along the way Pyle picked up the nickname 'cash and carry' which was apt because he went bankrupt several times.

The story of how Pyle, a 43-year-old entrepreneur with a chequered business record, ended up promoting Lenglen, at 26 the world's most celebrated sports star, is an unusual one even by tennis standards, and worth returning to. But let's pause for a moment and consider exactly how the genteel pastime of tennis on an English country house lawn turned remarkably quickly into global box office entertainment. The Lenglen–Pyle collaboration was by no means unique. Tennis players and entrepreneurs, some respectable, others less so, had been enmeshed together from the start. The origins of lawn tennis, after all, came from the desire of its inventor, Walter Wingfield, to make money.

A major reason why tennis spread so quickly across Britain and the world in the mid-1870s was that there were half a dozen manufacturers of sports equipment who had the expertise to deal with the explosion in interest that Wingfield's tennis sets had generated. Companies like Lilywhites (founded in 1853), Grays (1855) and Ayers (1810) were already in the business of supplying rackets, balls and other paraphernalia for the sports of real tennis and rackets. When Wingfield's sets proved a commercial success in 1874 and 1875, they saw no reason why they should not sell lawn tennis equipment as well. There were lucrative licensing deals to be done here but Major Wingfield preferred to carry on by himself, spurning any kind of commercial collaboration. He lost out on a fortune since the established sports companies simply copied his ideas without paying him any royalties. Between 1874 and 1900 over 100 companies making and selling lawn tennis equipment and dress were formed in London alone. Outside the capital, the business of tennis flourished too. In Shrewsbury, the county town of Shropshire, for example, Altree and Lea sold tennis markers, Majors of Mardol St supplied tennis jackets and J. Della Portas of Princes St sold their own tennis sets for 29/6.[2] Within a few years of play, the possibility of making serious money from tennis was apparent and the game attracted the attention of an astute business family from Manchester.

Slazenger started as an umbrella maker in the early nineteenth century but by 1881 the company had branched out and was registered as a 'gaiters and leggings' business. It was run by two of the younger members of the clan, Ralph Slazenger, then 36 years old, and Albert Slazenger, just 30. The two brothers noted the profits that were being made from lawn tennis in the south, and in 1883 moved the business to an old tea warehouse in Cannon St in London where they started specialising in the new sport. Ralph Slazenger, an easy-going, thick-set man with a strong sense of public duty – he would later become mayor of London – looked after production. The thinner, more intense Albert managed sales. Their first success was with tennis shoes, and at one point they had 16 different styles on the market. They then designed their own tennis rackets but found it difficult in the mid-1880s to dent the dominance of two rival companies, Ayres and Wisden. The Slazenger lawn tennis rackets were excellent but excellence wasn't enough. What the brothers needed was an endorsement.

The early Wimbledon champions had already appeared in several advertisements. Spencer Gore, the first Men's Singles winner in 1877, was pictured in newspapers and magazines with an Ayres tennis racket alongside the famous cricketer W.G. Grace wielding an Ayers cricket bat. Ralph and Albert Slazenger took this type of marketing to a new level. From Ayres they poached William and Ernest Renshaw, the great Wimbledon champions of the 1880s, and they built their products around them. Adverts for Slazenger's new 'Demon' racket, priced at one guinea, and their 'Renshaw', a bargain at 12/6, both carried William Renshaw's imprimatur. They sold out. By 1890, Slazenger had 16 tennis items on sale all endorsed by one Renshaw twin or the other. Twenty years later, the company would have 33 different rackets that you could buy in shops or direct from them in Cannon Street. These included, at the top end, the 'Doherty', endorsed by Laurie Doherty, and at the bottom the 'Colonial' and 'Kangaroo' rackets aimed at players in Australia. By then, however, Slazenger had turned its attention to a tennis item that was even more profitable.

In the late 1880s, Ralph and Albert grasped a crucial economic fact about the game. More money was spent on tennis balls than on rackets since well-made wooden rackets like the Demon, if kept carefully in a press, could last a lifetime while balls, however well they were made, lasted no time at all. Slazenger started manufacturing their own hand-sewn, flannel-covered rubber tennis balls in Woolwich in 1887. To ensure though that their balls stood out from the half-dozen similar ones on the market the brothers required an endorsement a little grander than that of a mere champion. They needed a major tournament to adopt their ball. The most successful tennis tournament in the world was the Championships at Wimbledon run by the All England Club and the Slazenger brothers decided to try and acquire Wimbledon's imprimatur. The club had been using an Ayres ball since 1879 and seemed happy with the arrangement. Slazenger looked for a way in and soon they found one, the secretary of the All England Club, Archdale Palmer, a retired judge with whom Ralph and Albert Slazenger cultivated a friendship.

At the brothers' suggestion, Palmer conducted a 'round-robin' among the top players asking them which tennis ball they preferred. Most opted for Slazenger rather than Ayres, although this was hardly surprising since champions like the Renshaw and Doherty brothers were being paid by Slazenger to endorse their products. Palmer was nevertheless persuaded of the merits of the Slazenger ball and presented a case for change to the All England Club Committee in the late summer of 1901. The committee agreed. The Slazenger ball was introduced at the Wimbledon Championships in the summer of 1902 and has been used ever since – the longest sponsorship deal in sport history and one of the most profitable. A few years after the ball switch was made, however, some awkward facts started to emerge.

Around the time the change was agreed, Slazenger had made a donation of £100 to the All England Club and two of the All England Club's Committee who made the decision turned out to hold Slazenger shares. Then the close relationship between Archdale Palmer and the Slazenger brothers came under scrutiny. After the 1901 championships, Palmer had written to Ayres congratulating them: 'The balls you supplied this year have given very great satisfaction and nearly every player has remarked on their quality.'[3] A few weeks later, he changed his mind and was pushing the Slazenger ball as the preferred player choice. What happened to produce this sudden conversion has never been revealed, but three years after the introduction of the Slazenger ball, Palmer resigned from the All England Club, bought a substantial house in Essex (which was later owned by another tennis fan, Cliff Richard) and became managing director of Slazenger where he stayed the rest of his working life. The Lawn Tennis Association launched an enquiry but no impropriety was found, although it was noted at the time that another tennis project Slazenger funded was the association's own journal.

Ayres never recovered from losing its ball deal with Wimbledon. The company limped along until 1940 when it was taken over by a thriving business which had since become one of the largest sports equipment manufacturers in the world: Slazenger. Ralph and Albert's success in winning the Wimbledon ball contract was 'probably the single most important event in the company's history'.[4]

The behaviour of the Slazenger brothers seems like sharp practice today, but it would not have been seen that way at the time. In the early years of the twentieth century, British capitalism was at its zenith and there were few constraints on commercial behaviour. Many companies behaved similarly. Two decades before, Ayres had kept their Wimbledon ball contract by offering to pay for a new grandstand. Ever since Walter Wingfield's lawn tennis sets were first offered for sale in March 1874, commerce and tennis had been intertwined and this was also true of the players.

The men who entered the first tennis tournaments in the 1870s and 1880s expected to be rewarded if they won with cash or silver cups that could be sold. These players were regarded as 'amateurs' because they did not need to rely on tennis for a living. 'Professional' was a term reserved for those who earned their livelihood from the game as groundsmen or racket stringers. The duties of these early lawn tennis professionals expanded in the last decades of the nineteenth century from ensuring that courts and rackets were in good shape to providing lessons in how to hit the ball. At the more prestigious tennis clubs this soon became their principal activity and by the turn of the century the best of these first lawn tennis coaches had developed a reputation as skilful interpreters of the game, people like George Kerr at the Fitzwilliam Club in Dublin, Tom Browne at the Lansdowne in the same city and Tom Fleming at Queen's in London whose protégé, Charles Herrion, would go on to write several best-selling guides to tennis playing in the 1920s.

The playing standard of some of these early professionals soon became close to that of the champions, but they were banned from official tournaments like Wimbledon because they were not gentlemen but artisans who were involved in tennis not out of love for the game but to make money. It all came down to class. The gentleman-amateur in tennis was someone who combined an 'upper-class ideal of chivalry and a new middle-class belief in the moral value of strenuous effort'.[5] What they did not exhibit was a lower-class need to earn money. Many of the early coaches like George Kerr and Tom Fleming were from working-class backgrounds and relied on income from tennis to survive. In Britain they were seen as servants, but other European countries were not so rigid, and at the turn of the century some of Britain and Ireland's top coaches, the best in the world at the time, were enticed abroad. Browne went to Paris. Fleming went to Vienna. Kerr ended up in Berlin. A generation of coaching expertise was lost, at least in Britain. It is hardly surprising, then, that Wimbledon would soon become dominated by players from America, Australia and France, all countries which took coaching more seriously than Britain and rewarded their coaches well.

The British tennis coaches that came after Fleming and Kerr felt they had little choice but to accept the distinction between gentlemen and professionals and work instead for gradual change. Dan Maskell was born into a working-class family in Fulham and went to work at The Queen's Club nearby as a ball boy in 1923 when he was 15 years old. In this alien world, he progressed by doffing his cap and embracing the style of the upper middle class. While still in his teens, he became one of the top coaches at Queen's and was then appointed the first professional coach at the All England Club in 1929 at the age of 21. He stayed 30 years. After the Second World War he achieved national fame as the voice of tennis on BBC television – he was particularly known for his catchphrase 'oh I say', the phrase he used as the title for the paperback edition of his autobiography published in 1989. In his television commentaries over the decades there was never a hint of dissent, but in his book you can sense shimmering between the lines Maskell's resentment at being treated as a servant by people who could not play the game nearly as well as he could, a resentment he could never express because his livelihood was at stake.

There is little doubt that Maskell was not just one of the best coaches between the wars but also one of the best players of the game. People who saw him on court during this time were convinced he could have beaten Fred Perry, Bunny Austin, perhaps even Bill Tilden or Donald Budge. He was never given the opportunity simply because they were amateurs and he was a professional. Instead he helped organise the first professional tournaments for coaches like him and ex-amateur players who wanted to earn money openly from the game. There had been competitions for professionals in Britain and Europe as early as 1910, but the first official world professional championship was organised by Maskell in London in 1927. It was won by him, as were many of the professional competitions held in Britain, Europe and America over the next 20 years.

The irony was that professional coaches like Maskell never earned anything like the top 'amateurs' from tennis. In 1911, when it was already clear that champions like the Doherty brothers were amassing a considerable income from the game, the Lawn Tennis Association in London decided to define exactly what players could earn from playing tennis and what was forbidden. This was the first real opportunity in the game to deal with a division that would go on to blight tennis for the next 60 years. The association could have chosen to banish the distinction between amateur and professional or copy the cricket compromise and allow both 'gentlemen' (amateurs) and 'players' (professional). Instead it reaffirmed its view that tennis was a game for amateurs only, and to make sure everyone understood it underlined the rules. Amateurs were prohibited from playing for prize money. They were not allowed to play in matches or demonstrations with professionals, nor could they sell any prizes they won, nor contribute to the press 'except with express permission' from their national associations. Any expenses they received should be the bare minimum.

If these rules had been rigorously applied over the next few decades, tennis would have been rescued from commercialism but destroyed as a global entertainment. Instead the rules were circumvented and sometimes simply ignored by the top players who became as entrepreneurial as Charles Pyle at receiving rewards from their sport. The masters were Bill Tilden and Suzanne Lenglen, and in the 1920s they developed what became known as 'shamateurism', the appearance of an amateur ethic concealing a considerable amount of money making underneath.

Tilden and Lenglen recognised that their star qualities were making fortunes for the people who ran tennis and the companies they were connected with. In 1919, when Lenglen made her debut at Wimbledon, it proved almost impossible to purchase a ticket. The more people who turned up to watch her the more money everyone in tennis made apart from Lenglen herself, at least officially. In New York, the new stadium at Forest Hills was built to accommodate the crowds who wanted to see Bill Tilden play, although Tilden himself received nothing from this financial bonanza, at least officially, because, like Lenglen, he was an 'amateur'.

In practice, Charles Lenglen ensured his daughter was well rewarded for her play and Tilden became adept at stretching the rules. Tilden's rackets were free, his living expenses paid, he drove an expensive Packard sedan paid for by Buick and he made 25,000 dollars a year from his newspaper columns. Tilden and Lenglen were by no means the only players who devised ways of receiving payment by exploiting the ambiguities in the amateur rulebook. In 1947, Norah Cleather published *The Wimbledon Story*, an insider's account of what went on in the Championships between the wars. Cleather, who was secretary at the club, admitted that many players resented the considerable profits that were being made out of their talent. They devised a 'thousand ways of cashing in on their popularity by indirect means'.[6] Very generous expenses were claimed. Thousands of pounds changed hands to endorse rackets. Money was slipped into jacket pockets in hotel suites. Exclusive interviews were given for cash. All these ruses were perfected by the top players but the masters were the Lenglens.

In the 1920s, Charles Lenglen became known to everyone by his persistent question, 'what is it worth?', and it was not only at Wimbledon that he cashed in on his daughter's box office appeal. Every summer, Suzanne Lenglen would embark on a grand tour of Europe. She stayed in the most expensive hotels with an entourage which included her parents, hairdresser, masseur and maid, as well as the London socialite, Lady Sophie Wavertree, for whom Suzanne had a deep affection. Many people at the time questioned how the 'amateur' Suzanne could finance these costly tours, but the most likely explanation lay with the final member of Suzanne's retinue, Lady Wavertree's lover, Francis Fisher.

Fisher was a New Zealander who had played tennis on the circuit before going into politics, at which point he became known as 'Rainbow Fisher' because he kept changing sides. In the early 1920s, he became a director of Dunlop, a Birmingham manufacturer of rubber goods who were looking for ways to challenge Slazenger's dominance in tennis. According to Teddy Tinling,

Francis Fisher's friendship with Suzanne could never be 'entirely divorced from the commercial interest' of Dunlop.[7] Fisher ensured that Dunlop tennis balls were used everywhere Lenglen played, particularly in a celebrated exhibition match in Cannes in February 1926 when she met the American champion Helen Wills for the first and only time. This contest between Lenglen, the current queen of women's tennis, and Wills, the young contender, attracted worldwide attention. Writers were given 15,000 dollars to report it. Tickets were going for 100 dollars each. Newsreel rights were auctioned off to the highest bidder. The match was awash with money. Lenglen won 6–3, 8–6, but it was the closest contest she had played since her epic Wimbledon final against Dorothea Lambert Chambers seven years before.

Despite her loss, it seemed likely that Wills, still only 21, would eventually take over as world number one and possibly as soon as the next Wimbledon Championships in a few months' time in July. But Wills missed this tournament because of illness and Suzanne Lenglen won the Women's Singles in 1926 with ease for the fifth and final time. Then, in a misunderstanding on Centre Court, Lenglen was criticised for keeping Queen Mary waiting and the English press turned against her. She was no longer their Wimbledon favourite. Her father's health at the time was poor and the family was running out of funds. If ever there was a time to cash in on her celebrity status, this was it.

The deal on offer from Charles Pyle was 75,000 dollars for a tour across the United States playing 38 matches against Mary Browne and starting in New York. Suzanne Lenglen signed a contract in August 1926 and was immediately banished from the official tennis world. Her membership of the All England Club, one of the perks for winning Wimbledon, was rescinded but she seemed content: 'Becoming a professional to me is an escape from bondage and slavery. No one can order me about any longer to play tournaments for the benefit of club owners.' Lenglen admitted that tennis had been great fun, but that it had become 'too exacting. I have done my bit to build up the tennis of France and of the world. It's about time tennis did something for me.'[8]

Whether the tour really did do anything for her apart from the money she earned is debatable. Certainly the tennis was undemanding. She won all her matches against Browne sometimes with the loss of only a few games, but the travel between venues was exhausting and unrelenting. Baltimore, Philadelphia, Buffalo, Cleveland, they criss-crossed the country sleeping in railway carriages and carrying with them a collapsible tennis court made of cork and rubber and covered with green-painted canvas. As professionals, they were not allowed to play in any tennis club affiliated to the United States Lawn Tennis Association and so they pitched up in arenas that were designed for ice hockey, basketball and dance bands.

With two clowns enlivening the intervals between matches, the Lenglen tour was the first to serve up tennis as a variety performance. The people who came to watch were different from the usual tennis spectators, more lower class. They loved the spectacle, at least on the east coast, but as the players headed west, ticket sales declined and gate receipts dwindled. Charles Pyle kept adding on more cities to meet his costs. New Orleans, Miami, a dip down to Havana, then north to Newark, Hartford and Providence, Rhode Island, and an audience of just 2,500. The tour ended in New York in February 1927 where it had begun four months before. Charles Pyle boasted that Suzanne had played to 'capacity or near-capacity throngs in every city she visited. The venture has been a financial success far beyond our expectations.'[9] He lied. She hadn't. It wasn't. It had demonstrated, though, that there was a new audience for the game that was not being reached by the established tennis world, although it seemed unlikely this new professional tennis would ever challenge Wimbledon, at least if it was run by Charles Pyle.

Pyle quickly moved on from tennis to American football. Lenglen went back to France. She worked for a Parisian fashion house and then ran a tennis school but was never accepted back into the amateur tennis world. When she went to Wimbledon as a spectator a few years later, she was not allowed in the players' box but had to sit in the public stands with her friend Dorothea Lambert Chambers, another great champion who had also been disowned by the All England Club because she had become Britain's first female professional coach.

The prospect of being barred for life from any connection with the official tennis world was the ultimate sanction the authorities had against top players turning professional. Many thought it was a small price to pay for earning honest money. In 1931, Bill Tilden set up his own professional tour which included Europe as well as the USA. He was joined by his fellow American Ellsworth Vines and, in 1936, by Fred Perry. It was a tough living. Conditions were primitive. They had to play night after night at different venues and were often required to share accommodation as well as the driving. It was usually late when they ended and difficult to find somewhere open to eat. But in six years as a professional on the road, Tilden earned 500,000 dollars. Vines and Perry weren't far behind.

Most of the Wimbledon champions in the 1930s, 1940s and 1950s joined Tilden's tour or tours run by his successors, Bobby Riggs and Jack Kramer. Like Tilden their amateur reputations– Riggs and Kramer were Wimbledon champions – ensured a regular flow of the best players, although not everyone took the professional dollar. Bunny Austin, the British number two in the 1930s, whose tennis achievements were overshadowed by Fred Perry, kept his City job and played as an amateur all his life. 'Lawn Tennis is not a career and does not bring a man to the happy harbour of financial independence', he once said, 'and for that reason I feel that one should beware of becoming too far ensnared in its toils. That a man should have to end his life as a professional, teaching others to play, is I think nothing short of a tragedy.'[10] Austin went on to join Moral Re-Armament, a curious spiritual movement which put individual change before social and political action. Perry went to Hollywood, married an actress and dined out with film stars.

Most of the professionals between the wars never achieved anything like the fame or fortune of Perry. Frank Donisthorpe played at Wimbledon as an amateur although he never did better than the third round. As a professional he won the second British professional championships held at the Gipsy Club in Highbury but the prize money was only a few pounds. Like many professionals who were not good enough to play in Tilden's tours, Donisthorpe became a coach. He is remembered because he was the first person to use an outsized, re-enforced wooden racket which he called Hazel.

Ted Millman was brought up in a colonial family in India and came to England in 1936 to make a living from tennis as a professional coach. He took over a struggling tennis club in Birmingham and made it profitable with exhibitions from the top professionals. In 1939, he arranged for Bill Tilden and three other players to appear at a local football ground and 8,000 people turned up to watch, a sign that professional tennis could attract crowds in Britain as well as America. After the war, Millman re-formed the professional coaches' association which had originally been founded by Dan Maskell and Charles Hierons in 1925 but had collapsed because of lack of support from the Lawn Tennis Association. Soon, the new coaches' association had several hundred members. But even with Maskell in the chair, it was still treated by the Lawn Tennis Association as 'the poor relation in the game.'[11]

This was a pity. The story of making money out of tennis is not simply one of sharp business people and star players fighting for their share of the spoils. It is also about coaches like Dorothea Lambert Chambers, Teach Tennant, Frank Donisthorpe, Dan Maskell and Ted Millman trying to earn a modest wage teaching the game they loved. The stars, entrepreneurs and coaches are not as far apart as they seem. With the exception, perhaps, of Charles Pyle, they all loved the sport as much as any amateur, probably more. It was their occupation and passion. They also shared something else that was a radical contribution to the sport, and in this Pyle was no exception. They brought new kinds of people into tennis, people who thought that Wimbledon was not for them but found a professional exhibition match in a sports arena near their home the key to a lifetime of enjoying the game.

8

Performers

At Waterloo station in the late morning of Monday 21 June 1937, there were queues already for the train to Wimbledon even though the scheduled start of that year's Championships was not until 2.00 pm. The day, weather forecasters had warned, was going to be 'rather warm' and the prospect of a packed steam train to the suburb, another queue for the trolleybus to the All England Club in Church Road and then another queue to gain admission to the ground was not something most fans were looking forward to, despite the enticing matches on offer. For the first time, however, there was an alternative.

On platform 16, Southern Railway had transformed a waiting room into a movie theatre. At the far end of the room there was an electronic television set powered by a cathode ray tube, one of only a few hundred then in existence. The programme due to be shown that afternoon was considered so experimental that there was no listing in that week's *Radio Times* as the technology might fail. It almost did, but the black-and-white pictures that flickered through that afternoon from Wimbledon's Centre Court were clear enough for viewers to see two men in white hitting a ball across a net. It was the first time a game of tennis had been televised.

Most of the officials at the All England Club in Wimbledon paid little attention to this experiment at the time. They were more concerned about the absence that year of Fred Perry. Perry had been the Men's Singles champion for the previous three years, but his defection to the professional game at the end of 1936 looked likely to dent Wimbledon's popularity. So there was considerable relief at the club when Monday morning saw the familiar queues snaking down Church Road. The crowds had come back confident that the 1937 Championships would throw up new performers to enthral them.

One promising new prospect was a young man from Oakland, California, who was rumoured to have the best backhand the game had ever seen. The 22-year-old Donald Budge did not disappoint. Over the next two weeks he lost only one set as his whiplash backhand destroyed his opponents, especially when they attacked him at the net. In the Men's Singles final he dispatched Gottfried von Cramm (who was playing, with considerable misgivings, under the Nazi swastika) almost as easily as Perry had done the year before. 'Gee whiz, I can't believe it even now', Budge told the press afterwards, 'I gave everything I had and was hoping and praying it was enough'. The papers certainly thought so. 'Few if any will ever beat Budge's great record having won the Championship with the loss of only one set', proclaimed the *Western Daily Mail*, 'he has established himself as the greatest amateur in the world'.[1] It was the start of a stellar tennis career for Budge that would result in him winning the first Grand Slam: the Australian, French, Wimbledon and American titles in the same year.

Despite the absence of Perry, 1937 turned out to be a good year for Britain. Dorothy Round, the daughter of a builder from Dudley, triumphed in an exciting Women's Singles final just edging ahead to beat the popular Polish player Jadwiga Jędrzejowska (usually called 'Jed' because her name was difficult for non-Polish speakers to pronounce). Bunny Austin reached the men's semi-final before losing in an epic struggle against von Cramm. Austin, though, is better remembered that year for his first-round match against the tall Irishman George Lyttleton-Rogers. It was not an exciting contest – Austin won easily – but it would change the game forever. It was the first tennis to appear on television.

The Championships had been covered by radio since 1927 when the BBC was allowed four experimental broadcasts live from Centre Court on condition that the corporation's regular sports commentator, Captain Teddy Wakelam, was assisted by Colonel R.H. Brand, a keen tennis player who had the trust of the All England Club. Over the airwaves, listeners heard Wakelam describe each stroke with precision. He said later that he found commentating on tennis 'much easier than any other sport' since he could 'see everything and was close to the action'. Radio coverage was extended in 1928 and 1929 to a couple of hours a day and within a few years the cut-glass tones of Captain Wakelam and Colonel Brand were being heard not just in Britain but on stations around the world.

The radio coverage at Wimbledon was seen as one of the great successes of the BBC's first decade of broadcasting, and when the corporation started experimenting with television, tennis seemed an obvious choice. In May 1937, six months after the first television transmissions from their studio in Alexandra Palace, north London, the BBC built a portable outside broadcasting unit to capture live pictures of the coronation of George VI. A month later, it was Wimbledon's turn.

To cover the tennis, the BBC positioned two cameras on Centre Court, one in a corner giving a close-up view of the match and the other at the opposite end giving a wider, more general shot. They were connected by a cable to a mobile control room built into a single-decker bus and stationed in the All England Club's car park. The plan was to transmit pictures 18 miles across London to Alexandra Palace where they would then be broadcast to the thousand or so electronic television sets in existence, most with a screen only twelve inches wide but set in wooden cabinets three times that size.

Unfortunately the connection from Wimbledon was more haphazard than from the coronation since there were more obstacles in the way. Not the least of these was Hornsey General Hospital in north London where high-frequency currents of diathermy, a treatment at the time given before surgery, interfered with the pictures. Fortunately the hospital agreed to suspend this treatment during transmission, and when the BBC's black-and-white pictures eventually appeared on television screens it was easy enough to distinguish the six foot seven inch Lyttleton-Rogers from Austin, who was only five foot nine. The sound was better than from most radios.

On that first Monday afternoon in June 1937, the few thousand people who watched at home or at special viewings in cinemas, central railway stations and department stores were given only 25 minutes of tennis, but it was enough. One reviewer noted that 'even the marks of the lawnmower were distinctly visible' while another said that the two players' movements about the court were clear enough 'after they became used to the strangeness of it all'.[2] The strangeness passed quickly because the cameras returned every day that fortnight to cover the entire Championships. In the second week the *Radio Times* felt confident enough to list it for the first time: 'The experiment of televising play on the Centre Court at Wimbledon by means of the radio link will be continued this week. Transmissions will take place every day with commentaries by F.H. Grisewood.'

The 49-year-old Freddie Grisewood was then in the middle of a long BBC career. Educated at public school and Oxford, his television commentaries from Wimbledon were one of the highlights of his life. His sister-in-law had been a top British tennis player in the 1920s and Grisewood himself was competent enough to once hit up with the Doherty brothers. In his autobiography published in 1952, he said he had tried to convey Wimbledon's 'unique charm'. A moment he had particularly enjoyed was the success of Dorothy Round and her 'gallant come-back' in 1937 to win the title. He hoped he would soon have the 'thrill of announcing to the world in general that a British player has become Champion again'.[3]

He never did. It would be another 24 years before a British player became a singles champion once more, and by then Grisewood had long given up tennis commentary to chair the popular radio programme, *Any Questions*. But he was at Wimbledon in 1938 and 1939 when the two BBC cameras were joined by a third which focussed on spectators and was able to capture the arrival of Queen Mary in the Royal Box.

Very little tennis was played in Britain during the war and none at Wimbledon, where the grass courts were turned into allotments and the ground became a farmyard stocked with rabbits, pigs and hens. The All England Club office was given over to military personnel and in early 1940, Air Chief Marshal Hugh Dowding – one of the key strategists behind the Battle of Britain – moved in. Perhaps because of some inside knowledge, Wimbledon was attacked by German bombs a few months later, on 11 October 1940. A corner of the Centre Court was struck destroying 1,200 seats although no person – or indeed animal – was hurt. A month later Dowding was removed from command. Wimbledon was never troubled again. When the Championships resumed in 1946, the destroyed seats remained out of commission and the ground was not fully repaired until three years later. With a shortage of essential items like lawn mowers, it was surprising that the 1946 Championships took place at all. But take place they did and television was there.

This time the BBC wasn't content to cover just the players and the Royal Box. The cameras would swing away during a pause in a match to catch film stars and ex-champions and to pick out the details that made Wimbledon special, like the white cloths covering picnic tables on the members' lawn which were adorned with iced cakes and cucumber sandwiches. In the early evening sunshine of finals day in 1946, the BBC filmed Alice Marble, the 1939 winner, interviewing the new champions, Yvon Petra from France and Pauline Betz from America. If the television pictures seemed to show that, despite the war, Wimbledon had changed little, it was clear the players had. Before the war, half of them were British. Now three quarters were from overseas, many from the USA.

Tennis had continued in America throughout the war, which was one reason why the top American players were more prepared for Wimbledon when it resumed than players from the British Isles. Many of the new American champions came from modest backgrounds. Jack Kramer, Bobby Riggs, Pancho Gonzales and Maureen Connolly all learned their tennis on the public courts of California and considered tennis not as an engrossing leisure activity but as a considered career choice. The potential of park tennis to produce a stream of hungry talent in Britain was ignored by the Lawn Tennis Association and was the principal reason why there was no British women's champion at Wimbledon between Dorothy Round in 1937 and Angela Mortimer in 1961, and no men's after Fred Perry in 1936 until Andy Murray in 2013. This absence of British champions, however, seemed not to bother spectators. They carried on with the Wimbledon tradition of adopting a charismatic foreign player as their own.

In 1948, their latest favourite was Jaroslav Drobny, the Czechoslovakian number one who beat Gottfried von Cramm and Donald Budge while still in his teens and became a national sports idol. Drobny's disenchantment with the new communist regime in Czechoslovakia led to his defection in 1949 with two shirts, a toothbrush and 50 dollars. When a wealthy cotton magnate from Cairo offered him the kind of job where he could play tennis full time, Drobny became an Egyptian citizen. Each year at Wimbledon, he would do well but then lose in an epic struggle against someone he was expected to beat. The spectators loved Drobny's stylish play, good looks, impeccable manners and his status as the perennial runner-up. Drobny also captivated viewers at home whose numbers were increasing every year. By 1948, Wimbledon was attracting a television audience of 200,000, almost as many as made it to the ground. Many were female, and the BBC coverage became known as 'housewives' fortnight'. Certainly more women than men watched Wimbledon over the next few decades, often with 'curtains drawn against the evening sun, Mum and the family peering at a black-and-white TV passing the salad cream and the Kraft cheese slice'.[4]

One woman who became a tennis fan, although she never expressed any desire for salad cream or cheese slices, was Judy Haines from Chingford in Essex. Judy had agreed with her husband Abbe to stay at home after the war despite Prime Minister Clement Attlee's appeal to women to return to the workplace: 'Abbe said I had a job of work at home, and I was very happy. I think Abbe deserves to be well looked after and a woman can't do this and go to work as well.' For the next two decades she brought up her family trying to 'make the best of everything in a time of endemic shortages'. She found being a housewife an undemanding occupation and poured her thoughts and energy into a diary which was highlighted by historian David Kynaston in his social histories of Britain after the Second World War. According to Judy Haines' diary, watching the tennis every year at Wimbledon was one pleasure she could rely on, although she was sometimes frustrated by the BBC scheduling. On Wednesday 5 July 1950, Judy noted her annoyance that the 'children's programmes including Prudence the Kitten interrupted a set which went to 31–29'.[5] That set was a men's doubles quarter final and involved Frank Sedgman and Budge Patty who three days later would contest the Men's Singles final when Patty was the unexpected winner.

If the BBC television pictures after the war generally pleased viewers like Judy Haines, the commentary took longer to sort out. One newspaper reviewer in 1949 claimed that the commentators showed 'less skill than the cameras. Several perform as though they were doing sound broadcast and repeat in words what we have seen the moment before with our very own eyes.' BBC executives were critical too, although they exonerated Grisewood's 'warm homely voice'. 'He doesn't add anything much to the picture but is worth retaining as the main lawn tennis commentator because of his manner.' Other potential commentators who were tried in the late 1940s were found wanting apart from Dan Maskell, then celebrating 20 years as the All England Club's professional coach. Maskell did 'very well. He steadily improved and while a little inclined to talk over rallies we strongly recommend him next year.'[6]

Maskell did come back the following year and stayed four decades, never missing a day's play. His approach – 'instead of describing in words a winner, I try and say why it was a winner'[7] – became the defining BBC tennis style. With a dulcet microphone voice and insider knowledge, Maskell captured the attraction of Wimbledon as a theatrical performance as much as a tough sporting contest, although the BBC initially thought he should lighten up a little. 'I am afraid', a producer wrote to him in 1951, 'you must have got rather tired of my reminding you of our half-witted viewers but it is of course a fact that only a minority have an informed appreciation of the significance of the Championships and after all our object is to widen the interest and bring it down to the level of the less knowledgeable'.[8]

To connect better with these 'half-witted' viewers, Maskell developed some of the first television catchphrases such as 'quite extraordinary' and 'peach of a shot' and the phrase that came to define him, 'oh I say', all enunciated in an upper-middle-class accent a long way from his humble origins. Watching the 1952 Championships for *The Observer*, Caroline Lejeune was a Maskell fan: 'Better than ever this year with just the right amount of informed and constructive commentary from Dan Maskell. Mr. Maskell knows a commentator's place as well as he knows tennis. It's a privilege to watch a championship match in his company.'[9]

In Chingford, Judy Haines seems to have liked Maskell too. In June 1954, she noted the 'good tennis and good sportsmanship. Wimbledon has kept me going this week', although on the final Saturday she was 'very sorry Louise Brough didn't beat that cocky little Maureen Connolly in the women's singles'.[10] Haines clearly did not warm to the diminutive Californian even though Connolly had become the first woman to win the Grand Slam the year before. Much of the British press, while applauding Connolly's achievements, shared Haines' lack of enthusiasm, saving their cheers that year for the bespectacled Jaroslav Drobny. 'In the tennis world, 1954 will be remembered as Drobny's year', gushed the London newspaper, *The Sphere*, 'like a fairy story, everything came right in the end'. It certainly did for Drobny who at 33 possessed enough tennis magic to confound the 19-year-old Australian prodigy Ken Rosewall and win the Men's Singles at his eleventh attempt. After the match, Drobny received a rapturous reception from the crowd, which 'could not have been greater had he been an Englishman'. In 1959, he took British citizenship and became just that.

Perhaps because it took Drobny so long to win Wimbledon, or maybe because the Egyptian arrangement was better than any he could obtain from playing for money, Drobny was one of the few

Wimbledon champions in the decades after the Second World War not to switch from amateur to professional. The professional circuit in the 1950s and 1960s was small but the rewards on offer tempted all the best players, especially those from poorer backgrounds. Most eventually succumbed. In 1955, a series of hard-fought contests between Pancho Gonzales and Tony Trabert, when they almost came to blows, attracted large crowds and removed any lingering concerns about the intensity of professional play. 'No one', pointed out tennis writer Joe McCauley, 'could doubt the genuineness of their meetings'.[11] But the next few years saw the fortunes of professional tennis fluctuate and it was only the signing of the Australian champions Lew Hoad and Rod Laver that kept the tours popular.

Some of the matches Laver, Hoad, Gonzales, Trabert and the other professionals played in were held in prestigious places like Madison Square Garden in New York, Marks Oval in Sydney and Wembley Arena in London, and these were televised by the American and Australian networks and by the BBC. Most professional matches in the decades after the war were away from the cameras. In venues across Europe, Australia and the United States there were occasionally capacity crowds of several thousand people, but usually a few hundred turned out. It was, as Jack Kramer, the most successful of the professional promoters, once put it, 'a tough way to make a buck' but this was how bucks in tennis were made.

Making money as an amateur was certainly possible if you were prepared to take part in the charade of 'expenses'. Despite the considerable cash flowing into tennis from television in the 1950s and 1960s, the sport remained trapped in the 'gentleman-amateur' bubble laid down by the Lawn Tennis Association in 1911. Players were still meant to perform simply out of love for the game. They did nothing of the sort. Top tennis by then was not only a sport but a televised entertainment and, as the South African player Gordon Forbes pointed out, entertainers do not entertain for free.

Forbes was never a champion, but in the early 1960s he did make the top 20 and in a final he once beat Rod Laver. Like most of the amateur players after the war, he adored the game but had no private income and could only afford to play if he was paid. This had to be done in secret. 'Each tournament would have a settling up day', Forbes recalled, 'the secretary got all shifty eyed and furtive and took one into a small windowless room, inserted his head into a wall-safe and withdrew a money box. Lips were licked while the box was unlocked, and a fat fresh slab of money was withdrawn.'[12] At the time, the going rate for players like Forbes was 75 dollars a week plus travel and board. The stars received much more. Since these payments were often on top of earnings from sports or tobacco companies, life as a champion amateur could be extremely lucrative. The masters were the Australians.

From upper-middle-class beginnings in Victoria in the 1880s, tennis had evolved into a more egalitarian sport in Australia than in the British Isles. In the 1950s, no other country had as many courts per head and the sport was relatively inexpensive to play. When most of the top American players turned professional after the Second World War, Australia took on the role of the leading amateur tennis nation due to the heroic efforts of one man, Harry Hopman.

Hopman was born in 1906, the son of a schoolmaster. He was good enough to reach the 4th round in Wimbledon in the 1930s and then trained as a coach while working as a sportswriter for the *Melbourne Herald*. It is for his coaching and not his journalism that he will be remembered. A strict disciplinarian, he devised a style of playing tennis that emphasised percentage play and control of emotion. The result was that his protégés, like Frank Sedgman, Ken Rosewall, Lew Hoad and Rod Laver, played with a rigour that ensured success but at the expense of expressing their personality on court. Hopman had an unrivalled ability to turn out champions in the 1950s and 1960s but it was underpinned by money. Many of his players were from working-class or rural families: their fathers were plasterers, electricians and grocers. They weren't in the least embarrassed about being paid to play and they all became adept at receiving every expense on offer. 'The Australian interpretation of amateur tennis', recalled one of them at the time, 'was the envy of the rest of the tennis world'.[13]

Even the Australians, though, were at the mercy of tournament officials who could treat them like performing animals. Service was expected, and not just on court. Arthur Ashe, one of the few top American players in the 1960s who remained an amateur, described this experience not unkindly as that of a 'tennis bum' totally dependent on charm, grace and favour. It was all enjoyable enough as long as you were winning. The 'bums' attracted supporters and hangers-on, young women with taste and rich men with connections who provided meals, cars and hotels in return for a share of the limelight and an occasional hit on court. This was the celebrity life, but the players were treated, as Jack Kramer taunted, like 'athletic gigolos'.

One player who did not mind how he was treated as long as the money rolled in was Mike Davies. Born in 1936, he learned tennis on public courts in Cwmdonkin Park in Swansea where he fell in love with the game. 'Nothing mattered except that I should play tennis every available moment', he wrote in his 1962 memoir, *Tennis Rebel*. 'When I lost I was literally furious. If you don't want to win it is not worth playing.'[14] Davies did want to win, badly. In the 1950s, he progressed from junior champion in Wales to British number one, but money was always a problem. He often hitch-hiked to tournaments, lived on a 'diet of potato crisps and Polo mints' and would sleep in dingy bed and breakfasts or once under a hedge. Slowly he learned to survive by finding out which tournament and which officials could be tapped for travel, accommodation and food and sometimes he was fortunate. On one occasion in the late 1950s, he played in Detroit where he was put up in a mansion with 'swimming pools, automatic garage doors, television and telephone in literally every room, concealed lighting, stereo sound equipment, playrooms as big as billiard halls and enormous bars stocked with every conceivable brand of liquor'. It was owned by a millionaire publisher called Wilkinson who 'always made his house available for visiting tennis players'.[15]

Most of the time though there were no millionaire mansions, and life on the road was tough. 'Only a very small minority of amateurs make much money out of tennis', wrote Bobby Wilson,

Davies' British rival, and there were a 'great many also-rans who see the world free of charge but who have nothing in the bank to show for ten years of hard physical endeavour'.[16] After a decade of playing tennis full time, Mike Davies had only a hundred pounds in the bank despite his best efforts to accept money wherever and whenever he could. He was grateful to receive an invitation from Kramer to turn professional and accept a 'guaranteed income of three thousand five hundred pounds a year' with possible bonuses, coaching and advertising work. He described his amateur tennis playing years as 'so much hypocrisy and nonsense'.

Davies was lucky. For many other successful amateurs the call from Kramer never came. Despite their talent, they didn't fit into his professional portfolio. These professional rejects remained amateurs, and when they began to lose matches they were dropped by their rich tennis friends quickly and ruthlessly. When his form on court started the slow journey down, Gordon Forbes asked these friends to help him find a job. 'Certainly Gordon, old fellow', was a typical response, 'I'll arrange for you to talk to Old Buster Miles. A great friend of mind. Jolly good chap really. We ride together. Loves his tennis too.' Forbes met several 'Old Busters' but none delivered. At the end of his playing career, he returned to South Africa and took a job as a salesman for a lighting firm.

Many of the top players in the 1950s and 1960s ended up in similar positions, particularly the women who were less in demand on the professional circuit. The clever ones retired early to train for a career. The remainder became tennis coaches. In 'A Fairly Regular Four', a short story set in the early 1960s, the novelist Frederic Raphael described a lesson with 'old Ralph', an ex-amateur champion who taught in a London tennis club. 'He was bent at the waist like some antique butler warped by deference. On the high-roofed court, he called you "sir".'[17] Ralph had been a Davis Cup player for England, but this had not provided him with any future income. Immediately after his last match for his country, 'he had been given the elbow'.

Old Ralph may be a literary exaggeration written 20 years after the time it describes, but not by much. While few of the last amateur champions ended up bent double teaching tennis to novelists, many suffered as a result of throwing in education at an early age to play tennis full time. This was the reality of tennis at the top level during the early televised years and it passed television by. The revelations by journalists and ex-players about 'amateur' tennis were aired in newspapers and books but were ignored by the BBC, which was concerned that any criticism of the game might mean losing their Wimbledon contract.

After 1946, Wimbledon had gradually become a 'must' for the BBC and the BBC a must for Wimbledon, a relationship that has continued ever since. Wimbledon treated the BBC generously. 'I assumed it was the deliberate policy of an amateur sport towards a public service', said one BBC executive at the time.[18] What he didn't say was that this was repaid by television coverage which never criticised the way the All England Club did business and never investigated the rotten state of the elite amateur game. BBC tennis viewers were treated to some magnificent tennis in these years but were kept in the dark about the shady dealings that kept it all afloat. There was too much at stake.

In 1954, the formation of Eurovision meant that the BBC was able to supply its pictures to eight countries on the continent including France, Germany and Italy who all paid handsomely. In 1961, 14 million viewers in Britain saw the Women's Singles final between two British women, Christine Truman and Angela Mortimer, and millions more watched in Europe. A year later, live pictures were transmitted by the Telstar satellite across the Atlantic to the lucrative American market for the first time. Tennis was awash with money. With the introduction of a second television channel in 1964, the BBC increased its coverage of Wimbledon to ten hours a day.

Growing up in the east Midlands in the 1950s and 1960s, the Championships at Wimbledon were an annual treat in Andrea Sanders-Reece's house that all the family looked forward to each summer: 'When my father died, the Rugby Round Table gave us a television and then every year for as many years as I can remember, our family life during the two weeks of Wimbledon ran to the rhythm of the tennis matches shown on TV.' Even when it was raining and repeats were shown, Andrea's mother was still captivated. 'Tennis was the common language in phone calls with my uncle and mum's cousin. The opening line was "Did you see ... ?"'[19]

Like many devoted fans, Andrea's mother didn't play tennis but she knew the game and recognised in the 1960s that Wimbledon was losing its best stars. The exodus of amateur players to the professional ranks reached such a level that the Championships every July started resembling a qualifying competition for Jack Kramer's tours. Open tennis was inevitable and the BBC started preparing the way by employing Kramer as a Wimbledon commentator in the hope too that his Californian sharpness would be a foil to the plummy tones of Dan Maskell. Internal memos from the time admitted that Kramer had been a 'controversial choice' because of his central position in the professional game, but his 'tremendous knowledge of tennis and its personalities won him wide popularity with the viewers'.[20] One viewer who was not happy was the retired civil servant Sir Henry French, who claimed in a letter to the BBC that he 'wielded a good deal of influence in sporting circles'. He told the corporation that he objected strongly to Kramer's speculation during the televising of the 1962 championship that the men's champion Rod Laver would soon turn professional. Kramer turned out to be exactly right, perhaps because he knew Laver would not refuse the deal he was about to offer him. The BBC never heard from Sir Henry again.

The top players who remained as amateurs in the mid-1960s were increasingly blatant about ensuring they were rewarded for their play. 'The players' tearoom during the Wimbledon fortnight', according to the well-informed tennis journalist Richard Evans, 'was an open market with tournament directors from around the world bartering for the services of "amateur" players. Top of the wanted list was Manolo Santana, the 1966 Champion, at 1000 dollars per week – under the table naturally.'[21] When deals like this were being done just a few seconds' walk from Centre Court, the All England Club realised the time had come to abandon its ban on professionalism, whatever the rest of the tennis world thought. With the Lawn Tennis Association's backing, it held a professional tournament over the August bank holiday in 1967 which attracted large crowds, and was won by Rod Laver with a standard of play much higher than at the official Championships a few weeks' earlier. A few months later, in December 1967, British tennis unilaterally abolished the words amateur and professional from its rules. The rest of tennis followed sheepishly a few months later. In April 1968, Ken Rosewall received £1,000 after winning the first amateur tournament to include professionals, the British Hard Court Championships at Bournemouth. The tournament was pronounced by newspapers like the *Birmingham Post* a 'resounding success'.[22] A new era of tennis was beginning.

It felt a brave move at the time, but in hindsight the money television was bringing in made it inevitable. Something, though, was lost with the transition of top tennis from amateur to professional. There were virtues in the old system despite the double standards. Unlike the professional game, amateur tennis did try and keep alive the enjoyment of playing tennis at the highest level for its own sake. Gordon Forbes describes a tennis life in the late 1950s where young men and women travelled from tournament to tournament living off expenses and patronage. The most important people were not officials or coaches but each other, as opponents, confidants, room-mates, friends and lovers. It was a vivid time of escapades and affairs where players competed fiercely on court in the day and then danced all night in exclusive clubs in Nice, Melbourne and Beverly Hills. Of course it was not quite like this. Memory can do odd things. Forbes kept a diary and he quotes from what he actually wrote at the time. There is one 'rather bitter little page' composed one night in Rome in 1956 in which he described his life as 'all just travelling, tennis and waiting'. He thinks back and admits that there were many moments like this, but what he prefers to remember is 'the fun and the laughter'.[23]

What he also remembers is that, despite the massive gulf in standard between elite and club tennis, the champions often turned up to play at local tournaments and remained members of their local tennis club. But these clubs themselves were changing during this time, changes hastened by television. The first era of televised tennis coincided with – and contributed to – a golden age of tennis playing at the grass roots.

9

Enthusiasts

On the west coast of Wales, half-way between Aberystwyth and Cardigan, is the seaside resort of Aberaeron. A pretty town of some 1,500 people, it has been voted the 'best place to live in Wales' and its fine Regency buildings, grouped around a central square, have been featured on stamps celebrating British rural architecture. Less celebrated but arguably just as important to the community is the Aberaeron Sports Club half a mile from the sea, which dates back to the late nineteenth century when the town was a busy fishing port. Tennis has been played here since 1882, and by the First World War the club had men's, women's and mixed teams in the tennis leagues of Cardiganshire. Team play has continued virtually without interruption since.

Sometime in the early 1950s, a 16 year old called Gareth Owen, who had been a keen junior member of the club, was invited to join the men's first team as the partner of Hubert Griffiths, then approaching the 'autumn' of his playing years. It was hoped that Gareth's youth and speed combined with Hubert's experience and 'killer instinct on the net' would provide the necessary balance, consistency and guile for the pair to win matches. So it proved. They quickly became one of Aberaeron's best pairs. 'He used to run miles to save my ageing legs,' Hubert Griffiths remembered, 'mind you I had to threaten him on many an occasion in a tight match at match point. Gareth used to try and finish in a blaze of glory by serving an ace but more often or not he served a double fault. That was the time I used to walk back and threaten him with my racket or the lashing of my tongue.'[1] For Gareth Owen, it is the away matches that remain in his mind. There was Ammanford, 'which seemed to have a carnival in progress whenever we played there,' Lampeter College, 'where would-be-vicars frolicked away the last of their youth,' Llandysul, 'where it never rained,' Aberystwyth, 'which had red ash courts and real changing rooms', Llandybie 'on the fringe of the anthracite belt where the only way to survive was to dig in', and Llanelli, 'who had grass and were better than us or so they thought'.

With the exceptions of Llanelli and Aberystwyth, with its 'real changing room', the facilities at the clubs Gareth and Hubert played against were basic. Few had showers and in one the players were encouraged after the match to wash in the nearby River Teifi. But then their own club in Aberaeron in the 1950s was hardly salubrious. The entrance was through a dilapidated kissing gate and the pavilion was a rusty zinc shed which served as changing room, grandstand and recreational area when rain stopped play.

Gareth and Hubert were a successful partnership for six years. 'The best partner I played with', said Hubert, 'happy memories' with the exception of one match when Hubert caught a ball in the stomach and was 'poleaxed'. Fortunately a doctor was playing bowls on a nearby green and prescribed an 'immediate injection of spirit' in the local pub. Everyone else joined them for a pint but it was the beginning of the end. Hubert would soon retire from matches and their partnership finished. Twenty-five years later, Gareth still recalled those games with Hubert not just for the sport but for the 'companionship, incidents and friendship'.

Their tennis experience is included in *Reflections on 100 years of Aberaeron Tennis 1882–1982*, a booklet written by Gareth Owen and published in 1982 to mark the centenary of the Aberaeron Sports Club.[2] It is one of several dozen similar histories celebrating their clubs' one hundred years of tennis playing. All the decades of the twentieth century are usually covered in these booklets but they are at their best in the 1950s and 1960s, a time far enough away to allow secrets to be revealed and yet near enough to be able to rely on first-hand accounts from retired members, although of course what is remembered and its significance will change over time.

Reading them today, the fond memories that are recalled by Gareth Owen and Hubert Griffiths turn out to be not so unusual.

As television was bringing championship tennis to a new audience, the 20 years after the Second World War turn out to be an exhilarating time for tennis players at the grass roots, especially those who played in clubs. In 1959, the number of tennis clubs affiliated to the Lawn Tennis Association reached 3,788, an all-time high as adult participation in tennis in Britain reached its peak. These years were a golden age of tennis playing, and not just in the British Isles. Club histories from Canada, Australia and the United States also show that the 1950s and 1960s were a treasured time. Long gone is the garden party atmosphere of the late nineteenth and early twentieth century, and gone too is the aspiration of the 1930s. After the Second World War, the members-owned tennis club relaxed into a style which would last until the advent of commercial rivals in the early 1980s and which can best be described as a celebration of cooperation, understatement and thrift.

This way of playing tennis reflected the spirit of the times. Post-war Britain was dominated by an austerity which lasted well into the 1950s. At the end of the war, there was a shortage of essential materials. The Lawn Tennis Association told clubs they had to do their own repairs and so the ethos of most suburban and small-town tennis clubs, like many sports clubs of the time, became DIY – do it yourself – as the booklet celebrating 100 years of the tennis club at Blundellsands, a northern suburb of Liverpool, proudly recounted: 'The wooden surround of the pavilion base had rotted as had the netting posts, and timber with everything else was on permit even until 1952. So the base of the pavilion was renewed with bricks from bombed buildings and a source of supply of concrete posts found for the netting.'[3]

The patching-up worked. Membership of Blundellsands Lawn Tennis Club quickly rose to 149 adults even when the annual subscription was raised to three pounds. Soon the scope of club activities extended beyond tennis. Formal dances were arranged at the Blundellsands Hotel while informal hops took place in the club pavilion when attendances were 'so good that substantial sums were transferred to club funds'. On wet evenings, there were darts, table tennis, bridge and mah jong; on Sunday afternoons, treasure hunts were organised around local villages which often involved 'getting lost in the wilds of Halsall and trying to decipher the names on old stone bridges over the canal'.

Many of these social events were courtship by another name. Blundellsands claimed it had 'more eligible bachelors than anywhere in the western hemisphere' and a 'bevy of female charm to match the Television Toppers'. This, perhaps, was the main reason why single members came to play from as far away as Liverpool city centre, an eight-mile train journey down the coast. One woman who met her husband at the club looks back on these times with fondness. 'I consider myself very fortunate', she recalled, 'to have belonged to the club during the fantastic 1950s'. She remembered most of all not the tennis but 'dancing the hot summer nights away to the beat of 12th Street Rag and going for a walk around the courts in the moonlight', even if such moonlight walks might mean waiting on Blundellsands Station for several hours for the early morning milk train home.[4]

Stories like this do tend to support the argument made by some historians that the tennis played at club level in Britain during this time was not a competitive sport open to anyone but a pleasant pastime restricted to the middle classes. Certainly the focus of the centenary booklets in these decades is on social activities rather than the actual tennis. Then again, there are only so many ways to describe a player's game, though the booklet about Cullercoats Tennis Club in north-east England does its best. John Miller, the 1950 Men's champion, was 'a pleasure to partner thriving on accuracy, touch and placing' while Ken Atchison played with 'an excellent almost error free game and a well disguised reverse spin service'. Mike Adams was a 'good all court player with excellent volleys' and Shirley Miller possessed a 'good service and accurate sliced shots deep in the corners'.[5]

These descriptions of play, though, could have been written about members of any tennis club in Britain or in most other countries at the time. 'Bill (Croskell) was a very cagey player who because of his inability to move freely around the court indulged in delicate drop shots and a tricky reverse spin serve which shot off at peculiar angles. Another member of a similar ability was Ted Reynolds a teacher at the State School. Between them, these two had every shot in the book and a few of their own inventions.' Bill and Ted were not from Cullercoats but from Frankston, 34 miles south of Melbourne, where tennis dates back to 1881.[6]

What makes clubs like Cullercoats and Frankston unique is the inclusion of other details which were incidental to the tennis but summed up the individuality of the club and its members. In Frankston in 1946, the club organised a series of exhibition matches in aid of the 'Food for Britain' appeal. In one the future Wimbledon champion, Frank Sedgman turned up and 'coped stoically with a rather damp and slippery grass court before a very appreciative gallery'. In Cullercoats, a decade later we learn not just about Mike Adam's excellent volleys but also about his 'waste-paper saving campaign' (although not whether it was successful). We find out not only about Shirley Miller's 'sliced shots deep in the corner' but about her decision to leave Northumberland to 'go and live in Gibraltar' (although we are never told why). Joy Lawson was a 'wonderful partner as the six different players who shared her doubles titles would testify' (although we never hear from any of them).

It is not play that stands out in these booklets but character. In the centenary account of Catford Wanderers Tennis Club in south London, Ken Thompsett, a 'county tennis player', is remembered for his 'masterly story telling'. Ken, a county councillor from 1947 to 1963, had a house backing on to the club and his 'yarns enlivened late night drinking. If one was awake at 2am, quite a common sight would be Ken in his pyjamas vaulting over his back garden and watering the grass courts.'[7] At Harpenden Tennis Club in Hertfordshire, Kim Grenside is described as 'never team material but played his tennis for fun and love of the game'. He spent all his weekends at the club and served as 'honorary secretary' for 20 years with an office in a shed next to the pavilion 'doing everything'. When he finally retired from the club in 1990, he was presented with 'a well-padded garden chair'.[8]

For Kim, Ken and many of the people who are featured in these booklets, the tennis club was one of the most important things in their life and the social jaunts they organised and the other activities in which they took part gave their lives meaning. Without the actual tennis though, these activities would have seemed empty. Sport was the reason they became members in the first place and what they had in common with everyone else. There is absolutely no reason – nor any evidence – to think that these club members did not take playing tennis in the 1950s and 1960s as seriously as any football, hockey or cricket player took their game. Ken, after all, was a county player and Kim truly loved competing.

After the Second World War, club tennis in Britain was pulled in two different directions. Many clubs removed participation barriers, reduced costs and promoted inclusivity, but some continued to see themselves as much as a social club as a sports club. Membership for these 'social' clubs was a status symbol and members needed to be the right sort. To make sure, new members had to take a 'playing in test' which tested more than their ability to hit a ball over a net. Julian Barnes captures this well in his 2018 novel *The Only Story*, which starts in suburban Surrey in the summer of 1963 when 19-year-old Paul Roberts is back from university with nothing to do. His parents suggest he joins the local tennis club. 'I went along and was invited to "play in". This was a test in which not just my tennis game but my general deportment and social suitability would be quietly examined in a decorous English way. If I failed to display negatives then positives would be assumed: this was how it worked … I reminded myself not to swear burp or fart on court.'[9]

Paul passed the test, but then he knew what to do. The question is whether such exclusionary tests, which only took place in a minority of clubs, had a disproportionate effect on the sport in general, whether the knowledge that there were tennis clubs which did not want working-class (or indeed black, Jewish or gay) members put off people who would have liked to take up the sport but were made to feel it was not for them. Tennis clubs in Britain during these decades were more conflicted about potential new members than Julian Barnes's novel implies.

Certainly to thrive in clubs like Cullercoats, Blundellsands, Aberaeron and Catford Wanderers you needed to be the 'right sort', but it is not clear what this actually meant. The most crucial ingredient seems to be not your social class but your ability to rub along, and skills in carpentry and decorating were appreciated just as much as the ability to do a proper set of accounts. What mattered above all was the desire to mix in. Roy Thorn joined Chesham Bois Tennis Club in Buckinghamshire in 1948 and was a member for 60 years. 'Membership fees were one guinea and the facilities were fairly primitive, with a single storey wooden clubhouse and only six courts – three grass and three red shale'.[10] 'People would just turn up and mix.' At least they did most of the time. Roy remembered one particular game in the early 1950s when this didn't happen. 'Four players were already there but they just kept playing.' He was left twiddling his racket and waiting for them to come off court and include him, but this never transpired. 'Once they had finished their two sets they all just packed up and left!' Roy raised the issue with the committee, and they decided to instigate 'club play', times when members were not allowed to organise their own games but had to play with anyone who turned up.

'Club play' was a common device at virtually all tennis clubs during these decades to allow people of different abilities to play together. It usually took place on Saturday or Sunday afternoons, and the tennis game played was doubles with the strongest player in a four paired with the weakest to ensure a reasonable game for all. One positive consequence of this, perhaps intended, perhaps not, was that it helped people from different classes and backgrounds learn the manners and etiquette of a club, how they could 'fit in'. The main opportunity for this was mid-afternoon tea when play stopped, and everyone ate and drank together. Decades later it is these teas that are remembered. At Dinas Powis Tennis Club in Glamorgan, they were laid out 'on a long trestle table with dishes of jam and plates piled high with bread and butter. There were also meringues, gateaux, and flans. Tea was served weak.'[11] For those on the rota, 'no mistakes were to be made regarding egg sandwiches' because Dr Bev (Lex Beveridge, the 'moving spirit of the club') liked his 'unadulterated. Heaven help anyone who committed the cardinal sin of adding mayonnaise.' After a mayonnaise-free tea – or perhaps they mean salad cream, as mayonnaise was not widely available in Britain until the 1970s – tennis carried on at Dinas Powis until the 'evening sun lit up the horse chestnut trees that surrounded the courts. We were still chasing balls as the last glint of sunshine disappeared behind the trees.'[12]

It is a deeply nostalgic image but there were changes ahead even in south Wales. As 1950s family Britain morphed into 1960s individualism, there was a growing division between the old hierarchy like Dr Bev and a new breed of members who were more permissive in their appetites. Richard Jeffrey, who joined the Dinas Powis club at this time, remembers this division erupting over a 'highly controversial men's night' with a stripper who 'may or may not' have been called Pandora. The venue was originally intended to be the clubhouse, but after protests it was moved to a local golf club where 'we made some money, had plenty of laughs and got some great gossip'. According to Jeffrey, this event symbolised a 'coming of age of a club that had until then been firmly locked in a Victorian time warp'.[13] What Dr Bev thought about it is not recorded.

By the middle of the 1960s, most private tennis clubs were learning to embrace bingo as well as bridge even if they drew the line at strippers. The gradual importation into the British tennis club of cultural forms that owed more to working-class than middle-class sensibility, pop music rather than jazz, polytechnic rather than red brick university, was spurred on by economics. In the 1960s, the number of affiliated clubs to the Lawn Tennis Association fell as the land clubs occupied was targeted for new development. Many ended up under car parks or blocks of flats. Some of their members moved to other clubs but some gave up tennis completely. There was greater social mobility in this time too, and this produced a larger churn of members than before.

Most private tennis clubs needed all the new members they could find, especially as they were also competing with another kind of tennis club that existed before the Second World War but came into its own at this time: the tennis club at work.

When Jesse Boot took over the small pharmaceutical business his father had founded in Nottingham in 1849, his ambition was to make it 'the chemist for the nation'. By the middle of the twentieth century this had been achieved in a way Boot could never have dreamed. By the time a Boots pharmacist discovered ibuprofen in 1961, one of the best-selling drugs of all time, the company already had shops in most high streets in Britain and Ireland and was set to expand overseas. Its headquarters, however, remained firmly in Nottingham. To attract talented scientists to the east Midlands, the company invested in one of the largest works' sports clubs in the country, including a thriving tennis section which dated back to the early years of the century. Jesse Boot had insisted on it.

In 1900, Boot was 50 years old and had severe arthritis which left him 'racked with pain' and often confined to a wheelchair.[14] He spent most of his time in the summer house he built on meadows on the south side of the city next to the River Trent which he named 'Plaisance'. To encourage his managers to visit him, Jesse Boot laid out a recreation ground in front of the house, paying particular attention to tennis. 'You will want a good man who understands tennis to look after all the tennis courts', he instructed his staff, 'they will be in use all the year around.' And they were. Before the First World War, tennis matches for Boots employees were arranged on most 'long sunny afternoons' with 'refreshments served to thirsty participants'.[15] In the years that followed, Boots became known not just for its medicines but also for its tennis. On summer evenings in the 1950s, the company's 24 grass courts and four hard courts were often fully occupied and it sponsored several successful men's and women's teams in the county leagues.

Boots may have given tennis a special prominence but it certainly wasn't the only Nottinghamshire employer who provided the sport for its staff. Dozens of other companies in the county invested in tennis courts at this time, from the giant British Sugar factory in Newark to the small printing works in Longsight. Nottinghamshire was not unusual. In Derbyshire, 20,000 people played on company courts in the 1950s. In Paisley, Clarks sponsored the Anchor Tennis Club for employees from their textile mills which had the 'best facility in the south-West of Scotland'.[16] On the Wirral near Birkenhead, Lever Brothers set up the Port Sunlight Tennis Club for their soap factory workers. In Bourneville in south Birmingham Cadburys had 60 tennis courts in the 1950s. The chocolate company regarded their tennis club as a way of breaking down the division between white- and blue-collar staff: 'we have helped extend play of once exclusive games like tennis where managers and workers meet as equals.'[17]

Another company that took tennis seriously was Midland Bank. After the First World War, the bank laid down three hard courts and four grass courts in New Beckenham on the outskirts of London. A pavilion was opened in 1921 with an exhibition of tennis by Dorothea Lambert Chambers, and one of the first presidents of the bank's tennis club was Alexander Goschen, a senior director at the bank. Betty Kendale, who joined the Midland straight from school in the thirties, became their star player and one year won the United Banks Ladies' Singles title. She carried on playing until 1961.[18]

The Midland Bank Tennis Club, now renamed after its parent company, HSBC, survives today as a one of Kent's more dynamic tennis clubs, but it is in a minority. The decline in work club tennis started in the middle of the 1960s. In counties like Derbyshire, colliery tennis leagues and miners' tennis clubs closed while in Nottinghamshire tennis clubs at small firms like Beeston Boilers folded when the company went out of business, as did the club at British Ropes a few years later when its three hard courts were turned into a car park. By 1969, even the Tennis Club at Boots had slimmed down to just twelve courts. Today it has only six.

Some of this reduction can be explained by the changing nature of work, but not all. The number of people who played tennis in private clubs fell in this decade too. The same was true in public parks and one statistic sums this up. In Birmingham, 71,000 tickets to play park tennis were sold in 1955–6. Seven years later, there were only 31,000. All across Britain there were similar stories as queues to play on a park court became a distant memory. To try and revitalise public court tennis the British Parks Amateur Lawn Tennis Association was formed in 1957 with representatives from park tennis associations in Sheffield, Manchester, Leeds, Bradford, Burnley, Dumfries, Glasgow, Nelson, Walsall, Bournemouth and Brighton. But the new association only lasted a few years. In the early 1960s, it was taken over by the Lawn Tennis Association and then forgotten about. Slowly the local park tennis associations disappeared too, and without an advocate many tennis courts in public parks fell into disrepair, their nets tangled and their tarmac cracked and broken. Few people cared. Like private tennis clubs and works tennis, the demand for courts so noticeable even ten years before had disappeared. Many people in 1960s Britain simply stopped playing the game.

Explanations for the loss in popularity of tennis during this time in Britain vary from the lack of attention given to the sport at the new comprehensive schools to the increased popularity of sports that could be picked up and enjoyed straight away like squash. Certainly there was a shift from playing social sports like tennis and cricket (which also went into decline) to individual pursuits like running, cycling and walking. But this shift was a sign of something else going on. The retreat from tennis mirrored a retreat from other forms of associational life. It wasn't just membership of tennis and cricket clubs that declined in this time but also membership of churches, trade unions and other voluntary groups. Longer working hours, growing domesticity, holidays abroad, increased private car ownership and not least the developing attraction of television changed the context within which people spent their free time. Tennis lost out. It seemed part of an older world of civic life, social improvement and suburban clubbability and unable to adapt to social change. In 1960s Britain and abroad, the sport didn't do enough to reach out to new constituencies and attract new people into the game who would bring energy, enthusiasm and ideas. In particular in Britain it missed out on a small but growing part of the population whose children would change British sport forever.

10

Immigrants

In the middle of Crouch End in north London – hemmed in by suburban streets, million-pound houses and a school proudly describing itself as 'truly comprehensive' – is an open expanse of woods and meadows that has provided exercise and enjoyment for local people since the 1920s. Every weekend the area's residents can be spotted here tending organic vegetables on their allotments, walking their Labradors and Labradoodles, or indulging in a game of cricket or tennis in one of the half-dozen clubs that jostle for territory here in this space known as Crouch End Playing Fields.

As you enter the fields from the main entrance in Park Road, the first tennis club you come to is called Georgians. It is a relatively new club with an array of clay, carpet and artificial grass courts painted in red, blue and green. The club house is well equipped with a coffee machine, bar and satellite television and there are four coaches who offer a wide range of courses to club members including cardio tennis, a Monday evening ladies session and a performance programme for talented youngsters. Fifty years ago, long before Georgians existed, the tennis played on this spot was more basic. In the late 1960s, there were four red shale courts here, all of which had seen better days, a dilapidated club house with no heating or showers and just one coach. That coach, however, was Cas Fish.

Cas Fish was an autodidact with a goatee beard and confrontational manner who first played tennis in his native Caernarfon in North Wales in the early 1950s when he was 15. The game quickly became his passion and teaching tennis to youngsters his life's work. For five decades, until his death at the turn of the twenty-first century, Fish gave tennis lessons which emphasised 'character, grit and courage' rather than sound technique and correct strokes, the conventional coaching goals of that time. Never the most tactful of souls, Fish also found plenty of time to take on a self-appointed role as the Lawn Tennis Association's 'most outspoken critic'. He constantly lampooned the British tennis establishment and dismissed most tennis clubs as 'social gatherings for middle aged people'. 'The wrong people are playing tennis in this country', he maintained. 'If we ever want to be good as a tennis nation we are going to have to find ways of getting the right people into the game.'[1]

In the autumn of 1967, Fish set out to do just that. On those four battered shale courts in Crouch End Playing Fields, he set up the Dolphin Squad which would meet on Saturday and Sunday afternoons throughout the year for fitness training and tennis drills. The squad would be open to any promising junior to join as long as they committed to 15 hours of practice a week and accepted that there would be 'no more parties and late nights, no more boy and girl friends'. 'You get up early in the morning and get in an hour or more practice before breakfast', he told prospective squad members, 'after school in the afternoon you head for the tennis court and play until you can't see the ball any longer, then you go home and do your school-work and somewhere along the way you fit in a meal'.[2]

It was a taxing regime with little space for fun, although there were few complaints from participants or their parents. The experience of playing in the Dolphin Squad was summed up by a comment Fish once made when they played another club. 'My boys and girls didn't come here to enjoy themselves', he said, 'they come here to win'.[3] And win they did, match after match after match. Soon Cas Fish was producing the champions he craved and his methods started attracting national attention. In the summer of 1969 one of the first invitations the British player Ann Jones accepted after winning the Wimbledon Ladies' Singles title in July was from Fish to come and meet his squad.

Word of Jones' impending visit spread around north London and one youngster who turned up to watch was a 15 year old from Wood Green called Raph Harvey. 'There were 20 boys and girls knocking up and doing drills with Ann', Harvey remembered, 'and I thought crikey these are brilliant. Everything I saw those boys and girls doing, I wanted to be like them.'[4] In time he would, although there would always be one major difference. Raph and the three school chums that came with him that afternoon were black and the Dolphin Squad, like most tennis in Britain at the time, was white. It was one more thing Cas Fish was determined to change. He picked out Raph and the other three enthusiastic black teenagers from the crowd and encouraged them to join his squad. Perhaps here was an untapped source of tennis talent which would produce the world-beater he longed for. He certainly had no competition from the Lawn Tennis Association which at the time had little interest in encouraging play in the growing British black community even among those who were developing a passion for sport.

There had been black people playing games in Britain at the highest level since the professional footballer Arthur Wharton appeared for Rotherham in 1889. But their numbers, like the total number of permanent black residents here, remained small until the Caribbean immigration to Britain after the Second World War. Between June 1948 when the *Empire Windrush* arrived in Tilbury dock from Jamaica, and 1962 when the Commonwealth Immigration Act imposed restrictions on immigration, some half a million West Indians moved to the UK for work, many responding to advertisements from London Transport or the National Health Service which advertised vacancies all over the Caribbean. The children these immigrants brought with them and the children they would conceive when they settled here changed the colour of British sport. From second- and third-generation West Indians in Britain came much of the talent that now dominates British football, athletics and boxing. In 1969, Cas Fish saw no reason why tennis should not be the same. He was sure his methods could persuade young black men and women with sporting ability to opt for tennis rather than soccer or running. Perhaps in time he could produce a British Arthur Ashe, the black American who was then one of the top tennis players in the world.

Neither Raph Harvey nor any of his friends seemed likely to be another Ashe. They were in their mid-teens when they joined the squad and too old to be moulded into champions. They could, though, be role models for their younger brothers, sisters, cousins and friends. Raph was certainly keen. In 1965, when he was eleven, he had left the hamlet of Bath in West Jamaica to join his mother who was working as a nurse in a north London hospital. At school he played football but he was small and wiry and not good enough for the team so he tried tennis: 'I used to borrow a tennis racket from the school sports room and the PE master encouraged me and I just turned out to be better than everyone else. A lot of people respected that.'

Tennis became his sport, and for several years in his teens he played every weekend and many weekday evenings with his friend Errol Francis, two years younger than him who had come to Britain from Jamaica a few years earlier when he was four. 'Errol and I never had much money, so we used to play with balls that were bald and stick newspaper in our shoes to cover over the holes. We used to come down and play until it got so dark we were playing at night. Errol didn't need to come as far as I did though because his school [that "truly comprehensive" one] was just next to the club.'⁵

None of the four black members of the Dolphin Squad ever became national champions, although some of the white boys did. 'The members of the squad who improved a lot quicker than me', Raph reflected, 'were the white guys who could afford individual coaching and lessons as well as playing in the group sessions. I didn't get any individual lessons which I would have liked but my Mum couldn't afford them.' One or two of the more talented white members of the squad now earn their living from tennis. Raph works as a bus driver.

When lawn tennis first developed as a national pastime in the mid-1870s, it was aimed at the white English upper middle class, but tennis didn't stay completely white for very long. The Wingfield sets sold not only in Britain but in the colonial outposts of the British Empire, and this is where people with black and brown skins first learned the game. In India, the new sport was not restricted to white ex-pats. Wealthy Indians were encouraged to take it up because the participation of locals in 'British' sports was seen as an indicator of the Raj's success. In 1884 a 'Hindoo player' named 'Ajax' came over to play in the UK and, although the All England Club decided he wasn't good enough to play at Wimbledon, he competed that summer in tournaments around the south coast. In 1908, a Sikh called Sirdar Nihal Singh became the first player of Indian origin to play at Wimbledon. By the 1920s Indians were competing at tennis at the highest level. In 1934 Leela Row became the first female player from India to win a match at the Championships. Players with darker skin though had a different experience.

In 1884, *Pastime* highlighted a notice at a tournament in Exmouth which said, 'no niggers allowed'. A decade and a half later, a report in *Lawn Tennis* about a tournament in Great Yarmouth ended with the sentence, 'there were also niggers'.[6] There is no reason to think these two instances were exceptional. Just like other sports of the time, lawn tennis treated black people as second-class citizens. But what the reports do confirm is that black people in Britain were interested enough in tennis to play in tournaments or at least pay money to watch them. Whether these people were residents, migrants or visitors remains unclear.

The black population of Britain in the late nineteenth century was centred in London and other port towns like Liverpool and Cardiff. Its people originally came mainly from the USA, the West Indies and Sierra Leone and they tended to be sailors or entrepreneurs with the occasional entertainer and minstrel. Tennis does not seem to have played much part in their lives. But around the turn of the twentieth century, they were joined by a steady stream of students from all parts of the British Empire and these young people had more time for leisure, including lawn tennis.

Norman Manley, who would become chief minister of Jamaica in the late 1950s, was a keen sportsman and won gold medals on the island for his schoolboy sprinting. It seems likely that such an athletic person with social aspirations would have tried tennis when he studied in Britain before the First World War, although there is no mention of the game in his biographies. Then again this is true of another celebrated Jamaican, the cultural critic and scholar Stuart Hall. Hall was a keen tennis player when he was a student in Britain in the 1950s and carried on playing most of his life after settling in this country. When he died in 2014, however, there was no mention of his love of tennis in his many obituaries.

It would have been odd if none of the Caribbean, black African and black American students who came here in the first decades of the twentieth century did not also try out tennis, especially as the game was then at the peak of its popularity. There are occasional glimpses of black tennis playing in other records of the time. The correspondence from the international students' hall of residence in Pelham Place in West London in 1916, for example, notes an outcry by overseas students when a tree was blown down destroying their tennis court.

Many black overseas students who came to Britain during the first few decades of the twentieth century would have picked up the game in summer jobs as ball boys at white tennis clubs. In countries like Trinidad and Nigeria, a tradition developed for these boys to be allowed to play at times that were too hot for members, although this wasn't true elsewhere. Nat Pithadia, whose parents emigrated from Gujarat to Uganda, played tennis in an Indian tennis club in Mbale in the 1960s. He remembered the 'black population was keen on football but had no interest in tennis', perhaps not surprisingly as they had no way of learning it. Albert Lester was a white teenager in Southern Rhodesia in the late 1940s and recalled black people being employed as ball boys and groundsmen at the local tennis clubs but never allowed to hit on court. 'There was apartheid and it applied in tennis as much as in all other aspects of life.'[7] In South Africa, the home of apartheid, the situation was more complicated.

Tennis had been played regularly by the white population in South Africa by the late 1870s, and in 1903 there were over 100 tennis clubs, all white but employing black and coloured people to look after members and ensure enjoyable play. As a result, the sport developed a presence in the non-white population, particularly among the coloured community.[8] One tennis match in particular attracted widespread attention. It took place in November 1926 at the Bantu Men's Social Centre which had been founded in Johannesburg a couple of years before to encourage recreational activities among black and coloured people. On the centre's main tennis court, G.H. Dodd, South African's top player, took on a 'coloured man called Smith', the first recorded case of a non-European meeting a white South African on court. 'Fine form was shown by Smith who actually took a set with his uncanny anticipation', reported the *Dundee Courier*, adding that for Dodd the game was an 'eye opener'.[9]

The match was never repeated as the white South African Lawn Tennis Association made clear its opposition to any more interracial mixing. But it does at least suggest that if one coloured player could take a set off the white national champion, tennis in the 1920s was well established in South Africa's coloured communities and perhaps in black communities as well.

After the Second World War, there were black and coloured tournaments all over South Africa and national organisations were formed to represent African and Asian players.

In 1949, a 21-year-old coloured musician called David Samaai came to Britain to pursue his musical studies and play tennis. He had been the coloured tennis champion of South Africa for four years but had not been permitted to compete with white players, and his game, as he told the *Gloucester Citizen*, had 'stood still'.[10] Playing in Britain gave him the stimulus he needed. By 1951, he had improved enough to reach the third round of Wimbledon before losing to the seventh seed, the Australian Ken McGregor, who that year reached the final. Subsequently Samaai returned to South Africa to teach but often spent summers playing tennis in Britain. Mike Davies, who was Britain's number one player from 1958 to 1962, remembers meeting him in a tournament in Bedford in 1955. 'I subsequently got to know David really well. Cultured, talented and a fine musician.' A couple of years later, Davies contacted Samaai when he played in South Africa and invited him to the club he was playing at but Samaai wasn't allowed in. 'The colour of his skin', reflected Davies sadly, 'made him a pariah.'[11]

In Jamaica another player described as 'coloured', B.M. Clark, was also good enough to play at Wimbledon after the First World War. Clark worked as medical secretary at the Island Board of Health but took time off to play tennis. He was Jamaican tennis champion for seven consecutive years and in 1920 achieved his greatest success when he travelled to Baltimore to win the American Tennis Association's Men's Singles championship. He was not the only player to be grateful for the association's commitment to multiracial tennis. The association was founded in 1916 by a group of African American businessmen, college professors and physicians and it would be their hard work over the next few decades that ensured many racial barriers in tennis were broken down.

Tennis had spread to the black middle classes in America in the late 1880s, but they were not allowed to join the prestigious country clubs in the white suburbs so they formed their own. Chautauqua, the first black tennis club in America, was established in Philadelphia in 1890 and other clubs in New York, Baltimore, Washington, DC and Alabama followed. By 1939, there were 150 black tennis clubs across the United States. These clubs were successful and the standard of tennis high, but there was little contact between them and the established white tennis world. The United States Lawn Tennis Association ran the major championships which were open to everyone in theory, but the only way to qualify was through regional tournaments in country clubs where the only black people allowed in were the hired help. The American Tennis Association represented any player who was excluded from the tennis mainstream in the USA, not just black people but all those who did not fit into the white protestant mode. It organised public parks programmes in which anybody could play, although most who did were black.

This was tennis apartheid. After the Second World War, two American Tennis Association officials, Drs Walter Johnson and Hubert Eaton, were determined to challenge this pernicious state of affairs. They searched for a player with enough talent to take on the white tennis establishment and at the black Cosmopolitan Club in New York they found her. In 1940, the Cosmopolitan had hosted a match between Donald Budge, the number one tennis player of the time, and Jimmie McDaniel, the American Tennis Association's champion. Two thousand people crammed into the club to watch, and although McDaniel lost 6–1, 6–2, Budge said afterwards that if he had been allowed to compete against white players, Jimmie McDaniel would likely be in the top ten in the world. It was too late for McDaniel and too late for Ora Washington, probably the best black player in the first half of the twentieth century, who was never able to test her talent against white female players. It wasn't too late though for a gangling 13 year old who had followed the Budge–McDaniel match with great interest. Althea Gibson had no money but the Cosmopolitan Club was impressed by her talent and she was allowed to become a member for free. There she was spotted by Johnson and Eaton who were convinced they had found the potential champion they were looking for.

Gibson had been born in South Carolina in 1927 in the plantation town of Silver. Her parents were subsistence sharecroppers and their parents had been slaves. If she had stayed in Silver, the young Althea would never have taken up tennis, but she was sent to relatives in Harlem, New York, when she was eight. Harlem at that time was home not just to the black poor like the Gibson clan but also to rich celebrities like the jazz musician Louis Armstrong and the boxer Joe Louis, who lived there because other parts of the city were not open to them. This meant that talented but penniless youngsters like Althea had successful black role models around them who they might bump into at the end of a block and who might give them a break. Althea was tall and strong and excelled at every sport, particularly paddle tennis, a form of the game that had developed in Greenwich Village 20 years earlier and was played in the street with a solid paddle. She became Harlem Paddle Tennis Champion and her talent at racket sports was apparent. She was introduced to Johnson and Eaton and in 1946 she became their experiment and weapon.

Hubert Eaton encouraged Gibson to return to the South to live with his family in the segregated town of Wilmington in North Carolina. There he taught her the correct way to hit a tennis ball and gave her the first proper schooling of her life. Meanwhile Walter Johnson lobbied the US Lawn Tennis Association to change their rules and admit exceptional black players directly into their national tournaments without having to qualify at regional championships in all-white country clubs. Althea Gibson was Dr Johnson's calling-card. Her talent was obvious to any but the most bigoted official. His plan succeeded, but it needed the help of Alice Marble.

Marble won Wimbledon only once, in 1939, although she would almost certainly have won more if war had not intervened. After the war, she found fame as a sports journalist and commentator and was one of the first white people to play exhibition matches with black players. In July 1950, in a carefully composed editorial in *American Lawn Tennis*, Alice Marble argued that keeping Althea Gibson out of the US Open was an affront to the standards of the sport. 'If tennis is a game of ladies and gentlemen', she wrote, 'it is time we acted a little more like gentlepeople and less like sanctimonious hypocrites ... I've never met Miss Gibson but to me she is a fellow human being to whom equal privileges ought to be extended.'[12]

It was a message that was reprinted with approval in newspapers and magazines across America and around the world. The United States Lawn Tennis Association caved in. Gibson was admitted to the major American tennis tournaments without having to qualify and everyone expected her to excel, but at first she struggled. She had never faced such strong competition before and was dependent on the help of tournament officials, many of whom were determined to keep her out. Gibson herself did nothing to win support. She was often rude to her opponents and careless with people who tried to become her friend. Not many did.

The top women players on the tennis circuit in the 1950s were like an extended family. Often they had been to the same school or played in the same club and they travelled as a group, hit with each other and played doubles together. Gibson did not fit into their cosy world and she found the other women unfriendly and at times hostile. As a result, her performances suffered and she never achieved the success predicted for her until she met another outsider, the British player Angela Buxton, who was Jewish.

Within two years of teaming up, Gibson and Buxton had won the doubles championships in Paris and Wimbledon. Buxton reached the Wimbledon Women's Singles' final in 1956, the first British woman to do so since Kay Stammers in 1939. A year later Gibson became the first black player to win the singles at Wimbledon, an achievement she repeated in 1958. The two young players inspired each other on court and off. When Gibson was in London, she stayed with Buxton in her small flat near Baker Street and Buxton's mother, Violet, would fend off the London press who camped outside looking for photos of the two glamorous tennis stars. There was a downside to this fame, at least for Gibson. Throughout her tennis career, she had to be constantly on guard against racial abuse.

When she started playing against white people in 1947, Gibson was harangued by chants of 'beat the nigger, beat the nigger',[13] and comments about her physical appearance and lack of femininity were not unusual. When she played at Wimbledon in July 1956, the crowd, according to the *Sunday Graphic*, showed a 'shameful' bias against her with an atmosphere that was 'tight-lipped and cold'.[14] Many Wimbledon spectators didn't seem to like her, although it wasn't clear whether this was because of her colour or manner or a mixture of both. Gibson's arrogant play, intimidating power and burning desire to win did not make her a natural favourite. The Centre Court crowd preferred their tennis players stylish, graceful and modest.

In the USA, Gibson's pride in her talent went down well. When she returned to America in 1957 as the first black Wimbledon champion, she received a ticker-tape welcome in New York, was interviewed on the *Ed Sullivan Show* and recorded an album with the Harlem Globetrotters. As she pointed out at the time, though, despite all this acclaim she was still a 'poor negress' who, when she travelled home to the American South, often couldn't find a seat in a restaurant or hire a room in an hotel because of the colour of her skin. Perhaps it is unsurprising that Gibson showed little gratitude. In the mid-1950s, American black men were still being lynched.

Today we are used to pushy players like Althea Gibson. We forgive their detachment, their tight entourage, their insistence on winning at all costs. We suspect it is not possible to be modest and unassuming and play at the very top level. Perhaps it never was, but it was always easier if you came from the right background or had the right skin colour to act as if nothing mattered, that the game was everything and the result little. Gibson was distrusted because she made no apologies for being black and successful and was often ungrateful to those who had smoothed her way. She was a pioneer who knew only one way in: to ram the door down.

It didn't make her life easier, though, when she refused to take on the 'black person's burden': to act as a representative for all black people in white society, particularly those like her from poorer backgrounds. Gibson did not participate in any of the civil rights campaigns of the 1960s when her support as the most famous black athlete of her generation would have been invaluable. As a result she was vilified by the black press. A few years after her success, however, another black tennis player emerged who would earn universal praise because he lent his name and reputation to causes a long way from the white lines of the tennis court.

Arthur Ashe's descendants came to America in 1735 on a slave ship where they were traded for tobacco. By the time he grew up in a segregated Virginia 200 years later, the family had prospered and Ashe's father was a police officer. One of his responsibilities was to look after a public park which had four tennis courts, and this is where his young son learned to play. Arthur's mother had died when he was six and sport became the young boy's life.

His talent was spotted and he was invited to join the tennis school that Dr Walter Johnson, Althea Gibson's mentor, had set up to find other talented black youngsters. It soon became clear he had the potential to emulate Gibson's success, but when Ashe started playing on the circuit in the mid-1960s there were few black players at the top level, despite Gibson's breakthrough ten years earlier. 'I played in clubs where the only blacks were waiters, gardeners and bus boys', he would say a few years later. 'The game had a history and tradition I was expected to assimilate but much of the history and many of those traditions were hostile to me.'[15] At the time though, it never seemed to bother him, and he became known for his composure on court and his studied politeness after a game.

His greatest moment came when he reached the Wimbledon final in 1975, four days before he turned 32. His opponent was Jimmy Connors, a 23-year-old white hurricane from Illinois. They were not friends. Ashe had never beaten him and Connors was expected to blow him off the court. Instead the crowd were treated to a masterclass in cerebral tennis. Between points, the black American closed his eyes and meditated. He then varied the spin and speed of the ball to confound and bewilder his opponent. At crucial points in the game, Connors simply did not know what to do next. Ashe won in four sets and his victory was greeted with noisy acclaim on Centre Court, perhaps making up for the coolness Althea Gibson had received on the same court two decades before. The elegant and stylish Ashe was one of the tournament's most popular winners for decades. What was less remarked upon at the time was a small gesture he made after he won. Arthur Ashe clenched his fist in the black power salute made famous by two American athletes, John Carlos and Tommie Smith, at the 1968 Mexico Olympics seven years before. It was a promise of activism to come.

Up to then, Ashe had tried to accommodate white hostility with careful courtesy and impeccable manners. 'Sure I get fed up with being the nice guy', he told a reporter in 1985, 'but back in the '60s if you were black and the first one you simply had to behave yourself'.[16] Now he no longer had to pretend. Until he died of AIDS in 1993, aged only 49, he devoted himself to social causes and was arrested twice on protest marches in Washington. Shortly before his death, Arthur Ashe said that coping with AIDS was nothing like coping with racism. 'Being black is the greatest burden I've had to bear.'[17]

In 1964, Ashe had refused to join in a tennis protest about apartheid in South Africa. In 1973 he went to the country to play in the South African Open – the first black man to do so – and also spent time in Soweto where he met political activists as well as black and coloured tennis players. On a trip to Cameroon, he spotted a talented eleven year old called Yannick Noah. Impressed by the young man's talent, Ashe arranged for him to move to Nice in France and become part of the French National Junior training programme. Noah went on to win the French Open in 1983, the first black man after Ashe to win a Grand Slam tournament, and he in turn inspired other black people in France to take up the game, one reason why the country became one of the top tennis nations in the 1990s for the first time in 70 years.

In sub-Saharan Africa today, several players have shown they don't need to emigrate to France to become tennis professionals, but none has yet broken into the top 200. Coaches like Ben Makhlouf, a Moroccan based in Senegal, believe it is only a matter of time: 'Our feeling is that if Africa can make it in football, why not in tennis?'[18] Certainly North Africa has had some success over the decades, with Egyptian and Moroccan players reaching the top ten in the world, although the sport in these countries has been the domain of the wealthy. The problem for young African tennis players today is the lack of support they receive as they make their way up the rankings playing for meagre prize money on the low-tier circuits. The only players south of the Sahara who have made successful tennis careers since open tennis in 1967 have been white players from South Africa.

In Britain, black players have not done a great deal better. Young British black men and women who are good at sports do not take up tennis. There have been over 50 black football players and athletes who have represented Britain in the last 20 years but only one black British tennis player, Heather Watson, has ever reached the top 50 in the world, and Watson had the considerable advantage of a father who was a millionaire. In British tennis, black players are noticeable by their absence. The astounding success of the Williams sisters at Wimbledon does not seem to have inspired a new generation of young black women in Britain to take up the game in the way it has in America.

The reasons are complex, but one that can be discounted is lack of interest. Surveys done in the last 20 years indicate that black people in the UK show, if anything, more enthusiasm for taking up tennis than whites.[19] Somehow this does not translate into active involvement. The expense of tennis is often cited as critical, not simply the cost of tennis rackets, balls and hiring a court but being able to fund a promising young child through the many years of coaching and practice required to enable them to become a professional. Other reasons advanced are the lack of role models in British tennis – not just players, but coaches and administrators too. Some academics have also cited the social obligations that come with tennis. Playing in a predominately white tennis club often involves connecting with people beyond the actual game, and people prefer to mix with people like them. All these factors contribute to a black absence at the heart of British tennis which isn't true in America. There is another reason as well.

Racism in tennis in this country has never gone away despite the acclaim given at Wimbledon to black champions. When Ashe was being cheered for winning the Men's Singles in 1975, Britain's number one player, Buster Mottram, was expressing political support for the openly racist National Front. Shortly before Serena Williams won her third Wimbledon title in 2009, BBC TV presenter Carol Thatcher referred on air to a black professional player as a 'golliwog'. Mottram was condemned and Thatcher was sacked but what goes unreported are the everyday experiences of racism from top black players not getting product endorsements, to those on the lower rungs of the professional ladder not able to find a family to look after them during a tournament.

The language used to describe top BAME (black, Asian and minority ethnic) players is also problematic. Black professionals like Jo-Wilfried Tsonga, Dustin Brown and Gael Monfils are described as 'naturally' athletic, the same word used to describe the black Australian player Evonne Goolagong in the 1970s. Serena Williams has also been singled out for her 'natural' advantages. This toxic use of the word 'natural' implies that black players have an unfair genetic advantage and don't need to work as hard as white players to become successful. BAME players are criticised for being 'lazy' and 'unpredictable' but rarely praised for their cleverness, composure and consistency, and yet these qualities are just as much part of their tennis as any white player. All this sloppy language and casual racism has a demoralising effect on talented young people who happen to be black. Jay Clarke, the brightest British black tennis prospect since Heather Watson, has said he receives some 15–20 racially abusive messages a month on social media, more if he wins.

In the autumn of 2019, Yemisi Ifederu from Mill Hill, north London, took up a tennis scholarship at Howard University, a renowned private university in Washington which has championed many black students. Her experience in Britain as a promising tennis junior over the previous ten years has been mixed. 'I was repeatedly called the N word during tennis performance practices. When my parents complained, the coaches said they didn't hear it! And even though I was beating everyone comfortably in group sessions they never allowed me to move up a grade.'[20] Her father, Boye Ifederu, had to step in repeatedly to challenge what he saw as unfair treatment of his daughter. 'They would expect my daughter to continue in sessions designed to drain her enthusiasm', he said, 'it makes you feel very bitter to clearly see the markings of discrimination.' This bitterness needs to be put into context though. The Ifederu family love tennis and have had many good experiences playing the game in Britain and abroad. Boye, a biochemist, took up tennis when he came here in his twenties from Nigeria and the social games with his work colleagues are one of the highlights of his week. Yemisi has travelled to Europe to play tennis and has won several trophies. Just like any white tennis family, tennis has contributed much to their life together.

The sport has also done something else. Tennis has given the Ifederus and other black sporting families a platform to contest racial stereotyping and discrimination and it has provided a public space where racism can be challenged and changed. Still, change is slow. Sport has been one of the predominant cultural forms in which Britain's black community, only 3 per cent of the population, have become the 'standard bearer of a new cultural and national identity'.[21] It is a pity that the one sport where this hasn't happened in Britain, as it has in France and the USA, is lawn tennis.

Fifty years ago, Cas Fish tried to produce the first British black tennis champion, but his Dolphin Squad never had enough resources. It was wound up in 1974, a year before Ashe's triumph at Wimbledon, and Fish went back to Caernarfon. After he left school, Raph Harvey earned his living for a while as a metal worker while his friend Errol Francis trained to become an architect. They would have gone separate ways but their love of tennis became the basis of a friendship that lasted over 40 years and they played in several different north London clubs together. 'There was no prejudice whatsoever', Raph reflected, 'we just fitted in. If there was a party we got invited.' It helped that they were both exceptional at the game and in time became one of Middlesex's top doubles pairs. 'Errol played on the left and hit the ball very hard. I played on the right and was a finesse player. We complemented each other pretty well and were partners for years and years. A few years ago, Errol got bowel cancer and had to stop playing. He died in 2017. I miss him.'[22] So do many other people in north London tennis, black and white.

11

Outsiders

The Dunbabin Road in Liverpool is a pleasant if nondescript thoroughfare that links Wavertree on the edge of the inner city with more affluent Childwall, the start of Liverpool's southern suburbs. For most of its perambulatory mile, the road is framed by mature trees and doused in the shadows of semi-detached houses. Many of these houses shelter behind a privet hedge or a car port and have at their back a large secluded space, sometimes big enough to accommodate a tennis court or two.

In the last hundred years, this area has been home to one of Liverpool's more prosperous communities. Today the Jewish population of the city is in gentle decline and numbers no more than 2,500 people, but in the 1920s there were four times this number and many settled along this road. Some of the Jewish institutions set up in this time remain today, like the King David School and the Childwall Hebrew Congregation, but others have gone including Harold House, a once thriving Jewish youth centre, and the equally popular Liverpool Jewish Tennis Club, the last Jewish tennis club in Britain.

Twenty years ago, the club's four tennis courts were in use six days a week. 'We were a flourishing family club with some 200 people', recalled one member, 'we had three artificial grass courts and one tarmac, several teams in the local leagues, and a busy social scene'.[1] The tennis club was Jewish but not exclusively so. Anyone could join, although it was closed on Saturdays and on Jewish holidays. It dated back only to 1955, although there were older Jewish tennis clubs in the city before the Second World War. The high point of the club in Dunbabin Road was in the late 1950s and early 1960s. One member was good enough to play in the mixed doubles at Wimbledon, but the club had many other less talented players at that time, including Helena Levy, an air hostess with British European Airways who was on the committee, and the Epstein brothers, Clive and Brian, who grew up in nearby Queens Drive.

The story goes that when Brian Epstein started managing the Beatles in 1961 he brought 'the boys' to the club, perhaps as part of his project to smarten up their dress and manners. This visit is not mentioned in any biography of the band nor in any press cutting of the time, but it may have simply been a fleeting occasion of no consequence when the Beatles were not well known and so not recorded by anyone. If it happened, it certainly didn't produce any great interest in tennis among the Beatles. The only subsequent enthusiasm for the game shown by the Fab Four seems to have come from George Harrison who was photographed playing tennis with Bob Dylan on the Isle of Wight shortly before the island's 1969 Pop Festival.

What isn't in doubt is the interest in lawn tennis shown by Jewish people in Liverpool and other cities in Britain, an interest which dates back to Victorian times. One early player was Samuel Montagu, a Liverpudlian banker who in 1885 became a Liberal MP. Even though he was a strict adherent of Orthodox Judaism, Montagu encouraged his family to play tennis on Saturdays as an acceptable alternative to croquet. This interpretation of Sabbath observance did not attract universal support. In 1898, the *Jewish Chronicle* reported with disapproval that a Sabbath spent in 'tennis, golf and bicycling is not ideal and does not smooth the rigours of the soul'.[2] One solution was to dedicate Friday afternoon to sport instead, and this seemed to work well in Victoria Park, east London, at the start of the century when Jewish schoolchildren were allowed to play sports on Friday, including tennis 'from 2.30pm until dusk'.[3]

In the first decades of the twentieth century, sport assumed a central role in Jewish life in Britain and was a pivotal factor in many social, cultural and political changes affecting the Jewish community. As David Dee, the historian of Jewish sport in Britain, has argued, sports like tennis and golf were a crucial area for the creation of an Anglo-Jewish identity.[4] They were certainly popular – perhaps a little too popular, as the Jewish community in Britain grew. Immigration from eastern Europe at the turn of the century increased the Jewish population from 60,000 in 1882 to 250,000 in 1914. More Jews took up golf and tennis and Jewish players started to be noticed on the golf course and tennis court and commented upon. From about 1900, Jews found their applications for membership at some private golf clubs refused while others introduced strict quotas. The arguments used to exclude Jewish people varied from them not being able to play on a Saturday, being too flashy or ostentatious and not understanding the notion of fair play. After the First World War, these poisonous tropes began to percolate tennis as well.

In 1925, the *Yorkshire Post* claimed that Jews would always remain ostracised by certain tennis clubs no matter how anglicised they were. In 1928, the *Daily Mirror* reported that Jewish tennis players in north London were 'complaining bitterly of their inability to get into the best lawn tennis clubs'. In 1936, Hazlewood tennis club in Winchmore Hill refused four applications from Jews to become members.[5] In Britain between the wars, Jewish men and women who wanted to play tennis were forced to abandon assimilation and create institutions of their own.

In 1922, a Jewish Tennis Club was formed in Liverpool, soon to be followed by clubs in Tottenham, Glasgow, Newcastle and two in north-west London, Chandos in Golders Green, and The Drive in Edgware. In 1927, the Waterpark Club in north Manchester was founded by Alfred Cassel, a Jewish builder, after the daughters of a friend were refused entry to other tennis clubs in the city. In the following decade, the Waterpark played an active part in the Northern Jewish Tennis Association, along with the Three Courts, another Manchester Jewish Club, the Greenwood Club in Sheffield and the Argosy Club in Southport. All those clubs have long closed, apart from Chandos and The Drive which are today two of the best places to play tennis in Britain. On their websites they no longer describe themselves as Jewish, although Chandos does record its proud hosting of a 1965 Davis Cup match between Great Britain and Israel.

Jewish tennis clubs from this time in Britain and elsewhere seem to have been divided over whether or not to use the word 'Jewish' in their name, perhaps because of concern that this might dissuade potential non-Jewish members: Jewish tennis clubs have always welcomed players from outside the community. There was also a fear that an obviously 'Jewish' club would become an easy target for antisemitism. Some clubs felt this was a risk worth taking, including a club that was set up in the mid-1920s in a city with one of the smallest Jewish communities in the UK.

On 17 December 1925, a dance took place at the Carlton Hotel in Belfast to raise money for a 'social tennis club aimed at younger members of the Jewish community'.[6] Two hundred people turned up, probably about a third of Northern Ireland's Jewish population at the time. They dined and danced away to the accompaniment of 'excellent music from Miss M. Cres's talented orchestra' and an 'exhibition of ballroom dancing by Mr. Jack Everard'. Enough funds were made on the night for the Belfast Jewish Tennis Club to open the following summer with their own tennis courts at the back of Ashfield Gardens, a cul-de-sac off the Antrim Road.

For the next dozen years the club prospered. In 1929, the *Northern Whig*, a non-sectarian Belfast newspaper of the time, carried a report about a successful home match in Ashfield Gardens against the Glasgow Jewish Tennis Club. Six years later, it printed a photograph of the smiling participants of an 'American' mixed doubles tournament at the club where players were paired at random. The newspaper was a little coy in its coverage about these pairings, but reading between the lines it does seem that a key role of the Belfast Jewish Tennis Club and the couple of dozen or so other Jewish tennis clubs dotted around the United Kingdom during the years between the wars was to enable young Jewish people to meet each other at a time when there was concern about Jews marrying out. Across the channel in Germany this concern seemed trivial compared with what the Jewish community was facing there.

The destruction of Jewish sport under the Third Reich is under-standably a side story in the main narrative of the Holocaust, yet it nevertheless represents an important loss in the expression of a community's identity and culture. Jewish tennis had flourished in Germany in the liberal Weimar Republic of the 1920s. There were one or two separate Jewish tennis clubs, but most Jewish players preferred to remain part of the established German tennis world since antisemitism in German tennis was then the exception not the rule. Many members of the country's most famous tennis club, the Rot-Weiss in Berlin, were Jewish as was Daniel Prenn, Germany's leading player.

Prenn was born in Vilna in Lithuania in 1904. After the Russian Revolution of 1917, the Prenn family feared persecution and moved to Berlin. Like Fred Perry, his contemporary from Stockport, the teenage Daniel first excelled at table tennis and was good enough to represent Germany in the 1926 World Champi-onships. Like Perry too, he switched to tennis and three years later led Germany to an unexpected victory against Britain in the Davis Cup which turned him into a national hero. In the next few years Prenn's tennis career was followed closely in the national as well as the Jewish press. In 1931 he was ranked the sixth best player in the world and even supporters of the increasingly powerful National Socialists called him 'our Prenn', although their affection would not last. That year Prenn, like many amateurs of the time, tried to negotiate a contract with a sports equipment company for work after he finished playing tennis. This was a clear violation of the amateur code, but similar deals had become an accepted practice for players at the end of their tennis career and the authorities usually ignored them. Prenn was singled out and suspended from tennis for six months in what seemed a clear case of discrimina-tion. Worse was to follow.

When the Nazis seized power in 1933, Jewish players were banned from representing their country and Prenn, Germany's best player for the previous five years, was dropped from their Davis Cup team.[7] Fred Perry and Bunny Austin wrote a letter of protest to *The Times*, but they received little support from the rest of the international tennis community and Germany was allowed to play in the competition without Prenn. Fearing what was going to happen next to even well-known Jews like himself, Daniel Prenn quit Germany. With the help of Jewish businessman Sir Simon Marks, a keen tennis fan who had an indoor court at his home in Maida Vale, Prenn settled in Britain and worked as an engineer after his retirement from competitive tennis in 1937. That year Germany played America in the semi-finals of the Davis Cup, which were held at Wimbledon, and a swastika flew over the All England Club to mark the occasion.

Despite widespread revelations about the Holocaust, Jews continued to experience discrimination in British tennis after the war, although it was more patchy. Jewish players in Birmingham reported difficulties joining local tennis clubs. Potential Jewish members of the Argyle Club in Southport, one of the top tennis clubs in the north-west, were turned down. 'Let them build their own clubs', said one Argyle member, 'they certainly have the money don't they?'[8] Jews interested in joining the tennis club in north London where I am now a member were told there was a club called Chandos just down the road in Golders Green which was 'more suitable' for them.

These experiences of exclusion were, however, less common than before the war and the 1950s saw the beginning of the end of discrimination against Jews in tennis in Britain if not across Europe and the world. By the end of the 1960s, Jewish players in my north London club were not just welcome as members but active participants in teams and committees. Most other tennis clubs in north London, which has a large Jewish population, were similarly grateful to their Jewish members. There were, though, one or two isolated examples in these times when tennis let Jewish players down once more, and because they involved top players they received widespread publicity.

Dick Savitt started playing tennis in a public park in New Jersey when he was 14 but took the sport seriously only in his twenties. His booming serve, classical backhand and competitive zeal quickly established him as a leading player, and in 1951 he became the first Jewish player to win the Men's Singles at Wimbledon. Savitt's tennis skills were never in doubt but he was an anxious, impatient man with a moody temperament and these traits did not endear him to spectators. One commentator even called him 'Wimbledon's gloomiest champion'.[9] It seems likely that Savitt's character contributed to what happened next, although it is always difficult to disentangle the personal from the political when considering prejudicial treatment, and it is too easy for those who have never experienced discrimination to condemn the manners of those who have.

After his 1951 Wimbledon victory, and despite being awarded the accolade by the *New York Times* of number one tennis player in the world, Dick Savitt was left out of the United States Davis Cup Team when they played Australia in the final later that year. The American team manager felt that Savitt was not a team player, but his exclusion led to a national discussion about whether he was being discriminated against on the basis of character or ethnicity, and if it is possible to distinguish between the two. What it also revealed was the extent of antisemitism in American tennis at that time, particularly in many of the prestigious country clubs where Jews were still barred from membership. Nothing was resolved about Savitt's exclusion and he quit tennis to become an executive in the oil industry. America lost a top player in his prime.

In the mid-1950s another talented Jewish player was almost lost to tennis, this time in Britain. Like Dick Savitt, Angela Buxton divided people. She was difficult and did not go out of her way to make friends or be charming to the tennis authorities. Norman Dale, a county tennis player of the time and Jewish himself, remembered her as 'simply not popular. She was very, very serious and dedicated to her tennis. People did not like that in those days.'[10] When Buxton was treated badly it was put down, like Savitt, to her personality not her Jewish identity.

She was born in Liverpool in 1934 where her father, Harry Buxton, was a successful businessman. At boarding school in North Wales in the late 1940s, the young Angela showed a natural aptitude for tennis. She became national junior champion and was tipped as a future Wimbledon contender. Angela was encouraged to move to London to aid her sporting development, and she settled in Hampstead and looked for a local club of a good standard where she could practice. Soon she found one.

Situated in extensive grounds off the Finchley Road, Cumberland Lawn Tennis Club offers some of the best tennis in London. In the 1950s, it had a dozen grass courts good enough to be used as practice by Wimbledon champions. Angela decided to join, expecting that her standard of play would make her application for membership a formality. She filled in a form which included her name, address, telephone number and religion and waited for her membership card to come through. It never did. When she asked one of the Cumberland coaches why, he told her she would never be allowed into the club because 'you're Jewish. We don't take Jews here.'[11] It was her first experience of discrimination but by no means her last. Two years later, now 19 years old, she played in a tournament at the Argyle Lawn Tennis Club in Southport. Before the competition, visiting players would usually hit up with members of the club, but when Buxton enquired, nobody would hit with her. She had to practice with a local journalist instead.

Angela Buxton made no complaint about any of this at the time. Nor did she complain when she went to the United States to play and was refused membership at the Los Angeles Tennis Club. She was never a crusader for Jewish rights and, if asked about it by journalists, said simply that it made her more determined to succeed. She developed a tough exterior and earned an undeserved reputation as a loner. The Lawn Tennis Association didn't help. It refused to pair her with other top British players in international matches and did not see her as a potential champion. It was true that she did not have the effortless talent admired by the British nor any forceful shots or obvious speed. But Buxton worked hard and often won matches where she was expected to lose. She had a desire to win that was alien to women's tennis in Britain in the early 1950s. The only person on the circuit she identified with was another pushy, unpopular young women who also had burning ambition, but who came not from Britain but from Harlem, New York and was not Jewish but black.

Angela Buxton met Althea Gibson on a tennis tour of India in 1955 and formed a friendship that would last 50 years.[12] They won doubles championships together, Gibson won the Wimbledon singles title twice and Buxton was a losing finalist. Angela Buxton would almost certainly have gone on to be a Wimbledon champion like Althea Gibson if she hadn't been forced to retire from tennis in 1957 when she was only 22 because of severe tenosynovitis. It was – and is – customary for the All England Club to reward British success at Wimbledon by offering life membership of the club. Despite Buxton's achievements in 1956 in the singles and doubles, she was put on a waiting list for membership even though other British players who were less successful than her, before and since, were offered full membership. This snub received national publicity in the summer of 1960 when it was exposed on BBC TV's new consumer programme *Watchdog*, which concluded that the only explanation was antisemitism. The All England Club has always refused to comment but Buxton herself has not been so reticent. 'It's an unfortunate example of how the British really treat Jews in this country', she told *The Times* in July 2019. 'It's perfectly ridiculous, it's laughable. It speaks volumes. There are so many players who didn't do anything like me and got membership.'[13] This is certainly true and it is regrettable that the club does not seem able to admit it made a mistake. Other Jewish players have since been admitted to full membership, so perhaps Angela Buxton's experience was just a blip. Certainly Norman Dale, who played for Kent around the same time and was once coached by Dan Maskell, never experienced any form of discrimination or exclusion in the game because he was Jewish. Neither did Albert Lester.

Albert was a *Kindertransport* child who arrived in Britain from Germany just before the Second World War while his parents escaped to Rhodesia. Now in his nineties, he has played tennis for over 75 years. The first British club he joined was the West London Tennis Club near Boston Manor station, now long gone.

'It was an entirely Jewish club', Lester remembered, 'with three courts and a nice club house. I used to drive out there in my red MG. The standard wasn't high but that suited me because I was never very good.'[14] Subsequently Lester played in non-Jewish clubs in London and Leeds and, despite a playing standard no better than average, he never had any problem joining, nor did he witness any antisemitism, though 'anyone who didn't know I was Jewish must have been blind, deaf and dumb.'[15] Lester's experience is heartening and certainly not unique. None of the other dozen Jewish players I have talked to in the last couple of years has ever had any problem playing tennis in Britain and abroad because they are Jews. I started wondering whether antisemitism in British tennis really had died out by the middle of the 1960s until I came across another example which occurred more recently.

Whitecraigs Lawn Tennis Club is situated in the affluent suburb of Giffnock, south Glasgow. Its parkland setting, extensive grounds and high playing standard make it a desirable place to play, the Scottish equivalent of London's Cumberland club. There is another similarity too. Whitecraigs also refused entry to a woman because she was Jewish, although this time not in the late 1950s but the late 1980s. Leonie Goodman, who lived just a few hundred yards from the club, applied to join in 1988 and 1990 but was refused membership without explanation, although she knew from friends that other applicants had been admitted and so the club was not full. She took Whitecraigs to court and the club admitted racial discrimination. They offered free membership for her and her family, paid all her legal costs and donated £1,000 to a local Jewish youth club. Her solicitor said she felt justice had been done and the Commission for Racial Equality claimed that her victory was 'an important win in this current climate of antisemitism which is sweeping Europe'.[16]

Justice has also been done to the memory of the Liverpool Jewish Tennis Club. After changing the court surface from shale to artificial grass in the 1990s, the club had a successful couple of decades, often hosting other events like a talk about Jews in English literature in November 2011 which 40 people attended.

The interest in tennis though dwindled, and in 2013 the club closed. It seemed likely the courts would be built over but a couple of years ago, a new club, the Carmel Sports Club, took them on and today offers football, dance and Pilates to juniors and adults as well as a full tennis programme. It is open on Saturdays and only one in ten members are Jewish, but in respect to its predecessor, the last Jewish tennis club in Britain, Carmel is still closed on two days a year, Rosh Hashanah and Yom Kippur.

12

Trailblazers

In the northern suburbs of Copenhagen, shortly before the stretch of coast known today as the Danish Riviera, lies the seaside town of Hellerup. Half a mile inland from the town's harbour, where chic apartments occupy the space once dominated by the Tuborg brewery, there is a three-storey building dating from 1927 which looks from the outside like a plain municipal warehouse. Inside, though, it is a riot of colour – vivid reds, orchid yellows, lush greens. One room is a gentleman's study with hand-painted Egyptian motifs on the walls. Another is a tearoom decorated with drawings from Bali. On the upper floor, large rectangular windows let in shafts of light which pour down into the open space beneath providing illumination for the principal activity here: the playing of tennis on an indoor court made of wood and covered in felt. It is one of the most beautiful places to play in the world.

The building, known as the Dansk Tennis Club, is a tribute to Leif Rovsing who commissioned, designed and decorated it after he was banned from tennis in 1917 for 'presumed homosexuality'. For half a century, Rovsing played here with friends from around the world until his death in 1977 when he left the club to a charity he had set up, the Danish Tennis Foundation. These days anyone can play between September and April for a few kroner which is donated to support one of the Foundation's central purposes: to oppose 'all kinds of prejudice'.

In a sport which was founded by mavericks and whose early players included socialists, feminists and other radicals, it is disappointing to discover that Rovsing is by no means the only person to have suffered because of his sexual identity. It is sad too to report that it wasn't until 1981 that the first top tennis players came out long after same-sex relationships were legalised in most tennis-playing countries. And it is salutary to remember that, despite countless rumours and gossip, in 2020 there is no openly gay man in the top 500 players in the world, although tennis is by no means the only sport where this is the case.

Perhaps, though, we are looking at this through the wrong lens. Ever since lawn tennis was first played in London in 1874, the role of men who have loved men and women who have loved women has been crucial to the game. Crucial too have been the qualities often associated with homosexuality and lesbianism in the twentieth century such as androgyny, a camp sensibility, sartorial distinctiveness and direct challenges to traditional definitions of gender. The number of top tennis people who have identified themselves as what we now call LGBTQ may be little more than a dozen but they include Bill Tilden and Billie Jean King, two of the most influential champions to have ever played the game; Teddy Tinling, the gay designer who changed the look of women's tennis; Eleanor 'Teach' Tennant, the Californian coach who opened up the sport to talented boys and girls from poorer backgrounds;[1] and Renee Richards, who in 1977 became the first transgender professional in sport. Before them all came Leif Rovsing.

Unknown outside Denmark, Rovsing has in recent years been rediscovered as a gay hero there.[2] He was born in 1887 to Marie Quist and her lover, Elif Rovsing, a wealthy Copenhagen merchant. Two years later, Elif formally adopted Leif and left him his fortune when he died in 1908. Leif was then in his early twenties and had enough money never to work so he chose instead to devote his life to his two consuming passions: tennis and the public defence of homosexuality.

Rovsing was never a truly great tennis player. In the first decades of the twentieth century, he won singles and doubles championships in Sweden and Norway as well as Denmark, but the standard of play in those countries was a level below that of the true tennis stars of the time who came from Australia, New Zealand, the United States and Britain, but not yet from Scandinavia. Rovsing was good enough, though, to play at Wimbledon in 1910 and he won the first two sets in his match against the British player L.E.

Milburn. He then faded badly and Lieutenant Milburn won the final three sets with the loss of only four games. Rovsing never came to the All England Club again but carried on playing in tournaments across continental Europe for the next decade, especially in Sweden where he became friends with King Gustav V.

Gustav had learned the game in Britain in 1876 when he was 18 years old. He was soon good enough to play on the French Riviera with the Renshaw twins and then the Doherty brothers, and to represent Sweden in the Davis Cup playing under the pseudonym of 'Mr G'. On a state visit to Berlin in the 1930s to meet the German Chancellor, Adolf Hitler, King Gustav insisted on seeing the Jewish player Daniel Prenn, then number one in Germany, as well. Soon afterwards Prenn was allowed to leave the country and it seems likely that Gustav intervened on his behalf, as he would a few years later for Gottfried von Cramm and Jean Borotra, two tennis champions imprisoned by the Nazis.

When Rovsing and Gustav met there was an age difference between them of 30 years, but they shared a love of tennis and something else as well. The tall, elegant Gustav, who always wore a pince-nez, never publicly admitted to any liaisons with men, but he did pay off a young restaurateur called Kurt Haijby in an infamous blackmail case in the late 1930s. Haijby was one of a number of the king's rumoured male lovers.

The much younger Rovsing made no secret of his involvement in same-sex relationships. Homosexual relationships were illegal in Denmark until 1933, but it is doubtful whether Rovsing's behaviour would have caused much concern if he had been discreet. As the decorations on the walls of the club in Hellerup show, discretion was not Rovsing's style. Not only did he openly share intimate times with young men, he also argued publicly for the advantages of homosexuality which was beautiful and pure, he claimed, hygienic and aesthetic. This unapologetic defence of what was then an illegal activity was a major reason in 1917 for Rovsing's ban from tennis clubs and tournaments in Denmark and abroad. 'Mr. Rovsing's morality is of such a nature', the Danish tennis authorities said, 'that it stands in open conflict with the task of all healthy sports, to promote bodily and spiritual health'. People with Rovsing's sexual preferences and conduct, they later added, shouldn't have access to players' changing rooms.

For eleven years Rovsing contested the ban. 'Life has no value for me without tennis', he claimed, as he fought the Danish authorities through the courts in a series of cases which became increasingly vituperative. In 1928, however, the ban was confirmed in Denmark's highest court 'for the protection of young members of clubs'. It was not the first time in tennis that a concern for minors has been used to justify homophobia.

When the pastime of lawn tennis became fashionable in 1880s Britain, it was snapped up by the new girls' schools as a potential attraction for prospective pupils and their parents. Most of the established boys' public schools, however, refused to include it in their roster of sports because they feared it would encourage homosexuality. Tennis was then seen by other sportsmen as a 'sissy' game liable to corrupt boys and hinder healthy male development. If it was going to prosper as a popular male sport, this stigma needed to be dismantled. It was a small step from being seen a sissy to being called a sodomite.

In late Victorian Britain, close male friendships were common, often with intense emotional bonds, but sex between men was illegal under the indecency acts. When concern about homosexuality rose in the late nineteenth century, it was made a specific criminal offence and, in 1895, Oscar Wilde was prosecuted and jailed. In his younger days, Wilde had been a keen tennis player. For tennis to survive as a male game, it needed to remove any suspicion of Wildean queerness and develop a masculine code as robust as that of the 'muscular Christianity' of rugby and cricket.

The solution came from the new skills that lawn tennis encouraged in its players. Other sports depended on force and aggression but tennis required discipline, control and restraint and these requirements fitted neatly into upper-middle-class masculine values of the time such as stoicism, magnanimity in victory and a desire to play games for their own sake and not for money. This approach to sport became known as the 'gentleman-amateur', and it was the conduct expected of men in the mixed tennis clubs that grew up around Britain that were fondly satirised in the short stories of Saki and the novels of P.G. Wodehouse. Even when the first champions like Herbert Lawford and the Renshaw brothers developed top spin that overcame the need for restraint in hitting the ball, the etiquette remained. William and Ernest Renshaw, the first great Wimbledon champions, were known not just for their aggressive play but also for their gentlemanly behaviour.

The problem was that while this passionless way of playing tennis like a gentleman dampened down accusations of sissyness, it also removed much of its entertainment value. Unlike other nineteenth-century sport crazes, lawn tennis attracted paying spectators who did not play themselves. The crowds who flocked to Wimbledon at the turn of the century wanted stars with more personality than the gentleman-amateur style of play allowed, and so a feyness crept into the game that was noticeable in the elegance and ambiguous sexuality of the Doherty brothers. After the First World War, a tennis player emerged from Philadelphia who took this fey behaviour much further because he understood that tennis at the highest level was as much theatrical performance as physical contest.

If Bill Tilden wasn't the greatest men's tennis player of all time – and many people think he was – he was without doubt the most entertaining. The Wimbledon spectators admired not just his sporting genius and swashbuckling style but his passion and theatricality. He brought playfulness into tennis, although it was the playfulness of a tiger toying with his prey. His style and manner, on court and off, were impossible to separate out from his homosexuality, which was clear to everyone around him although he never admitted it until he had long stopped playing. He was able to get away with camp behaviour partly because he was so good at the game and partly too because he was as much an artist on court as an athlete, and the arts were one of the 'few social worlds in the twentieth century that allowed for queer expression'.[3]

Tilden was born in 1893 in a Philadelphian mansion just a few hundred yards away from the prestigious Germantown Cricket

Club, one of the earliest places in America to offer lawn tennis. The young Bill, tall, intelligent, aristocratic but also shy and delicate, took to tennis straight away. He showed phenomenal talent but was never quite solid enough to win the major tournaments, at least at singles. When he was in his mid-twenties, he considered quitting the sport and resuming his studies at the University of Pennsylvania. Tennis was then a determinedly amateur sport and the dominant script for top male players was to have fun for a few years touring the world living on 'expenses' but then give up the game, take up a profession, earn proper money, marry and start a family.

As the queer studies researcher Nathan Titman has pointed out, Tilden's sexual preference for men ruled out much of this scenario.[4] Instead, like Leif Rovsing, Bill Tilden made a full-time commitment to tennis. He studied the game anew, invented new strokes, transformed the drop shot into a lethal weapon and spent hours experimenting with pace and spin. On Monday 21 June 1920, when he was 27 years old, he turned up at the All England Club a transformed player. Two weeks later he won his first Wimbledon singles championship, and for the next six years did not lose a match of significance anywhere in the world. Spectators loved his brilliance and showmanship. Tilden would rarely play the same shot twice. He threw points if he felt bored, glared at linesmen and corrected their calls. He would deliberately lose a few games so he could keep the crowd on the edge of their seats. The actress, Tallulah Bankhead, once 'chewed a pink rose down to the thorns in sheer nervous excitement' as she watched Tilden wrestle one more victory from what seemed clear defeat.[5]

Bankhead was not the only diva smitten. Katharine Hepburn and Greta Garbo were devoted fans too, and Tilden felt just as much at home on the stage and movie set as he did on the tennis court. He forged relationships with actors (many of whom were homosexual), put on his own plays (on which he squandered most of his fortune) and acted in Broadway shows and Hollywood films (although the reviews were never kind). It was at tennis that his talents truly shone.

After his success in the early 1920s, the American tennis authorities became worried he would revive the effete image of the game. Until he turned professional in 1931, Tilden did nothing to ease their anxieties. He spent time with the demi-monde in bars in Berlin and rarely disguised his enjoyment of the companionship of adolescents. As one tennis writer noted at the time, 'Bill was always interested in young players. He became very fond of boys and they of him.'[6] It was this 'fondness' that would eventually be his downfall.

On 23 November 1946, he was found in a car in California with a 14-year-old boy who reported that the 53-year-old Tilden had touched him. Tilden pleaded guilty and served seven months in prison. A few years later he was back in jail once more after being found with another young man of 17. Tilden tried to defend himself by claiming that tennis 'fosters intense relationships between men'. He argued that he found it difficult not to succumb because he suffered from a debilitating illness which attracted him to young people of his own sex.[7] Even at the time, when homosexuality was widely seen as a deep psychological flaw if not a genetic condition, Tilden's excuses for sexual abuse seemed flimsy. No tennis club would give him work as a coach. His name was removed from the records of Dunlop, his sponsor. His portrait was taken down from the Germantown club in Philadelphia. Apart from Charlie Chaplin, his famous fans deserted him. In 1953, Bill Tilden died in poverty in Los Angeles at only 60 years old, his exceptional contribution to tennis unacknowledged. His masterpiece, *Matchplay and the Spin of the Ball*, published in 1925, though, remained in print because it was – and is – the best technical book on how to play like a champion. Forty years later, the Australian Grand Slam winner, Rod Laver – like Tilden, another candidate for the greatest male player of all time – claimed 'we are all Tilden's disciples'.[8]

Two years before his death, one of Bill Tilden's great friends in tennis made his final appearance at Wimbledon. On Monday 25 June 1951, Gottfried von Cramm, then 42 years old, entered Centre Court for the last time dressed as always in immaculate long white trousers with his laminated wooden racket by his side. He was greeted by applause which equalled that shown to his opponent, the second seed Jaroslav Drobny, ten years younger and long a favourite of the Wimbledon crowd. In a tight match that lasted just under two hours, von Cramm lost to Drobny in three close sets. As he left the court to cheers from the spectators, he passed under the words of Rudyard Kipling exhorting competitors to treat triumph and disaster as 'two imposters exactly the same'. The words could have been written with von Cramm in mind. On this very court in the mid-1930s, he was the beaten finalist for the Men's Singles title three years in a row losing twice to Fred Perry and once to Donald Budge. Not once did von Cramm utter any complaint or regret. He was the most courteous competitor tennis has ever seen.

Despite early relationships with men, von Cramm married Elisabeth 'Lisa' von Dobeneck in 1930 and for a time they were Germany's most glamorous couple. It was the last years of the Weimar Republic, the twilight of the German avant garde. Androgyny was fashionable and there was nobody more androgynous than Gottfried and Lisa. There is a black-and-white photograph of them from this time standing side by side and looking into the distance with clipped blonde hair and identical smiles, almost indistinguishable. They were undoubtedly fond of each other but they loved and partied separately. While Lisa von Cramm frequented the desirable salons in town, Gottfried was most at home in the Rot-Weiss tennis club whose 16 pristine clay courts were located in the fashionable west Berlin suburb of Grunewald. There he played and dined with Bill Tilden, Daniel Prenn and King Gustav of Sweden and started an affair with an actor, Manasse Herbst. Von Cramm's playing style was elegant rather than aggressive, a textbook illustration of how to play a shot exactly in the right way. The only drawback was that he needed to be in the right position on court to do this. Donald Budge and Fred Perry were more flexible and could hit the ball on the run, a major reason why Budge and Perry were Wimbledon champions and von Cramm the perennial runner-up, a constant source of amusement to him.

Von Cramm's style and grace found favour with everyone, even among the Nazi regime although he was no Nazi. The story goes that Hitler phoned him before a Davis Cup match against Budge to wish him good luck and Hermann Goring, the second most powerful man in Germany at the time, offered to be his mentor if he joined the Nazi party. Von Cramm declined but would in the end need Goring's help. In 1938, he was arrested, questioned about his relationship with Herbst and thrown into jail. Goring intervened and von Cramm served only a year in prison, a difficult time but a lenient treatment compared to the many German homosexuals who perished in the death camps. He was, however, never the same tennis player again, and after the war his style of playing the sport as if it were still a garden party pastime had disappeared forever.

Partly because of the fate of Tilden and von Cramm and partly because the years after the Second World War saw a resurgence of traditional family values, top male tennis players of the 1950s and 1960s distanced themselves from any kind of gay or camp identity. Masculine stamina and restraint reasserted themselves as the dominant values in men's tennis, and playfulness and elegance were relegated to mixed doubles. This new style of male play was summed up in the character of Rod Laver, who was regal on court but modest off. He and the other top Australian players like Ken Rosewall and Lew Hoad exhibited, as Teddy Tinling mischievously noted, an 'admirable belief in sportsmanship and virility'. Like most of Tinling's observations, it was not entirely clear whether this was a compliment or not.

Cuthbert 'Teddy' Tinling was born in 1910 in Eastbourne. He was a sickly child and in adolescence was sent by his parents to the Riviera to recover his health. He never came back. In an extraordinary career as a confidant to the stars, player liaison officer for Wimbledon, spokesperson for women's tennis and spy for British intelligence, the tall, bald, bird-like Tinling was openly gay even when it was prudent to be secretive. He was helped considerably by his main profession as a dress designer. Fashion, like the arts, provided a relatively safe haven for homosexual men in the mid-twentieth century, and after the Second World War Tinling became the designer for several top female players at a time when women were struggling to develop their own distinctive appearance on court.

How tennis champions look has mattered ever since the Doherty brothers posed in a photographic studio in 1900, although it has not usually been male players who have taken sartorial risks but women. In the early 1920s, Suzanne Lenglen's designer outfits, corsetless dress, bandeaus and bobbed hair were loved by spectators and copied by women everywhere. The female tennis players who came after her extended the freedoms she pioneered – Ruth Tapscott and Joan Lycett left off stockings, Helen Jacobs wore a divided skirt – but without Lenglen's style or extravagances. When Alice Marble won Wimbledon in 1939, she wore a simple T-shirt and shorts and, after the war, shorts was the choice for most female champions. In 1947, though, Christian Dior introduced the 'New Look' in Paris which used glittering fabrics to emphasise the shape of the female body. Dior encouraged Teddy Tinling, who had dabbled with design before the war, to start reimagining tennis dress for women. Tinling had been one of Suzanne Lenglen's earliest confidantes and he searched for someone who could be the new Suzanne, at least in terms of look if not ability. Two years later, he found her.

In 1949, 26-year-old Gertrude 'Gussie' Moran, from Santa Monica, California, finally qualified for Wimbledon after doing well that year in tournaments in America. Playing at the All England Club had been her ambition ever since she gave up acting for tennis in her early twenties, and she approached Tinling to create a special tennis dress to mark the occasion. Tinling saw in Moran the 'provocative sexy bodyline' that reminded him of Lana Turner, a famous Hollywood actress of the time.[9] He designed a short dress of shimmering satin complete with 'frilly lace panties' which were visible every time Moran stretched for a shot. It caused a sensation. Gertrude Moran wore the outfit on the second day of Wimbledon in 1949 and photographers fought for close ups. 'Gorgeous Gussie', as the British popular press named her, was on the front page of every newspaper across the world. The tennis establishment hated all this. Tinling was accused of bringing 'sin and vulgarity into tennis' and was banned from Wimbledon for 30 years, but he was unrepentant. 'We changed the entire concept of how sports girls can look', he claimed. The scandal made his career but it did little for Moran. Her tennis floundered as did a putative career as a model. After two failed marriages she settled quietly in California and spent most of her remaining life teaching tennis to deaf children. In his many incarnations, Tinling thrived, but it was another of his designs 20 years later which caught the attention of the world's media once more.

In the autumn of 1973, the Wimbledon champion Billie Jean King was challenged by Bobby Riggs to a 'Battle of the Sexes' match in Houston, Texas. Riggs was a Wimbledon champion himself but 34 years before in 1939. He was now 55 years old but a few months ago had defeated Margaret Court, one of King's rivals, in a similar match. He used that occasion to berate women's tennis and boast he could beat any woman in the world despite his age. Ladies, he railed, should stay in the kitchen or bedroom and always support their man. 'The best way to handle women is to keep them pregnant and barefoot.'[10]

King felt compelled to respond to Riggs' taunts and agreed to take him on in front of a packed crowd in an astrodome in Houston on 20 September 1973. When the two players appeared, the surprise was that Billie Jean King matched Bobby Riggs for showmanship. When she came to Wimbledon in 1961 as a teenager, the then Billie Jean Moffitt was noticeable for her loud voice and fearsome play but not for any sense of fashion. The extravagant style King exhibited in Houston was due to Teddy Tinling. He had made her up like Cleopatra and she was carried into the arena by four bare-chested muscle men dressed as Egyptian slaves. When she took off her robes, she revealed not her usual bland sportswear but a Tinling-designed, glistening white dress with 'blue trim and rhinestones, a blue sweatband and bright blue tennis shoes'.[11] Riggs gave King a red lollipop. King gave him a live piglet wearing a pink bow.

In the match, however, Billie Jean King reverted to her usual seriousness and didn't allow Riggs' attempts at gamesmanship to divert her attention. Instead of being fooled by his lobs and drop shots, as Margaret Court had been, she stayed on the baseline, slowed her shots down and pushed and pulled Riggs around court. To the delight of the crowd, who were encouraged to cheer and boo throughout, King exhausted Riggs and ended up an easy and convincing winner. The game attracted 90 million television viewers across the world, the highest ever for a tennis match, and King claimed her victory was part of the feminist struggle of the time. After the match, she received letters from women saying that when she beat Riggs 'their lives changed. They demanded raises, demanded better working conditions and do you know what? They got them.'[12] It was a lesson she needed to apply to tennis.

By the end of the 1960s, it was clear that open tennis was not delivering the same reward for women players as for men. At the first open Wimbledon in 1968, Billie Jean King won £750 while Rod Laver received £2,000. In a tournament in Los Angeles organised by Jack Kramer, women received only one tenth of the prize money of men. Kramer claimed he was simply reflecting market demand. Most spectators, he argued, wanted to see men's tennis because it was more exciting. To counter this argument, women's tennis required someone with the authority of a champion and the determination of a fighter. Billie Jean King became the ringleader for the fight for an equal share of the spoils.

With the help of Gladys Heldman, publisher of *World Tennis* magazine, and Joe Cullman, chief executive of the tobacco company Philip Morris, King organised a separate women's tour in 1970 which developed its own market for women's tennis without comparison to men. She then joined other players to launch a political campaign to force the top tournaments in the world to pay women the same as men. This second aim was not finally achieved until 2007, when Wimbledon became the last Grand Slam tournament to concede to equal pay. But the Virginia Slims tour and the formation of the Women's Tennis Association in the early 1970s ensured that the gap between male and female earnings, if not extinguished, narrowed considerably. The top female tennis players became the highest paid sportswomen in the world.

It is difficult to overestimate the importance of Billie Jean King in all of this. Some of King's remarkable resilience and resolve came from her working-class background. Right from the start, she had to fight her way to the top even when she was a precociously talented teenager in California and beating everyone she met. But some of King's courage also came, at least it seems to me, from her sexual identity as an LGBTQ woman. It fuelled her feminism and helped her see her struggles as part of a wider fight for female power and control. Despite being happily married, King was involved for many years in a secret relationship with her secretary, Marilyn Barnett. In 1981, the relationship became public when Barnett sued for alimony. 'I had wanted to tell the truth', King has said, 'but my parents were homophobic, and I was in the closet. As well as that, I had people tell me that if I talked about what I was going through, it would be the end of the women's tour.'[13] The tour survived but the revelations about her sexuality cost King two million dollars in lost endorsements. Undeterred she fought on. Now in her late seventies, she still speaks out on behalf of women's tennis six decades after she first became a champion.

In 1981, another female tennis champion came out but in circumstances more of her own choosing. Martina Navratilova, who played a similarly powerful serve and volley game to King, had won Wimbledon twice in the late 1970s and had recently migrated from Czechoslovakia to the United States. She gave interviews to mark the occasion and admitted a relationship with the writer Rita Mae Brown. As a result she too lost sponsors, but many of these came back as Navratilova went on to win Wimbledon another seven times. Like Billie Jean King, it is difficult to overestimate the importance of Navratilova to women's tennis and women's sport. She reclaimed the women's game as a physical contest and struck the ball with venom, a link back to Alice Marble and Lottie Dod and a prelude to the Williams sisters. Much of Navratilova's confidence came from her ease and openness about her sexuality.

Despite press speculation that women's professional tennis in the 1970s and 1980s was dominated by lesbians, Navratilova argued that the percentage of gay women in women's tennis was no more than everyday life, although her estimate of 10 per cent was higher than most surveys show.

Whatever the numbers, the influence of lesbian women in tennis – from Toupie Lowther in the early twentieth century to Amelie Mauresmo a hundred years later – has been immense, especially because they have had to face regular taunts about their 'Amazonian' achievements. Perhaps this is one reason why most top female tennis players who have relationships with other women still continue to keep their sexual identity private. As the cultural studies academic and feminist, Elizabeth Wilson, has pointed out, labelling a woman athlete a 'dyke' was a means to discredit her and her achievements because a lesbian was not a "real" woman'.[14]

One female tennis player has put up with far more than jibes, and that's because she was originally not a woman at all but a man. Richard Raskind was born in New York in 1934 to Jewish parents who were doctors. He entered the family profession and qualified as an ophthalmologist but two things were more important to him than his medical practice. He loved playing tennis and he felt he was the wrong sex. His tennis was good enough to play the occasional tournament on the men's professional circuit, although he was never likely to trouble the top players. The feeling of fundamental discomfort with his male body never left him even on the tennis court. In 1975, when he was 41 years old, he had sexual realignment surgery in Morocco, changed his surname to Richards and first name to Renee, the French for 'reborn', and re-emerged as a woman. Soon after, a long-time friend invited her to play in the Tennis Week Open in South Orange, New Jersey and that's when the trouble started.

Twenty-five of the 32 participants withdrew from the tournament in a protest about Richard's presence in a woman's competition, although Billie Jean King supported her. It was the start of a tirade of objections from players and officials which culminated in Richards not being allowed to enter the US Open in

1976 without undergoing genetic tests to prove she was female. She did take one test which gave an ambiguous result but then refused to take it again and took the American tennis authorities to court.

On 16 August 1977, Judge Alfred Ascione found in Renee Richards' favour. He ruled that she was 'now a female' and that having to pass the test was 'grossly unfair, discriminatory and inequitable, and violative of her rights'.[15] Richards was allowed to play in the US Open the following year and, although she lost easily in the first round to Virginia Wade, she did make it to the final of the ladies doubles. She continued to play on the women's professional circuit for another half a decade, although she never came to Wimbledon. When she retired, Martina Navratilova employed her as a coach.

In 2012, Renee Richards gave an interview to *Slate* magazine saying that transitioning to a woman had given her an unfair advantage over other players. The only thing that prevented her becoming a female champion, she argued, was her age. 'I know if I'd had surgery at the age of 22, and then went on the tour', she said, 'no genetic woman in the world would have been able to come close to me.'[16] Whether that was true or not is difficult to know. Since Richards retired, there has been no other openly trans player on the professional circuit. There have also been no men who identify as LGBTQ, although a couple of retired players – Brian Vahaly from the USA and Francisco Rodriguez from Paraguay – have come out as gay in recent years. Neither reached the top 50 when they were playing. In a sport that has always attracted gay men, the absence of openly homosexual top players does seem odd.

One reason advanced is concern about losing sponsorship, although this seems unlikely these days. Another is the way men treat each other on the professional circuit. In tennis, as in most men's sport today, there is a 'persistent fear of homosexuality' often expressed when men are together at the start or end of a match.[17] 'I heard homophobic comments all the time in the locker room', Brian Vahaly has said. 'That was just part of the culture.'[18] There is another explanation too which is more prosaic. Many gay men do not come out until their late twenties, thirties or even forties. Some do not come out at all. Since most tennis careers are over by 30, perhaps professional tennis players are not so different from anyone else.

Stuart Hancock is in his early forties and works as a freelance composer from his home in Bedfordshire. He has played tennis for as long as he can remember. 'My parents met playing tennis and my brother and I were always around the game at tennis clubs, especially at weekends.'[19] Stuart now plays for clubs in London and Harpenden and, since 2013, in the Gay and Lesbian Tennis Alliance which organises tennis tournaments around the world for its 10,000 members, most of them men.

'I came out at the age of 28 to the surprise of a lot of people since I had girlfriends in the past. I am now number 66 in singles and 18 for doubles in the Gay and Lesbian Tennis Alliance's world rankings.' He finds tennis with other gay men as competitive as any. 'Probably the only difference, tennis-wise, in a gay tournament is that the handshake at the end of a match tends to be augmented with a hug or a peck on the cheek and there are some on-court outfits you wouldn't normally see!' In conventional tennis clubs, he has never experienced any homophobia. 'Tennis suits gay men very well', he argues, 'there are plenty who come to tennis later in life and been attracted by the accessibility, enjoyability and camaraderie of the sport. Tennis, to my knowledge, seems to fill that role in the gay community far more than any other sport does.'[20]

Perhaps that is why there are now over a dozen LGBTQ tennis clubs flourishing in cities around the world including Manchester ('Northern Aces'), Sydney ('Tennis Sydney') and London ('Tennis London International'). Most have the kind of anonymous name chosen when it was prudent not to attract public scrutiny, but a different approach is taken in Amsterdam. The LGBTQ club there calls itself 'Smashing Pink' and claims to be the largest in Europe with 240 active members, a third of whom are women. The choice of its name was crucial. 'Smashing Pink' makes public its members' sexual preferences and challenges the notion that tennis is played only by people with a conventional sexuality. 'We play tennis together, but the socialising after tennis is at least as important', says Eric van der Palen, one of the organisers of the club. 'We share a lot of our private lives. Smashing Pink feels like a family.'

It is a family that not only plays sport together but also takes political action, joining in events like Gay Pride Amsterdam, Pride in the Park and an LGBTQ Refugees Sports Day. For many Smashing Pink members, belonging to a gay tennis club is not a consumer choice but a political act. 'Visibility here is the most important thing', adds van der Palen, 'the wider tennis community is aware of the identity of our club. During participation of our club in the Dutch tennis league there are great conversations and connections. People from other clubs are really interested in who we are. The longer I am a member of Smashing Pink, the more I love our club.'[21]

It is a club that the gay Danish player Eric Rovsing would have adored, but when Smashing Pink was founded in 1996 he had been dead for 20 years. For most of his life, Rovsing continued his campaign to win acceptance of homosexuality in sport, writing books and pamphlets and giving talks and lectures in Denmark and abroad. For most of his life, too, he continued to play tennis on the beautiful court he had built in Hellerup, and the Dansk Tennis Club developed a deserved reputation as one of the most enjoyably decadent places to play tennis in the world.

13

Professionals

In 1968, I was 14 years old and obsessed with tennis. I had progressed from playing on public courts with boys from my council estate in Bracknell New Town to joining the local tennis club and playing with adults, many of whom were much better than me. On the club's three green tarmac courts, tucked away on a cul-de-sac behind Bracknell's new shopping centre, I played in the evenings until it was too dark to see the ball; in Saturday morning junior sessions run by the coach, a tall awkward man called Bill Jones; and on Saturday and Sunday afternoons with the senior members of the club who taught me doubles and middle-class manners.

Every year, Bracknell Tennis Club, like most of the tennis clubs in Britain at that time, was allocated a couple of dozen Wimbledon tickets from the Lawn Tennis Association, and every year the club organised a draw among its members for the chance to buy one of these desirable items. I was included in the Bracknell draw that summer of 1968 and, much to the annoyance of some older members, my name was the first to be picked out. This gave me an option to buy a Centre Court ticket for Monday 24 June, the first day of the 1968 Championships, for 32 shillings. This was a full two weeks' wages from my after-school job helping my father clean a local factory floor, but the chance to go to the temple of tennis was not to be missed, especially as that year the All England Club was admitting professionals for the first time. I would see legendary players like Ken Rosewall and Rod Laver return to a Wimbledon they had dominated ten years before until Jack Kramer's cheque book proved impossible to ignore.

My hero was Laver, a softly spoken red-head known as the Rocket, who came from a poor farming family in Queensland. In 1962, Laver had become the second man to win the Grand Slam:

Paris, Wimbledon, New York and Melbourne in the same year. Then he turned professional and was lost to most of his British fans as he played in American sports stadia for money rather than glory. He was now almost 30 years old. Could he do the Grand Slam again? I was about to find out, or at least I thought I was.

It was raining when I set off from Bracknell on the slow electric train to London Waterloo and it was raining after I changed to one of the fast electric trains from Waterloo that stopped at Wimbledon on its way to the south coast. It was raining while I waited at Wimbledon station for the special tennis bus to take me to the All England Club in Church Road and raining when I arrived on Centre Court at 1.00 pm, an hour before the scheduled start. The rain did not stop. Not a single ball was played that day, and Rod Laver never appeared. There was no refund, as there would be today, no ticket offered for the Tuesday or Wednesday. Two weeks' wages earned by scrubbing floors were, somewhat appropriately, washed away.

That year, I was just one of thousands of Wimbledon ticket-holders to lose out. The dismal clouds in south-east England in the early summer of 1968 caused severe disruption of play. It would be another 40 years before roofs were constructed first over Centre Court and then over Court One to ensure that at least the major matches would not be cancelled due to inclement weather. The constant downpours were one reason why this first open Wimbledon in 1968 was not the exceptional success it promised to be, even though it saw crowd favourites Laver and Billie Jean King crowned as men's and women's champions once more. But even with the sodden grass, dripping scoreboards and damp strawberries, there was an optimism about tennis again, or at least tennis played at the highest level. Much of this optimism came from television.

The year before, on Saturday 1 July 1967, the first colour television pictures in the world were broadcast from Wimbledon by the BBC to instant acclaim. The ball was clearly visible against the grass, which wasn't always the case on many black-and-white sets, and the combination of vivid pictures and, a year later, the return of the most talented players of the game highlighted tennis's advantages over other sports as a televisual offering. Unlike football grounds, golf courses, athletic tracks and cricket pitches, the tennis court was a perfect size for the television screen and the gladiatorial contest between two of the best tennis players in the world was completely in tune with television's thirst for character, conflict and drama.

One thing the new colour pictures could not deliver, however, were regular victories by British players. Apart from the unexpected triumph of Virginia Wade in 1977, which produced choruses of 'For She's a Jolly Good Fellow' in front of a bemused Queen Elizabeth, Wimbledon in the 1970s, 1980s and most of the 1990s was notable for its absence of British players in the final rounds of the singles. This made little difference to the television viewing figures, which kept going up. In 1981, they topped ten million in the UK alone, and between 1969 and 1989, 30 per cent of the British population said they enjoyed watching tennis, less than athletics but more than rugby or golf. Professionalism was bringing in new spectators, as Gordon Forbes noted in 1978: 'Tennis has changed. It has come into money and gone public. It's the day of the superstar, the supercoach, the how to books, the tennis universities and the tracksuits with stripes down the side. And a whole new set of people follow the game.'[1]

The cleverness of Wimbledon and the BBC during this time were that the regular fans who had followed the tournament for decades were not neglected. The look was still retro. Colour television pictures showed lush grass courts with players dressed in white. Male contestants were addressed by their surname while female contestants were addressed as 'Mrs' or 'Miss' and expected to curtsy to the Royal Box. Line calls were made by unpaid officials, often retired military men, who were expected to make instant decisions about whether a fast ball was in or out, decisions which were more than occasionally wrong. All these gave Wimbledon a period feel as if it was a Noël Coward comedy set in the 1930s.

In Rugby, Andrea Sanders-Reece's mother kept watching every year even though Andrea and her two sisters had long left home:

'She used to spend hours discussing the games in phone calls with her cousin, Mamie, who had met her husband Lou at their work's tennis club. My mum had her favourites and loved a bit of drama on the court. Ilie Năstase comes to mind.'[2] In 1973, Ilie Năstase, from Romania, entranced spectators and viewers in a memorable men's final with the American Stan Smith which went to five sets, with Smith just edging victory. Smith was a throwback to the unemotional Australians of the 1950s and 1960s but Năstase represented something new, a tennis artist who dealt out magical shots while often playing the clown. Occasionally his playful character turned dark, and his nickname in the British popular press would be switched from the 'Bucharest buffoon' to 'Mr Nasty'.

Another tempestuous champion of these times was Jimmy Connors, a lower-middle-class boy from St Louis, Missouri, who became known as the first tennis punk. Connors used one of the new Wilson tubular steel rackets to strike the ball on the rise hard and flat. His double-handed backhand was as fierce as his competitive nature, and the year after the Năstase-Smith tussle he bulldozed an ageing Ken Rosewall in a brutally one-sided 1974 Wimbledon final that represented a changing of the tennis guard.

Throughout their tennis careers, Connors and Năstase were repeatedly warned and fined as their antics unfolded in front of millions of television viewers. At that time, the BBC was particularly proud of its new courtside cameras which caught the 'tensions and emotions of the players'.[3] But these close-up shots also captured anger as well as heartache, temper as well as triumph, and they provided the clearest sign that tennis at the top level was changing.

In 1923, in his last year as secretary of the All England Club, George Hillyard had advised players new to Wimbledon of the 'immense importance of good manners on court not only on account of the dignity and prestige of the tournament but for your ultimate happiness and satisfaction'.[4] Fifty years later, Connors and Năstase rewrote Hillyard's recommended etiquette. They cast the tennis star as antihero battling against the remnants of the old tennis establishment propped up by officials who pretended little had changed since Hillyard's day. These two oppositional players brought in new kinds of fans. Connors and Năstase may have been uncouth but their passions were in harmony with the times, especially in Britain as punk rock skewered traditional British reserve. Anger became all the rage, as another champion would demonstrate a few years later.

It is the paradoxes that stay in the mind. John McEnroe was one of the smartest people to play championship tennis but could behave so badly you felt there was something not quite right with him. He could hit the ball with devastating pace yet he kept faith with slow wooden rackets while everyone else embraced fast graphite or steel. He sprayed shots around the court with spins and speeds which came sizzling off his racket but which often defied logic. His left-handed serve had so much swerve that it was, as the actor and tennis fanatic Peter Ustinov memorably described it, like 'hitting a ball around the corner of a building'. Kenneth Williams, another popular entertainer who was mad about tennis, watched on television at his flat on Tottenham Court Road and praised the 'genius stored in that delicate frame of my beloved John McEnroe'.[5]

Looking back now, it is easy to see that McEnroe was a throwback to the geniuses of the amateur game, professional tennis's genuflection to a bygone age, the last champion to play top-level tennis as if he was taking a year off college, as indeed he initially was. In this he resembles Bill Tilden, the 1920s Wimbledon champion from Philadelphia. Both were sons of self-made men, a businessman in Tilden's case, a lawyer in McEnroe's. Both went to private schools and top universities. Both shared a love of performance. Tilden was devoted to the theatre while McEnroe played in a rock band. Unfortunately the sounds McEnroe brought to tennis courts around the world weren't all contained in the headphones of his Sony Walkman. 'You are the pits of the world', he shouted at one umpire. 'Answer my question. The question, you jerk', he said to another. 'You cannot be serious', he screeched to everyone.

It is tempting now to be charitable about McEnroe's behaviour in his tennis matches in the 1980s, particularly as his subsequent broadcasting career has gone a long way to establishing him as one of the cleverest people ever to play the game. We can see that his rage emerged from a perfectionism that wasn't simply about winning but, like Bill Tilden, about trying to play the right shot at the right moment. Most top players control this anger because it makes them play badly, but for a few it does the opposite. McEnroe's tantrums often produced his greatest tennis.

McEnroe was appallingly bad and yet also uniquely thrilling. His outbursts at Wimbledon seemed to reflect a change in society where individualism and ambition replaced collective effort and community spirit. McEnroe, with his branded T-shirts, sponsored tennis shoes and iconic headband with visible logo, was the harbinger of the new consumer age.

One of his earliest deals was with Nike when the company was a fledgling operation in Oregon. Phil Knight, Nike's chief executive, was looking for the kind of athlete who exemplified his new company's outlaw image, someone who broke the rules and won. McEnroe was a perfect fit. Nike's advertisements in the early 1980s used John McEnroe's rebellious image to give the company anti-establishment credibility as it rolled out its sportswear remorselessly across the world. McEnroe's ads helped Nike appeal to the 'individual' at the very same time as it sold identical tennis shoes to millions of suburbanites worldwide. There was, after all, no one more individual than John McEnroe, a white suburban boy from the affluent quarter of the New York borough of Queens.

If McEnroe was the first tennis player to become a global brand, he was matched in business acumen by his great rival, Bjorn Borg. Born in Sodertalje in Sweden in 1956, Borg was an angry young man until his coach, Lennart Bergelin, transformed him into a glacial spirit who won Wimbledon five times before he was 26. Borg first appeared at Wimbledon in 1973 when he was 17, and his long golden hair encouraged scenes reminiscent of Beatlemania ten years before. Everywhere he was pursued by mobs of teenage girls. He signed up with Mark McCormack's International Management Group and McCormack used Borg's natural talent, learned composure and Scandinavian looks to turn him into a worldwide sporting celebrity. At the peak of his fame in 1979, McCormack licensed Borg's name to 39 different products worldwide, from Saab cars to suntan lotions, chocolate bars and Vidal Sassoon jeans to headbands labelled 'Tu Borg' advertising beer. There were even rumours of Bjorn Borg bread. Along with McEnroe, Borg transformed tennis in the 1980s into the new cool, the game that pop stars and prime ministers wanted to play and everybody wanted to watch.

Borg and McEnroe retired young and spectators were hard-pressed to keep their affection for the game in the years ahead. With the exception of Andre Agassi, the Wimbledon champions who followed lacked star appeal. Two of them, Steffi Graf from Germany and Pete Sampras from the USA, each won singles titles seven times but they were less global icons and more geeks next door. The British press categorised them as passionless machines. 'Are robots killing tennis?' said the *Evening Standard* before the 1994 Championships, and their chorus of disapproval was joined by Ilie Năstase who claimed the 'new players don't have charisma'.[6] Without champions who could offer something more than mere brilliance, tennis started losing out to other sports. David Beckham became the Bjorn Borg of his generation, the sports star who could best sell the new brands of the 1990s. Tennis seemed so last decade until it was rescued by two women who were intensely watchable, although for different reasons.

The display of the body, particularly the female body, has been a prominent part of lawn tennis from its earliest days. In the 1920s, two young English women, Evelyn Colyer and Joan Austin, wore short skirts and were known as 'babes'. In the 1940s Gussie Moran's frilly knickers were worldwide news. In the 1970s the American player, Anne White, was banned from wearing an all-white body suit at Wimbledon because it 'drew attention to the sexual area'. Around the same time, the feminist Billie Jean King defended the right of players to display their bodies. 'Tennis is an erotic sport', she claimed, 'and television has increased this appeal with its constant close ups. Every beautiful woman has the right to promote her assets.'[7] In the late 1990s, a Russian player used her 'assets' to make a fortune.

Anna Kournikova never won a major championship, although she did reach the semi-final of Wimbledon in 1997 when she was 16 years old. This exceptional start did not develop into winning tournaments, partly because of injury, but this mattered little in terms of her income. With clear skin, blue eyes and an hourglass figure, Kournikova was the blond sensation from the *dacha* next door and this was enough to make her a celebrity. She was the female tennis player the fans wanted to see, and at the start of the twenty-first century she appeared in countless advertisements, most notably the 2000 Berlei sports bra campaign with the slogan 'only the ball should bounce'. David Beckham had shown how an athlete's commercial appeal can be enhanced by appropriating rather than shying away from sexuality. Anna Kournikova took this further. Despite criticism from officials and tennis commentators, she posed in swimsuits and bikinis for sport weeklies and men's monthlies and made more money than many women who were champions.

Kournikova was a media sensation, but at the turn of the century it was the male players that drew the crowds. The women's professional game was thoughtful, considered and a little dull. For fans like Martin Amis, this meant there was time to appreciate the subtleties of tennis compared to the 'power struggle of athletic machismo' the men's game had become.[8] Certainly public park and club players, men as much as women, could learn more from watching top women play than watching the men. But learning to play better was hardly the reason people tuned in to the tournament every year. The benefit of tuition cannot compare with the thrill of narrative. Women's tennis at the time was no longer dramatic or exhilarating. Most female players rarely seemed to take any risk. Kournikova was not a risk-taker, at least not on court. Her game was a model of sombre concentration. In the summer of 1997, sitting in front of my television set, it was not Kournikova's debut at Wimbledon that astonished me but that of another teenager, all arms, legs and awkwardness. In the Championships that year,

Venus Williams did not advance beyond the first round, but she seemed destined to change women's tennis for ever.

She and her sister Serena grew up in the 1980s in the southern Los Angeles city of Compton, immortalised by the rap group N.W.A. in 'Straight Outta Compton'. Their father, Richard Williams, ran a security business but was always on the look-out for business opportunities and noticed that female tennis players like Billie Jean King and Chris Evert were earning a considerable fortune from the game. in 1976 Evert had become the first woman to win more than a million dollars in a single year. Williams thought his daughters should be able to do the same. Under his strict supervision, he taught Venus and Serena to play tennis on public courts near their home in Compton, then the fourth most dangerous city in the USA. At eleven, Venus was good enough to be on the front cover of a national tennis magazine and Jack Kramer said she would be a champion. Her father predicted that ten-year-old Serena would be even better, and he negotiated a deal with Reebok which allowed him to move the family to Palm Beach in Florida and employ the best tennis coaches around. Venus Williams grew into a tall young women with the 'shambling grace of a pool shark'.[9] Three months after I saw her on television, she made her debut in the 1997 US Open in Flushing Meadows and reached the final. She was just 17 years old.

Unlike the studied composure of other players, Venus Williams oozed passion. She transformed women's tennis by not playing safe. Her desire was always to go for a winner even if it meant occasionally losing to players with half her talent. Mostly, though, she triumphed. Her haughty style and angular power combined with the fastest serve the women's game had ever seen brought back to women's tennis the visceral quality of Martina Navratilova, Alice Marble, Suzanne Lenglen and Lottie Dod. She made women's tennis exciting again. In 2002 she was the number one player in the world. At number two was her sister Serena, who would do everything Venus did only better.

It is difficult not to credit Richard Williams for much of the astounding success of his two daughters. They were both natural athletes, but without his vision and drive it is doubtful whether they would have ever left Compton. On 14 September 2003, one of their half-sisters, Yetunde, who stayed living in the city, was shot dead by gunmen near the same public tennis courts where the Williams' sisters had learned to play the game. This kind of tragedy rarely happened in Palm Beach.

The parental support provided by Richard Williams was vital, but in the history of tennis it was by no means unusual. Williams is just one of a long line of parents who devoted their lives to making their children champions, a line which stretches back to Charles Lenglen in the 1920s, whose power over his daughter Suzanne eventually led to a break in relations between them. Many other parent–child collaborations ended badly. One top player was whipped on bare legs by her father in the 1970s. Another would later describe his father's coaching regime in the 1980s as a 'glorified prison camp', while yet another had to take out a restraining order against her father in the 1990s due to his constant verbal abuse.

What has received less attention is where this intense relationship seems to have been entirely beneficial. Jimmy Connors would not have been a tennis star without the drive of his mother, Gloria. John McEnroe would have quit tennis earlier without the level-headed diligence of his father Patrick. When Andy Murray had his first success at the United States Junior Championships in 2004, there was one person at his side, his mother Judy. In the years that followed, Judy Murray was a familiar sight in the stands watching her son play. Without her presence, it seems likely that he would not have become a champion. There has never been any break-up between them, perhaps because Judy Murray has known when to retreat. 'I'm the pushy mother. I know that's what people think', she wrote in 2008, 'but anyone who knows me can tell you I am not pushy at all. I have learned over the years to keep my mouth shut.'[10]

One of Murray's contemporaries is the Croatian player Ivan Dodig. After he had beaten Dodig rather easily in the US Open in August 2012, Andy Murray told the *Guardian* that when Dodig first became a professional tennis player, he had slept under bridges and on train stations because he did not have enough money for a bed for the night. 'Eventually people break through because they are hungry', Murray claimed, and 'don't have anything else to fall back on.'[11]

Well, very occasionally they do, but mostly they don't. Tennis players take a huge risk in turning professional. The chances of earning a stable income, even if you show exceptional promise as a junior as Murray did, are small. Professional tennis has some of the most extreme levels of income inequality in the sporting world and Murray is at the top of a steep pyramid. The best 250 women and 350 men make a good living, but most of the other 14,000 or so people trying to play tennis full time scrape by. Half earn no money at all as they tour around the world on Challenger or Futures circuits, one or two levels below Wimbledon, competing in tournaments that take place in anonymous leisure centres in front of a smattering of spectators.

In the summer of 2019, Andrew Watson was in the top 15 in Britain, and ranked around 650 in the world. 'You learn quickly the cheapest way to get to a tournament', he told the BBC, 'and you find somewhere where you can wash your clothes cheaply too, the nearest launderette or bathroom. You have to make the semis every week to make money. A lot of talented people give up and go into coaching.'[12] In the mid-1980s there was a proposal to equalise out the rewards of the game by taxing top players like Murray so that players much lower down in the ratings like Watson could receive enough money to keep going. It never looked likely to succeed. 'The average players wanted socialism, a welfare tennis state', commented Jack Kramer at the time, but the 'big stars and their agents wanted to freelance like movie stars'.[13]

The investment required for a player today to have even a small chance of making it to the top is huge, the main reason why tennis champions now rarely come from poor families as many did in the 1950s and 1960s. You have to take up tennis before you are five years old and have parents who can afford or know how to raise the hundreds of thousands of pounds to turn you into a possible contender, with no guarantee you will ever make a living out of the game, let alone a fortune. In a few countries like France, the Czech Republic, Russia and the United States, there are schemes and scholarships, public and private, to grab young talent and ensure family money is not essential for success. In most other countries this isn't the case. This is one unforeseen and regrettable consequence of the triumph of professionalism. There are others.

Fifty years ago, the top 'amateur' tennis players were under far less pressure than their equivalents today. They could choose which circuits to play, the European clay spring season, perhaps, or the British grass summer tournaments, the country clubs of the American east coast, the hot hard courts of California, the winter in Australia. Only at Wimbledon and Forest Hills (where the US Open was played until 1978) did everyone turn up. Today, the top tennis players compete with each other for eleven months of the year in tournaments around the globe. They stay cocooned in an entourage of physiotherapists, dieticians, hitting partners and boyfriends or girlfriends. They are obsessed with their sleep, glued to their smartphones and rarely see anything of the country in which they play apart from airport lounge, air-conditioned limo, hotel suite and tennis court. Some have long since left their home to live permanently in the USA or low-tax havens like Switzerland, Dubai or the Bahamas. 'I don't think tennis players are from anywhere anymore', claimed Roscoe Tanner as early as 1980.[14] 'Deep down nobody gives a shit about anybody else', John McEnroe pointed out the following year.[15]

The game itself has changed too. Towards the end of the twentieth century, new carbon fibres produced lighter, stronger rackets while new strings allowed more spin. All this rendered net play hazardous and so the baseline game became dominant once more. Grass was abandoned at championship level apart from Wimbledon, and there a new mixture of rye grass, introduced in 2001, slowed the game down and ensured that volleying became the exception not the rule. Elite tennis is now dominated by supremely fit athletes backed up by half a dozen therapists who ensure that all injuries are dealt with quickly and efficiently.

Such support does not come cheap, which is one reason why top players like Rafael Nadal come back from injury relatively quickly whereas those at the bottom of the pyramid are a torn ligament away from retirement. It has also brought one unexpected benefit. Extraordinary players like Roger Federer and Venus and Serena Williams now play much longer than any champion has done for the last hundred years.

With an average age of 38, all three turned up at the All England Club in July 2019 for the Wimbledon Championships. The men's final between Federer and the 32-year-old Novak Djokovic was one of the best for many years. I was one of ten million people in Britain who saw this thrilling contest on their television sets at home. Eighteen BBC cameras at the tournament transmitted live pictures to many more millions worldwide. During Wimbledon fortnight every year, I usually watch the tennis on television, but on the first Wednesday of the 2019 tournament, half a century after I made my original pilgrimage, I returned to Church Road to see how much had changed, one of 500,000 people who visited Wimbledon for that year's tournament. The grounds were more packed than I remembered. Every patch of concrete and grass was occupied by throngs of fans and dozens of culinary diversions. Henman Hill, the mound of grass named after Tim Henman (Britain's most successful player of the late twentieth century, who never won Wimbledon but reached the semi-finals several times), where people without Centre Court tickets watch the action on a giant television screen, has become the visual focus of the tournament. The private enclosures and corporate hospitality tents, so dominant a decade or two ago, are now tucked discretely away.

The top players in the world now play all their matches on the half a dozen show courts for which you have to obtain tickets well in advance. But there are over 200 other entrants in the Men's and Women's Singles alone, and for the first few days of the Championships many of them ply their trade on the remaining eleven courts, which are included in the price of general admission and where you can just queue up to watch. On these courts you are much closer to the players. You feel the vibration of the racket swiping at the yellow ball. You watch fear and desire dance around the players' faces. You are just a few feet away from victory or defeat. Half of them will not be here tomorrow. This is a sporting contest you can smell.

It is here you appreciate just how fast the ball is going. On television, the wide master shot makes tennis appear easier than it is. Even on the show courts, most seats are well above the players and the birds-eye view makes the ball appear impossible to miss. On the eleven back courts you realise this is all an illusion. Serves regularly come down at over 120mph and these young men and women have split seconds to react and yet their reaction has to be controlled and precise. I queued up at court 15 and after half an hour or so squeezed in to watch two men, Benoît Paire from France and Miomir Kecmanović from Serbia, hit the ball with such sustained coordination and elegance that it took my breath away. To be able to do this not once or twice or three times but hour after hour requires years of dedication and denial usually at the expense of anything else. The consequence of this, American novelist David Foster Wallace once argued, is that professional tennis players in the twenty-first century are 'totally present' but don't appear to be able to think.

This may be true of young players starting out, but it does tend to vanish as players mature. Many now use the time between matches and tournaments to grab the education they forfeited. To listen to after-match interviews with champions like Andy Murray, Roger Federer, Angelique Kerber and Venus and Serena Williams is to appreciate a keen intelligence that goes way beyond the game. Their politics does too. The Williams sisters have toured Africa promoting women's rights. Federer is known for his philanthropy. Kerber is an ambassador for UNICEF. Murray has worked tirelessly for many charities. For every retired player who has conservative political views there are many others like Martina Navratilova who speak out for progressive causes.

As for Wimbledon itself, while nobody can pretend that it is not a bastion of privilege, subtle marketing and design has kept much of the original garden party style intact, while the snobbery and class consciousness that were pervasive in the late twentieth century now seem less apparent. As a spectator experience, Church Road compares favourably with Wembley, Twickenham and Lords because it is a sporting space in which men and women have an equal share. Wimbledon may well be a 'bearer of class myths ... attuned to a reflexively conservative political discourse',[16] but it doesn't feel that way. It feels a little like a slightly staid version of Glastonbury.

In July 2019, players from 49 different countries entered the Wimbledon singles and they brought their fans with them. On the outside courts in that first Wednesday of the Championships, English was often not the first language I heard and whiteness of skin was nowhere near as dominant as it used to be 20 years ago. There was also an easy camaraderie among tennis fans here which seemed to bridge differences of class, gender and race particularly on Henman Hill. There, I noticed half a dozen lairy lads sharing cans of Red Stripe and chatting amiably to three middle-aged women from the Home Counties as they waited for Novak Djokovic on the big television screen above them to change ends. Now this all may be a façade. Wimbledon may indeed be a pastiche of tradition that shelters a calculating money-making machine, but it could have been worse.

A few months before the first open championship at Wimbledon in the summer of 1968, a professional tennis tournament took place on an industrial estate in Kansas City. The lawn tennis scoring system, which had remained virtually unchanged in the game since the 1870s, was dispensed with. Games were abolished and each set extended to 31 points. The players were not in white but in colour-coordinated clothing. 'Roger Taylor wore fire-engine red', recalled tennis writer Richard Evans. 'Pierre Barthes wore blue and John Newcombe's shirt and shorts could best be described as the colour of rust.'[17] The crowd was encouraged to shout when they felt like it and the court was next door to a slaughterhouse so the 'smell of cattle' wafted around the arena. This could have been top tennis in the 2020s. There are some things to be grateful for.

14

Amateurs

On Sunday 11 June 1972, a most unusual tennis match took place. On a specially constructed court on the back lawn of the Manor House Hotel in Leamington Spa, four of the town's top tennis players took on four players from Edgbaston Priory tennis club in Birmingham. The men were dressed in 'breeches, blazers and boaters'.[1] One or two of them had even grown a moustache for the occasion and practised underarm serves. The women were resplendent in crinolines: long heavily boned dresses made of cotton and satin which came with bustles, bodices and matching bonnets. Music from the band of the Royal Tank Regiment turned it into an appropriately festive occasion.

The eight players did their best. Using pear-shaped wooden rackets which dated from the nineteenth century and in front of an appreciative crowd of several hundred people, many of whom had just enjoyed a celebratory lunch at the hotel, they played a set or two of mixed doubles in the style of a hundred years ago while trying not to collapse with laughter. One person who enjoyed watching was Ann Jones, Wimbledon champion three years before. Another was Peter Gem, the only living descendant of Harry Gem in whose honour the match was taking place.

This celebration of lawn tennis in Victorian times was organised by the tennis historian Tom Todd on behalf of the Lawn Tennis Association and the local council. It was intended to mark the centenary of the tennis club set up at the hotel by Harry Gem and Augurio Perera in the 1870s. Todd was convinced this club dated from 1872, which would make it the world's first tennis club and Gem and Perera the first people to play lawn tennis. It was a bold claim at the time and it has turned out not to be true. The latest research shows it is unlikely Gem and Perera's club started playing lawn tennis until the summer of 1874, a few months after Walter Wingfield had invented the game in London.[2]

Harry Gem and Augurio Perera may not have been, as Todd thought, the first people to play lawn tennis but they were certainly early players of the game. Even if 1972 wasn't their club's centenary, and the club probably wasn't the first to play lawn tennis but more likely the third or the fourth, everybody on that Sunday in June seems to have had a good time. Todd was particularly pleased that Peter Gem was able to attend. He had been looking for someone who could represent Harry for a while and was about to give up before discovering Peter in Oswestry in Shropshire, where he was headmaster of the local grammar school.

Tom Todd was grateful too that the eight people who volunteered that Sunday to play tennis dressed up in Victorian clothes embraced the event with such *éclat*. The four local players were members of Leamington Lawn Tennis Club situated a couple of miles away from the hotel off the Rugby Road. This club was not the same as Harry Gem's original club, which only lasted 22 years before it went bankrupt, but it was a club that in 1972 Harry would have had no trouble recognising. The rackets used were made from the same wood as Victorian times. The balls were white, as was the tennis dress worn on court, even if the hemlines were a little shorter than in Harry's day and the women players no longer wore corsets. The grass courts were much the same too and so were the people who played at the club, at least in terms of their social class. The first two members of Harry Gem's club in 1874 worked as doctors in the Warneford Hospital in Oxford. Ninety-eight years later, Leamington Lawn Tennis Club had several medics among its members as well as lawyers, architects and surveyors, although there were no vicars. There were, though, plenty of estate agents.

Anne Tyler remembers the Leamington Lawn Tennis Club well. In 1972, she was 16 years old and the club was an essential part of her teenage life. Her mother played for the teams and her father would go on to be chairman of the club. Both parents took part in the Harry Gem celebrations that June. 'It was a big event', she recalled, 'they even had a rehearsal a few days before. Mum kept moaning that her movement was somewhat restricted due to the full-length frock but the actual tennis wasn't bad at all. It was all very exciting.'[3]

The Tyler family had moved to Leamington in 1968. Anne's parents had met playing tennis so they were delighted to find a tennis club just down the road from their new home. 'There were grass and shale courts, and a rickety old club house with wooden beams and a makeshift bar that the adults took turns to run. I played a lot of sport at school but belonging to a tennis club gave you a social life outside school with boys as well as girls.' At the club was a coach originally from Iran who all the young members adored. 'He picked me out to play in tournaments which I loved because I was competitive even at that age. I really wanted to win. I still do.' Summers for Anne and her friends in the early 1970s meant entering tournaments across the West Midlands as well as playing in intercounty matches at Keele University. 'Five of us travelled together and our parents sorted out a rota apart from one of us whose parents didn't have a car. But it didn't matter. She didn't feel at all disadvantaged.'

About the same time as Anne was travelling around Warwick-shire to compete in junior tournaments, I was doing the same in Berkshire and Oxford. At Bracknell Tennis Club, I had been welcomed as a new member and soon was good enough to play for the adult teams. I have a picture from that time, not a proper photograph but a press report from a 1971 edition of the *Bracknell News* which is illustrated with a 'recent photo of Bracknell Tennis Club's senior men's team'.[4] In the photograph, six of us gaze at the lens without a smile as we hold our wooden rackets solemnly out in front. We are all in white apart from me, the youngest member at 17 years old. I am wearing a white tennis jumper which has a striking red and blue stripe, a Christmas present from my mother who thought the tennis club's all-white rule pompous and silly. Looking at the photo now, I remember three of the men. There is Bob Prior at the back, a landscape gardener with a looping gait and private income. Next to him is Denis Salter, an architect who resembled the actor Terry-Thomas and was full of brio. And in the middle is Colin Harris, the chairman of the club who ran a local hospital for people with severe learning difficulties and whose patrician manner concealed an uncommon kindness.

Almost all the adults at Bracknell Tennis Club in the early 1970s were as middle class as the men in my team, whether professional, clerical or commercial. Many lived outside the town in the prosperous villages of Warfield and Crowthorne, where the original inhabitants of Bracknell had fled in the late 1940s when the new town was proposed. Perhaps because I was good at tennis, or perhaps because class distinctions in places like Bracknell were more fluid than elsewhere, my working-class background and my lack of tennis-playing parents did not seem to matter. Several club members looked out for me, including Colin who was my doubles partner for a couple of years.

Unlike Anne Tyler's friend in Leamington, my parents did have a car, but they both worked full time and weren't available to ferry me around. So in the summers of 1971 and 1972 I hitchhiked to junior tennis tournaments in Caversham, Maidenhead, Newbury and Oxford. This mode of transport did not go down at all well with the parents of the boys with whom I played, and they never extended any invitation to come back for tea or stay over. Many of the boys knew each other from public school and most had individual coaching, something my parents could not afford. In those dandelion days of my late adolescence my game deteriorated and I lost confidence. After a disastrous defeat in the 1972 Berkshire Junior Championships to a long-haired boy from a Quaker boarding school I had beaten easily a couple of years before, I stormed out of the ground, threw my Dunlop Maxply racket over a hedge and resolved never to play tennis again. I was 18 years old.

Twenty-five years later, just as New Labour was taking power in Britain, I returned to tennis and discovered my time away was not so unusual. Two in five of all British tennis club members in the 1990s were over 30, and this was even more true of the club I joined in north London. It was full of men and women who had played as juniors and then given up because work and family pressures in their twenties and thirties had taken over. What was glorious for me about coming back to tennis was discovering the passion I felt for the game as a teenager re-emerge, but this time in a more appropriate key. Tennis, as *The Field* pointed out a century ago, is a game 'well-suited for middle aged gentlemen'.[5] For middle-aged prime ministers too. Tony Blair was occasionally seen in those Labour government days playing tennis at the David Lloyd club in Finchley with his friend and tennis partner, Lord Levy, no doubt with plain clothes police officers watching nervously in the wings.

The sport Blair and I experienced in Britain in the late 1990s had changed in ways that Harry Gem would no longer have recognised. Technology had turned the racket into a ball-swiping machine. It was no longer made of heavy wood but light carbon fibre, with strings that generated far more pace and spin. With these rackets, ordinary club players could hit the ball much harder than before and several of my new young male friends at the club served faster than many female players at Wimbledon. The ball itself was now yellow and tennis dress was black or green or blue or mauve, anything but white. International brands like Nike, K-Swiss, Reebok and Adidas had supplanted the Fred Perry tennis shirt and Dunlop green flash tennis shoes of my youth. Grass and shale, the dominant court surfaces for most of the twentieth century in Britain, had been largely replaced by artificial grass, artificial clay and various types of hard court including tarmac, cement and acrylic. Virtually every club had floodlights and tennis was now played on autumn and winter evenings as well as spring and summer days, and sometimes, as in my club, in a giant balloon that turned outdoor courts into indoor spaces. By the turn of the twenty-first century, tennis at grass-roots level in Britain was a different game from the tennis I learned to play 35 years before. The culture and the etiquette had changed as well, although this took longer to appreciate.

In the late 1980s, the sociologist Donal Muir spent seven years studying a tennis club near his home in Tuscaloosa, Alabama. It was clearly work he enjoyed since he also played at the club three times a week. In between his own games, Professor Muir noted down strategies players would use to avoid going on court with people they did not want to play with. The strong players would turn up at pre-arranged times, sit in different places in the club house and see who else was around before changing into their kit. They turned down invitations to play from people not as good as themselves with an 'apparent callousness' which Muir found surprising, but this did not seem to bother the weaker players. If they were then asked to join the stronger players on court because someone had dropped out, they considered it 'an honour' and accepted in a style which bordered on 'self-flagellation'.[6] Yet these weaker players were not from any Alabama underclass but were doctors, architects and lawyers who had considerable status in life outside. Inside the club, though, this meant little. All that mattered was how good you were at the game.

Professor Muir's findings may have been based on research in Alabama in the 1980s but they seemed equally true of my club in north London in the first decades of the twenty-first century, and probably in most other tennis clubs worldwide as well, apart from the few where social position and connections remain more important than tennis talent. In my club today, it is often infuriating to see the lengths the better players go to to avoid playing with people they consider not on their level, but there is also something refreshingly honest about this discrimination. It is an exclusion based not on class, colour, age or character but simply on ability. It is often accompanied by an attitude common in tennis but rare in most other social interactions. What you do or who you are is unimportant compared with how you play the game.

Paul Monaghan is one of the most successful architects in Britain. In 2015 his firm won the Sterling Prize. Yet few people at his tennis club in London know anything about his work. What they are interested in is not his achievements but how well he serves. 'At the club I am "Paul who plays tennis" and I often have no idea what the people I play with do either. They are just friends who I am on the tennis court with and that makes it relaxing and enjoyable especially with a few drinks afterwards. We never mention work. It simply doesn't matter.'[7] This lack of interest in other members' jobs and social status is a radical shift in the culture of tennis playing in Britain. In the 25 years I had been away from the game, the tennis club had changed from being a place that provided a social network and affirmed middle-class identity to somewhere simply to play sport. Other changes have happened that were not so positive.

In the early 1970s in Bracknell, the central focus of the tennis club was 'club session' on Sunday afternoons, where adroit manoeuvring by that week's organiser allowed players of very different abilities to enjoy social games together. Fifty years later, these sessions, along with the formal teas and the socialising that accompanied them, have been relegated in importance. Once they were something that drew a club together, the beating heart of the British tennis club. Now many larger clubs include club session as an option for the weaker players in a smorgasbord of discrete tennis experiences. They had little choice, because in the 1980s the British tennis club faced real competition for the first time.

In 1982, David Lloyd, one of Britain's top players a decade before, opened his first commercial tennis centre in West London. With its emphasis on indoor courts, state of the art gyms and heated outdoor swimming pools, it reinvented the tennis club as a sports supermarket with a variety of consumer options from which members and their families could choose. The only thing they did not need to bother about was the time-consuming running of the club, because this would be done by paid staff who were answerable not to the members but to David Lloyd Ltd. Joining a David Lloyd tennis club was as easy as signing up for a gym, and just as popular: there are now more than 100 named after him throughout Britain, Europe and India, although he has long since sold them on.

This new, privatised tennis experience at a David Lloyd club chimed with the times. Many people with middle-class jobs in the last two decades of twentieth-century Britain saw their incomes rise but their leisure time shrink. They did not want to spend precious hours painting clubhouses, sorting out club accounts or playing doubles with people not as good as them. Tennis in the 1880s was attractive to the professional classes because it could be squeezed in around clients. One hundred years later, David Lloyd centres offered a similar deal: an hour or two of guaranteed tennis with your own choice of partner which could be arranged well in advance. There were no entry requirements, no social obligations and no problem about becoming a member as long as you could afford the monthly subscription, although as this was well over a hundred pounds, players with a low income were effectively kept out. Many of the players who did join, however, felt there was something missing.

David Obodechina-Joseph came to London from Lagos with his parents in 1991 when he was 15 years old. He had played in tennis clubs in Nigeria at a high level and looked for a similar experience here. 'I tried four clubs. One was unfriendly, another had a coach who said he could get me to play with the best players if I paid him! I then joined a David Lloyd club but it didn't have the proper tennis club atmosphere I had grown up on back in Lagos. I didn't feel as if I belonged.'[8]

David eventually found this sense of belonging in a club named after the local Methodist church, although very few Methodists were still members. 'Race was never really an issue although once when I wanted to play for the county the person in charge said I couldn't because I was not born here which wasn't true. That was definitely racism but it was one of the few occasions in tennis I have been treated differently because of the colour of my skin.' The one thing that David felt was missing in private tennis clubs in Britain at the start of the twenty-first century – and still missing 20 years later – was their lack of interest in reaching out to new kinds of members. 'Most of them don't have outreach programmes and they are missing black and low income youngsters. On their websites I didn't see anyone like me there. That's very important. When I don't see a black face, I think that's not for me.'

David Obodechina-Joseph's experience is backed up by research done by the sociologist Robert Lake in a tennis club in suburban London in 2005. Lake spent nine months there, befriending members, observing behaviour and playing for the seventh team. Although the club had made considerable efforts to reach out to new people, including hiring coaches and establishing links with local schools, there remained 'pre-conceived' notions of social status and behavioural norms which determined who felt at home in the club and who was ignored. The culture of the club was still 'almost entirely inaccessible to new members', he concluded in an article entitled 'They Treat Me Like I'm Scum'.[9]

Lake's research was impeccable, but it seems to me that the club he chose was – and is – not typical in Britain today, or at least not typical of the dozens of clubs I have played tennis in over the last two decades. Lake's club is larger than most with 500 members. It has seven men's teams, several grass courts and an historic tradition of people playing at Wimbledon. Most clubs in Britain are only half that size, dispensed with grass courts decades ago and never had any member who reached Wimbledon standard even in the early years of the last century. Most clubs in Britain, too, with a few exceptions like Hurlingham (old money) and Queen's (new money), no longer have any waiting list. They grab any new member that comes along, suggesting lessons if their standard is poor and doing their best to keep them. They have to if they are going to survive.

In 2019, there were some 700,000 people who played in the 2,880 odd private tennis clubs in Britain, but there were another two million who preferred to play their tennis in public parks. On a Sunday afternoon that spring, I went for a stroll in Clissold Park in Hackney, north-east London to see what state the park's tennis was in. Next to a couple of ponds where it was forbidden to feed the ducks, I found eight tarmac tennis courts laid out in a line. The courts were in good condition. The nets did not sag. The green tarmac was not broken. They were all occupied.

I noticed one young teenager playing with his girlfriend and I stopped to watch. She was winning easily and her boyfriend took it with good humour. On the next court were two men in their forties who were involved in an intense game with little quarter given. At the end were four older people playing doubles.

Their standard was not high but there was little doubt they were enjoying themselves. They grimaced as shots went out and cheered when they hit something well. I wondered how long they had been playing together, perhaps a decade, perhaps two, and I started imagining how much this Sunday game meant to them. Public parks are where I learned to play and if there were courts like these near where I live now, I wonder if I would bother with a club. The trouble is that few of the other tennis courts in the 2,300 public parks in Britain today are in such a good state. Many have nets full of holes or surfaces so poorly maintained they are dangerous when it rains. Outside the major cities, you are lucky to find any at all.

It might have been so different. In cities like Liverpool and Sheffield there were parks tournaments organised up to the 1990s, usually in conjunction with a local newspaper, and they attracted hundreds of entries. The finals of the London parks tournament, which was sponsored by the *Evening News*, was held at Wimbledon. It has stopped too. The cumulative effect of cuts made to local authority budgets by conservative governments from 1979 to 1997 left councils with little money to maintain tennis courts that were often built 70 years before. The Lawn Tennis Association could have stepped in. Every year it receives tens of millions of pounds from the profits of Wimbledon to invest in British tennis. But in the last decades of the twentieth century, the association focussed its resources on the top junior players, most from private tennis clubs, in an effort to find new British Wimbledon champions. Although the association's policy changed in the late 1990s to concentrate on people from lower-class backgrounds, still little money seems to have filtered down to public park tennis which is the place most people without a family background of tennis learn to play. In March 2010, the House of Commons All-Party Parliamentary Group on Tennis castigated the Lawn Tennis Association for its squandering of the Wimbledon bonanza. 'Public park tennis in Britain', Baroness Billingham, the chair of the group, remarked, 'remains woefully underfunded'. In other countries, this is not the case.

The Czech Republic has continued that country's fine tennis tradition, which dates back to the late nineteenth century, by making sure that every small town has three or four public courts with inexpensive coaching widely available. In the late 1950s, the sport in Czechoslovakia became a priority for the communist government after they decided that tennis was no longer 'bourgeois'. The result was a dozen international champions, from Helena Suková to Ivan Lendl, although that stream has dried out a little in recent years as Russia and other eastern European countries have caught up. At the start of the twenty-first century these countries took over from the USA as the dominant nations in women's tennis, while Australia and Britain, both countries with a strong tradition of the women's game, slipped behind. Then there was France.

Philippe Chatrier was French junior tennis champion in 1946 but never made it as a senior player. He turned to sports journalism and tennis administration instead. From 1973 to 1993, he was president of the French Tennis Federation and it is for these 20 innovative years he will be remembered. What Chatrier focussed on was not the talented few but the total number of people who played and how this could be increased. He integrated private tennis clubs, indoor sports centres and municipal courts, lowered the cost of playing tennis and ensured that every village in France had at least one tennis court that was available to anyone who wanted to play. His mission was to make tennis in France as popular as it was in the 1920s, and he succeeded. In 1974, there were 2,700 tennis clubs in France and 7,500 courts. Nine years later, there were 7,300 clubs and 18,000 courts. The number of people playing tennis tripled.

Chatrier, a 'strange complex man with the mentality of a dreamer',[10] died in 2000, but the increase in tennis playing in France which he inaugurated continues. In 2018, there were almost five million people who played tennis in France on 31,000 courts. In Britain, with a similar population, only three million people play on 23,000 courts. France has 7,700 tennis clubs, Britain 2,880. The French learn tennis with the help of 14,000 coaches. Britain has only half that number. In 2019, there were 16 French players in the top 100. Britain had four.

One of Chatrier's important innovations was to turn tennis in France from a summer sport to an activity played all year around. He encouraged, cajoled and bullied local authorities to build more indoor courts and there are now 9,000 of them all over the country. The Lawn Tennis Association in Britain decided recently to make indoor courts a priority, but they have some catching up to do. Presently there are only 1,500 and in many places in the country you have to travel over an hour to play in one. This is disappointing, particularly as Britain was the first country to play tennis indoors when the disused roller-skating rinks of the late nineteenth century were converted into tennis courts as rinking went out of fashion.

Apart from the lack of indoor courts, though, there are some hopeful signs today for tennis at the grass roots, at least in Britain. The public courts in Clissold Park in Hackney are in a good state because they are run by Hackney Tennis, a not-for-profit organisation which offers all the advantages of a private tennis club – match play, tennis leagues, a tennis pavilion – while also allowing anyone to come along and play. This public–private partnership has been copied in several other parks in London and beyond in different forms, and for the first time in decades park tennis in a few places is beginning to thrive.

Leah Hartshorne, a mathematics teacher in her thirties, came back to tennis in 2018 after not playing for 16 years. She wanted to play singles in her local park in Manchester but there was a problem. 'There are almost no public courts with facilities. How can I perform at my best when I need a wee! One time I saw a couple renovating their house and I had to ask to use their toilet as I couldn't start a three set match needing the loo.'[11] Very few of the public courts Leah has played on have 'facilities'. Virtually none have floodlights. There are some publicly owned indoor courts in south Manchester and they are 'brilliant but very expensive at peak times and oversubscribed so hard to book'.

One thing though that Leah did not have to worry about was finding people to play with. Her games were facilitated by another admirable initiative, Local Tennis Leagues, which was started as a hobby a few years ago by Nigel Billen and Sally Kinnes, two journalists who played on their local public courts in Highbury Fields, north London and wanted to find new opponents. There are now 160 leagues nationwide. 'What was striking was that there was this huge demand for competitive tennis', they say, 'the leagues were something that was fun and simple to organise but taken seriously enough to be worth doing'.[12]

There is little doubt that projects like this and half a dozen others funded by tennis charities and the Lawn Tennis Association have done something to bring in new kinds of players to tennis in Britain. The association's disability tennis programme, for example, now has 12,500 participants every month. The difficulty is that, unlike other sports like badminton or squash, tennis has a high entry point. For beginners to enjoy even a basic game requires coaching and coaching is expensive. Until the Lawn Tennis Association starts using some of the largesse it receives from Wimbledon each year to subsidise coaching in public parks, tennis in this country will always be, as Leah says, 'simply not accessible to the poor'.

There is, however, another form of grass-roots tennis that is thriving in twenty-first century Britain and beyond, and while the people who play are not usually poor, they are people who 20 years ago would have thought that tennis is not for them. In the late nineteenth century, the Northern Championships, held in alternate years in Liverpool and Manchester, was known as the 'Wimbledon of the North' and entered by all the top players. One of the early winners of the Men's Singles was William Wilberforce who was then 19 years old. The *Manchester Guardian* thought his victory prophetic. Lawn tennis, the newspaper, claimed was turning into a sport which favoured the young: 'It will no longer be a game which a fairly active man can reasonably look forward to playing long beyond his fortieth year.'[13]

It was one of the *Guardian's* less accurate predictions. Tennis is now played across the world by many millions of people well beyond their fortieth year. Vivienne McNaughton is in her early seventies and playing the best tennis of her long tennis life. She first played in her village in Yorkshire in the late 1950s on a grass court in her back garden. These days she captains the Middlesex Women's Over 70 team and in 2017 they became national champions 'against all expectation. There is nothing better than winning when you don't expect to.' She wonders, though, how long she can carry on playing at a level that gives her pleasure. 'Most of the people I play with are a lot younger. I don't think I could bear people saying they don't want to play with me because I am not up to it. I am still trying to improve, ridiculous at my age! The trouble is I have run out of role models. I am the oldest now.'[14]

Elsewhere, though, there are plenty of women and men in their seventies and eighties who still play tennis, some at a high level. The most popular tournaments organised by the International Tennis Federation across Europe and America are those aimed at people over 65, and the British Veterans Championships held at Wimbledon every August now has a section for people over 85. One person who won't be entering is Albert Lester, who lives in south London, but that's not because he doesn't qualify – Albert was born in 1928 – but because all his tennis life he has never wanted to play in matches but simply knock up with friends. 'I used to play at the net until I was 75 but now play at the back. Until I was 90, I used to play every Tuesday, Wednesday and Friday mornings and on Sunday as well.' These days he just hits a couple of days a week with another guy who, at 78, is a 'youngster compared with me'. The day after his 90th birthday, he was playing with three friends at his club and noticed that all the other courts were empty. 'The friends said lets go back to the clubhouse and they were all there with a special cake and candles to celebrate my 90th and the fact I was still playing the game I have played all my life.' That is something well worth celebrating.

Conclusion

In August 2009, *The September Issue,* a documentary film about the American edition of *Vogue,* was released in cinemas around the world. The central character was editor-in-chief Anna Wintour, 60 years old and known for her bobbed hair and intimidating presence at catwalks worldwide which had earned her the nickname 'Nuclear Wintour'. Wanting to see a softer side of one of the most powerful women in fashion, the director, R.J. Cutler filmed Wintour playing tennis at an exclusive New York club. During a break in the game, Cutler took the opportunity, away from the pressurised world of *haute couture,* to ask what single thing would most improve her life? Anna Wintour replied immediately. It would be, not the perfect little black dress, nor a luxurious Park Avenue apartment, nor even darker sun-glasses, her trademark accessory. The single thing, she said, that would most improve her life was a 'better backhand'.

Any attempt like this book to make connections between tennis, politics and society should always keep in mind that the principal desire of most tennis players is not for any understanding of the game or its history but simply to hit a better backhand. Better backhands, though, are not so easily isolated from the social context of the game. They take years of practice and many hours of coaching. Like Anna Wintour, I am still having lessons on how to hit a topspin backhand five decades after I was first shown the shot by Bill Jones, the coach of Bracknell Tennis Club.

The challenge of tennis is the same as that discovered a century and a half ago by the four men who played it at the Prince's Club in London in May 1874. Tennis looks simple but turns out to be difficult, not just to play well but to play at all. To become a decent park player yet alone a club champion you have to master difficult shots like the backhand, and this mastery takes time and costs money. It is the main reason why people from low-income families are excluded from the game: it is not the racket or the balls that are expensive but the number of lessons you need. So the apparently uncomplicated wish to develop a better backhand is enmeshed in politics. As this book has tried to demonstrate, this is true of every aspect of the game.

In the spring of 1943, Second Lieutenant William Plumer Jacobs returned home to Clinton, South Carolina on leave from the American infantry. In a few months he would go back across the Atlantic to join the Allied campaign under Dwight Eisenhower to invade Italy starting at its southern tip. But before this, there was something else he needed to do. Plumer Jacobs was a keen tennis player but also a keen Presbyterian. His great grandfather, who he was named after, had turned the small town of Clinton in the 1860s into the 'Presbyterian Center of the South'. Like another tennis-obsessed lieutenant, Robert Osborn in the late nineteenth century, Plumer Jacobs decided to try and integrate his religion with his passion for the game and write a guide to playing tennis that was informed by his faith.

The result was *Tennis, Builder of Citizenship*, a curious combination of conventional tennis tips, moral exhortations and folksy homilies like this one: 'There was a young man who was completely engulfed in self-pity. Tennis has enabled him to forget himself at least while he is on court and if he does not become a champion he will in other activities in life. Tennis is a game which strengthens weakness by overcoming fear.'[1] A few pages later, just to make sure his readers appreciate the point, he lists a few more of the sport's virtues: 'Tennis leaves the contestant little time for hesitation. It is a matter of action quickly or never. That is why tennis is such fine medicine for lowly spirits. It brings a new outlook, eliminates the defeatist attitude and inferiority complexes. That is how it makes men.'[2]

About the same time as Plumer Jacobs was penning this tribute to the game he loved, another tennis fanatic, Teddy Tinling, was working for British intelligence and found himself in Algiers with time on his hands. With the capture of Tunis in May 1943 and the surrender of Rommel's army, the Allies' North African campaign had achieved complete success. What better way to relax before the coming assault on Italy than an exhibition tennis match to raise money for the Red Cross? Tinling proposed the idea to General Dwight Eisenhower, the supreme commander of the Allied Expeditionary Force. He received a curt reply. The match was not going to happen, Eisenhower said, because 'this is a man's war and tennis is a women's game'.[3]

These two conceptions of masculinity espoused by Eisenhower and Plumer Jacobs have both had a strong currency in the history of tennis. From the sport's earliest days, boys who played the game were regarded by men like Eisenhower as effeminate, a stigma that has proved surprisingly difficult over the decades to shrug off. To counter these continual accusations of 'sissyness', other men like Plumer Jacobs have emphasised its mirror image. Tennis is a tough and exacting game that is worthy of male involvement, a sport that 'makes men'.

This book has taken another perspective. What I have suggested instead is that tennis has encouraged a different kind of sporting masculinity than that desired by Plumer Jacobs or derided by Eisenhower, a masculinity that has always had to adjust to the presence and power of women and has often been influenced, although this has been rarely acknowledged, by gay male culture even if the actual LGBTQ presence in top tennis today seems slight.[4]

This challenge to conventional sporting masculinity is one reason why tennis seems to me to be a radical sport, but there are others as well. In this book I have argued that the struggle of the early women players to keep the sport aligned with the men's game is one of the first examples of sporting feminism.[5] I have put forward the thought that Wimbledon, despite being run by people from the 'least progressive echelons of British society',[6] has encouraged a new form of spectatorship that has crossed racial and national boundaries in a way other sports could do well to emulate. All these seem to me truly radical achievements. There is more.

One of the main accusations made against tennis in Britain and abroad is that it has been a sport dominated and controlled by the privileged. I have tried to show that this perception masks a hidden history of working-class involvement in tennis in Britain, most notably public park tennis in the 1920s and the Labour Party tennis clubs in the 1930s.[7] Indeed, the Workers' Wimbledon tournaments from 1932 to 1951 gave a glimpse of a tennis culture run on socialist and cooperative lines and compared well with the shamateurism of the top game at the time and the status-driven stuffiness of many tennis clubs during these decades. Similarly, the story of the Jewish tennis clubs, the mainly black American Tennis Association and the recent LGBTQ tennis clubs in cities around the world have all provided powerful images of tennis as a sport that encourages inclusion and the participation of all. Tennis has also provided a site for struggle against racist and antisemitic practices, and it has forged an honourable record of ridding itself of much of this kind of pernicious discrimination, although there is still some way to go.

All this, I contend, adds up to a sport which can claim over the last 150 years to be as much a force for social change as one that upholds a class-ridden sense of entitlement. And there is still more. The one institution that historians, journalists and tennis authorities have targeted as a citadel of reaction rather than a location for innovation has been the private tennis club in Britain, which has been the model for many tennis clubs across the world. Much of this criticism has been deserved. Many clubs have a history of turning in on themselves in smug complacency rather than looking outwards to bring new kinds of people into the game. But what this ignores is the honourable role tennis clubs have played in maintaining a grass-roots culture of participation that is organised and run by sportsmen and women themselves.

At their best, tennis clubs have kept alive the spirit of voluntary endeavour that was common in society when tennis started back in the 1870s but is much rarer today. The British tennis club has given tennis a particular character of modesty, courtesy and kindness still shown throughout the world whenever the game is played and exemplified by a single word: 'sorry'. It is also one of the few places in contemporary capitalist society where commercialism has been kept at a distance. In 2020, most clubs have shed their old obsession with social position to develop a culture where status in a club is earned over months and years either on court, by helping run the club or by sheer character. What you do does not matter. I believe that the tennis club in Britain and abroad is not the 'exclusionary haven of conservatism' portrayed by many social historians and novelists.[8] Rather, it is somewhere that has pioneered new ways for men and women to share public space together, even if the men and women who have benefitted most have been overwhelmingly middle class.[9] Despite the exclusions (often more apparent than real) this book has documented, the members-owned voluntary tennis club has been, on balance, a progressive institution that deserves to be celebrated before it is lost for ever.

For many years I wondered why I was drawn to tennis, as it seemed the antithesis of my youthful commitment to socialism and change. I used to think it was a perversity in me, a desire to betray my class, a need to escape, somewhere I was happy to sell out my principles in exchange for new friends and a new life. I now know all this is not true. I feel at home inside tennis clubs not because they are agents of the status quo but because hidden underneath their outward conformity is an anarchic generosity. Club tennis in Britain and abroad remains a civilised way of taking pleasure in the company of strangers. It is also the easiest place to develop a special relationship that exists in some other sports but reaches an intensity in tennis, where your opponent becomes one of your most intimate friends.

In his 1998 memoir, *The Tennis Partner*, the writer and professor of medicine, Abraham Verghese, captures this intensity well. In a new job in El Paso, New Mexico in the early 1990s, Dr Verghese arranged to play tennis with one of his medical students, David Smith, who was, like him, a fanatical player but a good deal better. Smith turned out to be 'without question the perfect partner. But like a boy eager to turn a first date into a romance ... I worried that I had blurted out too much, exposed myself and, though he denied it, he had agreed to play out of politeness. Still, when we parted at the tennis club, I felt we had found a sense of connection.'[10]

That same sense of connection was experienced by Vivienne McNaughton when she joined a tennis club in London in the 1980s and discovered a new tennis partner. 'We were completely inseparable. People thought we were having an affair. It was a time in both of our lives when our personal relationships were awry so we met when both of us had space for a very close friendship.' Their partnership lasted a dozen years and even though they no longer play together, they remain the best of friends, although as with any close friendship there have been moments of tension. 'I wouldn't say our tennis matches were made in heaven. I once stormed off court in a semi-final after a row about me intervening to volley. But overall we spent a lot of time just the two of us travelling to matches and there were lots of opportunities for proper talking and intimacy.'[11]

This possibility of deep comradeship with a tennis partner, which often develops in tennis clubs, is one more reason that tennis deserves to be treasured by the Left as much as the Right, one more reason among many.

Timeline of (Lawn) Tennis

1874 (February), Pimlico, London	Major Walter Wingfield receives patent for his 'new and improved portable court for playing the Ancient Game of Tennis' and publishes *The Major's Game of Lawn Tennis*.
1874 (March), Pimlico	Wingfield places ads in *Court Journal* and *Army & Navy Gazette* to sell his new lawn tennis sets.
1874 (May), Knightsbridge, London	First public exhibition of lawn tennis takes place at the Prince's Club. Other exhibitions that month also happen at the Polo Club and Richmond Cricket Club.
1874 (Summer), Leamington	Harry Gem and Augurio Perera set up Leamington Lawn Tennis Club, probably the first club in the world completely dedicated to lawn tennis, although the version they played was slightly different from Wingfield's. In the next 15 years, some 300 tennis clubs are formed in Britain, the USA, Australia, South Africa, Germany, India and several other countries, and they ensure that tennis survives as a popular sport played across the world.
1874 (July), Bad Homburg	First lawn tennis match played in Germany at the Royal Victoria Hotel.
1875 (May), Marylebone, London	The Marylebone Cricket Club (MCC) publishes its rules for lawn tennis, making significant improvements to Major Wingfield's rules (which he accepts) but keeping his hourglass court.
1876 (August), Massachusetts	First tennis tournament in the USA.
1876 (December), New Orleans	First tennis club in America.
1877 (June), Wimbledon	Henry Jones, Julian Marshall and John Heathcote modify the MCC rules for the first Wimbledon lawn tennis tournament. They replace the hourglass court with a rectangle and introduce the scoring system still used today.

1877 (July), Paris	Decimal Club founded, probably the first tennis club in France.
1877 (July), Wimbledon	The final of the first Wimbledon tournament, contested by 22 men, is won by Spencer Gore, a local surveyor.
1877 (Summer), Dublin	The first Irish championship is held at the Fitzwilliam Club.
1878 Melbourne	First tennis court in Australia is laid out at the Melbourne Cricket Club.
1879 (Summer), Dublin	First women's championship is held at the Fitzwilliam Club.
1881 (August), Newport, Rhode Island	First US Open played at Newport Casino and organised by the United States Lawn Tennis Association formed in New York earlier that year.
1883 London	Slazenger move from Manchester to the City of London to become one of the most successful companies supplying tennis equipment in the history of the game.
1883 Birmingham	Public tennis courts laid out in Cannon Hill Park, perhaps the first in the world.
1883 (Autumn) Cannes	Wimbledon champion William Renshaw starts the tradition of British tennis champions playing the winter months on the red clay courts of the Riviera.
1884 (July), Wimbledon	The first of William Renshaw's three triumphs against Herbert Lawford, considered some of the most exciting Wimbledon finals ever played. Renshaw wins the Men's Singles seven times. Lawford wins only once.
1884 (July), Wimbledon	Maud Watson becomes the first women's Wimbledon champion.
1885 Lahore	Punjab Lawn Tennis Championships take place, the first tennis tournament in India (tennis had been introduced here ten years before).
1886 (July), Wimbledon	Blanche Bingley (Hillyard) wins first of six Women's Singles titles.
1887 (July), Wimbledon	Lottie Dod wins her first (of five) singles at the age of 15, still the youngest Wimbledon champion ever and one of the best, if not the best, female tennis player.

1888 (January), Barons Court, London	Lawn Tennis Association (LTA) formed at The Queen's club. William Renshaw elected first president and Herbert Chipp first secretary.
1888 (August), Exmouth	First battle of sexes game between Ernest Renshaw and Lottie Dod.
1891 (May), Paris	First French Open initially just for French residents (open to everyone in 1925).
1893 Bristol and Nottingham	The Bristol tobacco company Wills offers lawn tennis for its workers about the same time as Jessie Boot provides tennis for his in Nottingham.
1898 Barons Court	LTA agrees to represent women's as well as men's tennis.
1900 (July), Paris	Laurie Doherty wins gold at the 2nd Olympic Games. He goes on to become one of Wimbledon's most popular champions, and with his brother Reggie is responsible for bringing back the crowds and ensuring tennis survives to become a popular sport watched across the world.
1900 (August), Boston	First Davis Cup between the USA and Britain (won by the USA).
1901 San Francisco	Golden Gate Memorial Tennis Center opens, and goes on to become arguably the most famous public tennis courts in the world, responsible for several champions.
1902 (July), Wimbledon	Ayres, who had supplied balls for the Championships since 1879, is replaced by Slazenger in somewhat dubious circumstances.
1905 London	Workmen's Act accelerates building of public courts in Britain.
1905 (July), Wimbledon	May Sutton from California becomes the first women's singles' winner from outside the British Isles. Two years later Norman Brooks from Australia becomes the first men's.
1905 (November), Melbourne	First Australian Open championships, the last of the four championships which today add up to the Grand Slam. It is now played in January.
1907 (June), Wimbledon	Charlotte Cooper (Sterry) wins last of her five Women's Singles titles and is still the oldest woman to win at 37.

1908 (July), Wimbledon — Sirdar Nihal Singh becomes first player of Indian origin to compete at Wimbledon.

1909 (July), Wimbledon — Arthur Gore becomes the oldest singles winner at 41.

1910 London — *Lawn Tennis for Ladies* by Dorothea Lambert Chambers, seven times Wimbledon champion, published.

1911 Barons Court — LTA lays down the rules for players to remain amateurs and bans professionals from the game, a ban which lasts until 1968.

1913 (February), Wimbledon — Suffragette attack on centre court.

1913 (March), Paris — International Lawn Tennis Federation (ILTF) formed with twelve national members. It takes responsibility for the four Grand Slam tournaments.

1913 (July), Wimbledon — Women's doubles and mixed doubles championships added.

1917 Copenhagen — Leif Rovsing banned from tennis because of 'presumed homosexuality'.

1919 (June), Wimbledon — Suzanne Lenglen wins her first of five Women's Singles titles in a memorable final against Dorothea Lambert Chambers.

1922 Liverpool — First Jewish Tennis Club formed in Britain. By the 1950s there were three dozen similar clubs in Britain and probably as many elsewhere.

1922 (July), Wimbledon — All England Club moves from Worple Road to Church Road mainly to accommodate crowds who want to see Suzanne Lenglen play.

1924 New York — US Open moved to the West Side Tennis Club in Forest Hills, New York, mainly to accommodate the crowds who wanted to see Bill Tilden play. It stayed there until 1978 when it was relocated to the USA National Tennis Center at Flushing Meadows in Queens.

1925 New York — *Matchplay and the Spin of the Ball* by Bill Tilden published, perhaps the best technical book about tennis ever written.

1926 (February), Cannes	Helen Mills (Moody) plays Suzanne Lenglen at the Carlton Club, perhaps the most renowned tennis match ever played.
1926 (October), New York	Suzanne Lenglen's first professional game at Madison Square Garden.
1927 (March), Reading	Reading Labour Party Tennis Club formed, the first socialist tennis club in Britain if not the world.
1927 (October), Barons Court	First world professional tournament at The Queen's Club organised and won by Dan Maskell.
1932 (September), Reading	First Workers' Wimbledon held in Caversham.
1933 Berlin	Daniel Prenn, Germany's top player, is left out of his country's Davis Cup team because he is Jewish.
1935 (June), Brixton	Fourth Workers' Wimbledon held at Brockwell Park.
1936 (July), Wimbledon	Fred Perry wins the last of his three Wimbledon titles before turning professional to join Bill Tilden's tour.
1937 (July), Wimbledon	First live TV broadcast of tennis by the BBC.
1937 (July), (Wimbledon)	Donald Budge from the USA beats Gottfried Von Cramm from Germany in the final of the Davis Cup, another candidate for best ever match.
1938 (September), New York	Budge wins the US Open and becomes the first man to complete the Grand Slam (Rod Laver did it again in 1962 and 1969).
1939 Paris	The ILTF moves from Paris to Wimbledon. It is now based in Roehampton, represents 211 nations and is known simply as the ITF.
1939 (June), Portsmouth	Eighth Workers' Wimbledon held at the Canoe Lake courts.
1940 New York	Donald Budge plays exhibition match against the black American champion Jimmie McDaniel at the Cosmopolitan Club.
1940 (October), Wimbledon	Centre court bombed.

1946 (November), California	Bill Tilden arrested with a 14-year-old boy in his car, the end of a glittering tennis career from perhaps the best man ever to play the game.
1949 (July), Wimbledon	Gussy Moran's knickers designed by Teddy Tinling causes a sensation.
1950 USA	The first of Jack Kramer's professional tennis tours begins which would eventually lead to open tennis.
1950 (September), Forest Hills	Althea Gibson becomes first black player to play in grand slam after intervention of Alice Marble.
1951 (June), Hollywood	Alfred Hitchcock's *Strangers on a Train* is released, not the first or last film centred around tennis, but the best.
1951 (July), Wimbledon	Dick Savitt becomes first Jewish champion.
1951 (August), Wimbledon	Last Workers' Wimbledon championship.
1953 (September), New York	Maureen Connolly becomes first woman to complete a Grand Slam (Margaret Court did it again in 1970 and Steffi Graf in 1988).
1954 (July), Europe	Eurovision sends first live pictures from Wimbledon across Europe.
1956 (July), Wimbledon	Despite being a losing finalist in the singles and winning the women's doubles the British Jewish woman Angela Buxton is put on the waiting list for membership of the All England Club. Sixty-four years later, she is still waiting.
1957 (July), Wimbledon	Althea Gibson becomes the first black person to win Wimbledon.
1960 Cleveland, Ohio	International Management Group is founded by Mark McCormack. It is now the most powerful organisation in tennis.
1967 (July), Wimbledon	First colour TV pictures broadcast from Centre Court. First metal tennis racket appears.
1967 (December), Barons Court	The LTA and the All England Club abolish the distinction between amateur and professional.

1968 (April), Bournemouth	First major tournament of open tennis won by Ken Rosewall.
1970 New York	The Virginia Slims tournament launched, the first ever women's tennis tour.
1970 (September), New York	First time tie-break used in a grand slam tournament.
1972 (September), New York	The Association of Tennis Professionals (ATP) is set up by Cliff Drysdale, Donald Dell and Jack Kramer. It is now based in London and is the main body organising men's professional tennis.
1973 (June), Wimbledon	The Women's Tennis Association (WTA) is formed by Billie Jean King. It is now based in Florida and is the main body organising women's professional tennis.
1973 (September), Houston	Fifty-five-year-old ex-Wimbledon champion Bobby Riggs plays 29-year-old Wimbledon champion Billie Jean King in a 'Battle of the Sexes' match in front of 30,000 people. Ninety million people tune in on television worldwide, the most watched tennis match ever.
1975 (July), Wimbledon	Arthur Ashe becomes the first black man to win the Men's Singles after a masterly display against the overwhelming favourite Jimmy Connors.
1977 (August), New York	A New York state court rules that transsexual player Renee Richards can play in the women's events at the US Open. First graphite and fibreglass rackets appear.
1980 (July), Wimbledon	Bjorn Borg and John McEnroe play a tie break in the fourth set of their final which goes to 18–16 and is the most thrilling 20 minutes of tennis ever.
1981 New York	Billie Jean King and Martina Navratilova come out as the first openly lesbian top tennis players since Toupie Lowther in 1902. To date there have been no male players who have come out as gay while still playing at a top level.
1985 (July), Wimbledon	Boris Becker becomes youngest ever Men's Singles winner at 17 years old.

1986 (July), Wimbledon	First use of yellow ball at Wimbledon to help TV viewers.
1988 (September/ October), Seoul	Lawn tennis readmitted to the Olympics after 64 years. Wheelchair tennis introduced into the Paralympics after first being played in the mid-1970s.
1990 (July), Wimbledon	Martina Navratilova wins Women's Singles for record ninth time.
1996 Amsterdam	Smashing Pink founded. It is now the largest LGBTQ club in Europe, perhaps the world.
2000 Russia	Anna Kournikova's 'only the ball should bounce' advertisements start a trend where some players earn far more from endorsements than from winning tournaments.
2002 (January), Melbourne	Wheelchair tennis introduced into the Australian Open, the first Grand Slam tournament to include the game.
2002 (July), Wimbledon	Serena Williams wins her first Wimbledon on way to becoming arguably the best female tennis player ever, although Maureen Connolly, Suzanne Lenglen and Lottie Dod are also strong contenders.
2003 (July), Wimbledon	Roger Federer wins first Wimbledon on way to becoming arguably the best male tennis player ever, although Rod Laver, Bill Tilden and Donald Budge are strong contenders too.
2007 (July), Wimbledon	Wimbledon becomes the final Grand Slam tournament to give equal prize money to women.
2008 (July), Wimbledon	Rafa Nadal beats Roger Federer in final, another candidate for best tennis match ever.
2013 (July), Wimbledon	Andy Murray becomes first British man to win Wimbledon since Fred Perry. He wins again in 2016.
2019 (July), Wimbledon	Novak Djokovic beats Roger Federer in the Men's Singles in one of the most thrilling finals ever.

Notes

Introduction

1. George Hillyard, *Forty Years of 1st Class Tennis* (London: Williams & Norgate, 1924), p. 147.
2. Ibid., p. 147.
3. See Robert Everitt and Richard Hillway, *The Birth of Lawn Tennis* (Kingston Upon Thames: Vision Sports Publishing Ltd, 2018), p. 331.
4. See, for example, C.J. Bearman, *An Examination of Suffragette Violence* (Edinburgh: Edinburgh Historical Review 120, 2005), pp. 365–97.
5. See for example Richard Holt, *Sport and the British* (Oxford: Oxford University Press, 1989), pp. 145–6.
6. David Foster Wallace, 'How Tracey Austin broke my heart', in *Consider the Lobster* (London: Abacus 2005), pp. 142–3.
7. Steven Connor, *A Philosophy of Sport* (London: Reaktion Books, 2011), pp. 12–14.
8. Holt, *Sport and the British*, p. 367.
9. Bruce Tarran, *George Hillyard* (Kipworth Beauchamp: Matador, 2013), p. 59.

Chapter 1

1. *Morning Post*, May 4, 1974.
2. The present singles tennis court is a 78 feet by 27 feet. The net is 3 feet 6 inches at the posts dipping to 3 feet at the centre. It is not an hourglass but a rectangle.
3. *The Sporting Magazine* 33(11), 1793.
4. John Lowerson, *Sport and the English Middle Classes* (Manchester: Manchester University Press, 1993), p. 3.
5. Robert Lake, *A Social History of Tennis in Britain* (London: Routledge 2015), p. 16.
6. Alan Dale, *A Marriage Below Zero* (Ontario: Broadview Press, 2017), p. 254.
7. The book had been published separately the previous month as *The Major's Game of Lawn Tennis*, and then went through five different editions between 1874 and 1876 when it was renamed *The Game of Sphairistikè or Lawn Tennis*.

8. Major Walter Clopton Wingfield, *The Major's Game of Lawn Tennis* (London: French & Co, 1874), pp. 7–8.
9. It wasn't just the conservative establishment who bought them. One early buyer was the Countess of Waldegrave, who had strong links to the Liberal Party, and an enthusiastic early player was Herbert John Gladstone, a radical home secretary in the early years of the twentieth century who was responsible for the Workman's Compensation Act of 1906 and the Children's Act of 1908.
10. *The Field*, 1 December 1874.
11. *Morning Post*, 21 May 1874 and *Sporting Gazette*, 31 October 1874.
12. Heiner Gillmeister, *Tennis: A Cultural History* (London: Leicester University Press, 1997), p. 181.
13. Jean Coulter, *The Port Elizabeth Lawn Tennis Club Century* (Port Elizabeth: Port Elizabeth TC, 1979), p. 7.
14. Julian Marshall, *Tennis Cuts and Quips* (London: Field & Tuer, 1884), p. 7.
15. *The Field*, 16 January, 1875.
16. The plaque should have said 1859 not 1865.
17. Everitt and Hillway, *The Birth of Lawn Tennis*, p. 112.
18. Quoted in Gillmeister, *Tennis: A Cultural History*, pp. 179–80 from an original document held in Leamington Public Library.
19. Myra Hunter, *100 Years of Tennis in the West of Scotland* (Glasgow: West of Scotland LTA, 2004), p. 121.
20. Robert Durie Osborn, *Lawn Tennis, Its Players and How to Play* (London: Strahan & Co., 1881), pp. 11–12.
21. Ibid., pp. 11–12.
22. Everitt and Hillway, *The Birth of Lawn Tennis*, p. 256.
23. Osborn, *Lawn Tennis, Its Players and How to Play*, pp. 11–12.
24. See John Tosh, *Manliness and Masculinities in 19th Century Britain* (London: Routledge, 2016), chapter 5.

Chapter 2

1. Henry James, 'In Warwickshire', *The Galaxy*, July 1877, pp. 672–5.
2. See Susan Elks, 'Tennis Fashions in the Frame', in Ann Sumner (ed.) *Court on Canvas* (London: Phillip Wilson, 2011), pp. 125, 130.
3. Julian Marshall, *Annals of Tennis* (London: The Field, 1878), p. 42.
4. See John Tosh, 'Middle-class Masculinities', in Michael Roper and John Tosh (eds) *Manful Assertions: Masculinities in Britain since 1900* (London: Routledge, 1991); and Leonore Davidoff and Catherine Hall, *Family Fortunes: Men and Women of the English Middle Class, 1780–1850* (London: Routledge, 2018).
5. This was partly due to the influence of the women's exercise movement of the time, particularly in schools like Cheltenham

Ladies College where the formidable headmistress, Dorothea Beale, abolished croquet because it encouraged 'physical deformity and idleness'. See Jennifer Hargraves, *Sporting Females* (London: Routledge, 1994), p. 63.

6. Quoted in Everitt and Hillway, *The Birth of Lawn Tennis*, p. 69.
7. Hargraves, *Sporting Females*, p. 54.
8. *Daily Telegraph*, 12 May 1881.
9. Alan Little, *Maud Watson* (London: Kenneth Ritchie Wimbledon Library, 2002), p. 3.
10. Dorothea Lambert Chambers, *Lawn Tennis for Ladies* (London: Methuen, 1910), p. 39.
11. Charlotte (Cooper) Sterry, 'Lawn Tennis for Ladies', in Arthur Wallis Myers, *Lawn Tennis at Home and Abroad* (London: George Newnes, 1903), pp. 120–4.
12. Blanche Hillyard, 'Chapter for the Ladies', in Herbert Wilberforce *Lawn Tennis* (London: George Bell, 1889), p. 53.
13. *Theatre*, 1 August 1881 quoted in Everitt and Hillway, *The Birth of Lawn Tennis*, p. 67.
14. Quoted in Helen Wills, *Fifteen Thirty* (London: Charles Scribner's Sons, 1937), p. 285.
15. Lottie Dod, 'Ladies Lawn Tennis', in J.M. and C.G. Heathcote, *Tennis, Lawn Tennis, Rackets, Fives* (London: Longmans Green, 1890), pp. 307–15.
16. A Wallis Myers quoted in Jeffrey Pearson, *Lottie Dod* (Birkenhead: Countrywise, 1988), p. 27.
17. *The Field*, 28 March 1874.
18. *The Field*, 25 July 1874.
19. *The Times*, quoted in Alistair Revie, *Wonderful Wimbledon* (London: Pelham, 1972), p. 11.
20. Wilfred Baddeley, *Lawn Tennis* (London: George Routledge, 1903), p. 62.
21. *Pastime*, 14 January 1885.
22. See Kathleen McCrone, *Sport and the Physical Emancipation of English Women, 1870–1914* (London: Routledge, 2014), pp. 154–92.
23. *Pastime*, 14 January 1885.
24. Herbert Chipp, *Lawn Tennis Recollection* (London: Merritt & Hatcher, 1898), pp. 119–21.
25. Baddeley, *Lawn Tennis*, p. 62.
26. Quoted in Osborn, *Lawn Tennis, Its Players and How to Play*, p. 30.
27. Pearson, *Lottie Dod*, p. 28.
28. See Duncan Grant *On Sterility in Women* (London: J. & A. Churchill, 1884).
29. Chipp, *Lawn Tennis Recollections*, p. 113.
30. Dod, 'Ladies Lawn Tennis', pp. 307–15.

31. Chipp, *Lawn Tennis Recollections*, p. 114.
32. Suzanne Rowland, 'Fashioning Competitive Lawn Tennis', in Robert Lake (ed.) *Routledge Handbook of Tennis* (London: Routledge, 2016), pp. 173–83.

Chapter 3

1. See https://en.wikipedia.org.wiki.talk.Birkenhead school. Accessed 28 August 2019.
2. K. Clifford Cook, *Birkenhead Lawn Tennis Club Centenary* (Merseyside: Birkenhead LTC, 1992), pp. 1–3.
3. F.G. Aflalo (ed.), *Sports of the World* (London: Cassell 1903), p. 404.
4. Andy Lusis, *Tennis in Robin Hood's County* (Nottingham: Andy Lusis, 1998) p. 20.
5. *Shrewsbury Journal*, 9 June 1886, quoted in John Henshaw, *Passing Shots* (Shrewsbury: Shropshire Tennis, 2003), p. 14.
6. Lowerson, *Sport and the English Middle Classes*, p. 8.
7. John Buchan, *The Thirty Nine Steps* (Edinburgh: Birlinn, 2011), p. 107.
8. F.G. Aflalo (ed.), *The Cost of Sport* (London: John Murray, 1899), pp. 291–6.
9. *Jesmond Lawn Tennis Club* (Jesmond: Jesmond LTC, 1983), p. 7.
10. Tony Thatcher, *Tennis Tea and Tradition* (Ojai Valley: Ojai Valley TC, 2000), p. 26.
11. *Historical Highlights of the Seattle Tennis Club* (Seattle: Seattle TC, 1983), p. 19.
12. P.G. Wodehouse, *Love Among the Chickens* (London: Herbert Jenkins, 1921 [1906]), p. 69.
13. E.M. Forster, *Room with a View* (London: Penguin, 2012 [1908]), p. 179.
14. Winifred Holtby, The Crowded Street (London: John Lane, 1924), pp. 52–3.
15. Quoted in Ronald Lerry, *Cradle of Lawn Tennis* (Birmingham: Stanford & Mann, 1948), p. 83.
16. Quoted in Robert Lake, 'A History of Social Exclusion in British Tennis', in Lake (ed.) *Routledge Handbook of Tennis*, pp. 460–9.

Chapter 4

1. Quoted in Elizabeth Wilson, *Love Game* (London: Profile, 2014), p. 44.
2. Quoted in Rowan Ricardo Phillips, *The Circuit* (New York: Farrar, Strauss & Giroux, 2018), p. 114.

3. Quoted in Alan Little, *The Golden Days of Tennis on the French Riviera* (Wimbledon: Wimbledon Lawn Tennis Museum, 2014), p. 27.
4. Quoted in Wilson, *Love Game*, p. 45.
5. Chipp, *Lawn Tennis Recollections*, p. 23.
6. Holt, *Sport and the British*, pp. 144–5.
7. *The Times*, 22 August 1919. In 1937, the All England Club acknowledged its debt to the Doherty Brothers by naming a gate after them.
8. Ted Tinling with Rod Humphries, *Love and Faults* (New York: Crown, 1979), p. 20.
9. Quoted in Max Robertson, *Wimbledon 1877–1977* (Old Woking: Gresham Books, 1977), pp. 38–9.
10. Lambert Chambers, *Lawn Tennis for Ladies*, pp. 9–13.
11. Quoted in Robertson, *Wimbledon 1877–1977*, pp. 38–9.
12. Lambert Chambers, *Lawn Tennis for Ladies*, p. 12.
13. See Chapter 7.

Chapter 5

1. Richmal Crompton, *William Again* (London: George Newnes, 1923), p. 41.
2. Phil Lynch, *A Centenary History of Bromley Wendover Lawn Tennis Club, 1906–2006* (Kent: Bromley Wendover LTC, 2006), p. 15.
3. Marian Coles, *Felixstowe Lawn Tennis Club 1884–1984* (Felixstowe: Felixstowe LTC 1984), p. 20.
4. Edith Wharton, *The Age of Innocence* (New York: D. Appleton & Co, 1920), p. 143.
5. *Lawn Tennis and Cricket*, January 6th, 1904, quoted in Lake, *A Social History of Tennis in Britain*, p. 74.
6. A.J. Aitken, *Lawn Tennis for Public Court Players* (London: Methuen 1924), p. 1. The figure of 500,000 park players was first estimated by the *Daily Herald* in 1921.
7. Quoted in Claire Langhammer, *Women's Leisure in England 1920–1950* (Manchester: Manchester University Press, 2000), p. 80.
8. Lerry, *Cradle of Lawn Tennis*, p. 127.
9. Ibid., p. 127.
10. Aitken, *Lawn Tennis for Public Court Players*, p. 3.
11. See Langhammer, *Women's Leisure in England 1920–1950* and John Bale, *Sport and Place* (London: Hurst, 1982).
12. Martin Smith, *Advantage Harpenden* (Harpenden: Harpenden LTC, 2005), p. 51.
13. Andy Lusis, *Tennis in Robin Hood's County* (Nottingham: Andy Lusis 1998), p. 35.
14. George Orwell, *Coming Up for Air* (London: Victor Gollanz, 1939), p. 11.

15. Keith Browning, *Advantage Telford* (London: Telford Park LTC, 2000), p. 10.
16. G. Owen, *Reflections on 100 Years* (Aberaeron: Aberaeron LTC, 1982), p. 7.
17. Ibid., p. 7.
18. *Surbiton Lawn Tennis Centenary Handbook* (Surbiton: Surbiton LTC, 1981), p. 6.
19. Coles, *Felixstowe Lawn Tennis Club 1884–1984*, p. 20.
20. See Joyce Kay, 'Grass Roots: The Development of Tennis in Britain 1918–1978', *International Journal of the History of Sport* 29(18), 2012, pp. 2532–50.
21. Ross McKibbin: *Classes and Cultures: England 1918–1951* (Oxford: Oxford University Press, 1998), p. 361.
22. Holt, *Sport and the British*, p. 126.
23. Quoted in Helen Walker, 'Lawn Tennis', in Tony Mason (ed.) *Sport in Britain* (Cambridge: Cambridge University Press 1989), p. 251.
24. Owen, *Reflections on 100 Years*, p. 7.
25. K. Clifford Cook, *Birkenhead Lawn Tennis Club* (Merseyside: Birkenhead LTC, 1992), p. 7.
26. McKibbin, *Classes and Cultures: England 1918–1951*, p. 369.

Chapter 6

1. Barbara Humphries, *The Roots of Labour in a London Suburb: Ealing in the 1930s* (London: Labour Heritage, undated), p. 7.
2. *Daily Herald*, 3 July 1933.
3. *Labour*, June 1934.
4. Fred Perry, *Autobiography* (London: Stanley Paul, 1984), p. 10.
5. Ibid., p. 108.
6. *Tribune*, 6 August 1937.
7. *Reading Citizen*, 12 August 1937.
8. Ibid.
9. *Portsmouth Evening News*, 6 June 1938.
10. Ibid., 31 May 1939.
11. *Daily Herald*, 22 May 1935.
12. Lionel Winyard, *Programme, Workers Wimbledon* (London: British Workers Sports Association, 1947), p. 3.
13. F. Pethick-Lawrence, *Fate Has Been Kind* (London: Hutchinson, 1943), p. 26.

Chapter 7

1. Quoted in *Sports Illustrated*, 12 September 1982.
2. Henshaw, *Passing Shots*, p. 14.
3. Quoted in Everitt and Hillway, *The Birth of Lawn Tennis*, p. 374.

4. Brian Simpson, *Winners in Action* (Fakenham: JJG Publishing, 2005), p. 53.
5. Richard Holt and Tony Mason, *Sport in Britain 1945–2000* (Oxford: Blackwell, 2000), p. 36.
6. Norah Cleather, *Wimbledon Story* (London: Sporting Handbooks, 1947), pp. 173–80.
7. Tinling with Humphries, *Love and Faults*, p. 31.
8. Quoted in *Sports Illustrated*, 12 September 1982, the best of many accounts of the Pyle tour.
9. Ibid.
10. Quoted in Kevin Jeffreys, 'The Triumph of Professionalism in Lawn Tennis', *International Journal of the History of Sport* 26(15), 2009, pp. 2253–69.
11. Ted Millman, *A History of Professional Tennis* (London: Professional Coaches Association, 1984), p. 26.

Chapter 8

1. *Western Daily Mail*, 3 July 1937.
2. See Dan Maskell, 'Televising Tennis', in Max Robertson (ed.) *Encyclopaedia of Tennis* (London: Allen and Unwin, 1974), pp. 188–192.
3. F.H. Grisewood, *The World Goes By* (London: Secker & Warburg, 1952), p. 243.
4. Holt and Mason, *Sport in Britain*, p. 55.
5. All quotes from David Kynaston, Austerity Britain 1945–1951 (London: Bloomsbury 2007), p. 526.
6. BBC Written Archives, Caversham, 'Wimbledon 1949'.
7. Dan Maskell with John Barrett, *Oh I Say* (London: Willow Books, 1988), p. 296.
8. BBC Written Archives, 'Wimbledon 1951'.
9. *Observer*, 13 July 1952.
10. Quoted in David Kynaston, *Family Britain 1951–1957* (London: Bloomsbury, 2007), p. 393.
11. Joe McCauley, *The History of Professional Tennis* (Windsor: Short Run Books, 2000), p. 16.
12. Gordon Forbes, *A Handful of Summers* (London: Heinemann, 1978), p. 153.
13. Norman Cutler, *Inside Tennis* (London: Evans Bros, 1954), pp. 185–95.
14. Mike Davies, *Tennis Rebel* (London: Stanley Paul, 1962), pp. 16–17.
15. Ibid., p. 89.
16. Bobby Wilson with John Cottrell, *My Side of the Net* (London: Stanley Paul, 1964), p. 95.
17. Frederick Raphael, 'A Fairly Regular Four', in Giles Gordon and David Hughes (eds), *The Best of Best Short Stories* (London: Minerva, 1995), pp. 394–400.

18. Quoted in Lake, *A Social History of Tennis in Britain*, p. 135.
19. Email correspondence with Andrea Sanders-Reece (London, August 2019).
20. BBC Written Archives, 'Wimbledon 1962'.
21. Richard Evans, *Open Tennis* (London: Bloomsbury, 1988), p. 13.
22. *Birmingham Daily Post*, 29 April 1968.
23. Gordon Forbes, *A Handful of Summers* (London: Heinemann, 1978), p. 155.

Chapter 9

1. Owen, *Reflections on 100 years of Aberaeron Tennis 1882–1982*, p. 22.
2. Ibid., p. 24.
3. *Blundellsands Lawn Tennis Club Centenary 1880–1980* (Liverpool: Blundellsands LTC, 1980), p. 11.
4. Ibid., p. 15.
5. *Cullercoats Lawn Tennis Club* (North Shields: Cullercoats LTC, 1993), pp. 65–84.
6. *The Story of Frankston Tennis Club* (Franston, Vic.: Frankston TC, 1989), pp. 7–12.
7. Denis Costello, *A History of Catford Wanderers Lawn Tennis Club 1914–1998* (London: Catford Wanderers LTC, 1998), p. 4.
8. Smith, *Advantage Harpenden*, p. 28.
9. Julian Barnes, *The Only Story* (London: Jonathan Cape, 2018), p. 6.
10. *A History of Chesham Bois Lawn Tennis and Squash Club* (Amersham: Chesham Bois LT&SC, 2008), p. 19.
11. John Pikoulis (ed.), *Dinas Powis Lawn Tennis Club* (Dinas Powis: Dinas Powis LTC, 2001), p. 63.
12. Ibid., p. 66.
13. Ibid., p. 55.
14. Stanley Chapman, *Jesse Boot* (London: Hodder & Stoughton 1974), pp. 166–7.
15. Christopher Weir, *Jesse Boot* (Nottingham: Boots Company, 1994), p. 51.
16. Hunter, *100 Years of Tennis in the West of Scotland*, p. 63.
17. Quoted in Kay, 'Grass Roots: The Development of Tennis in Britain 1918–1978'.
18. Phil Lynch, *From Banking Halls to Grass Courts – a Centenary History of HSBCC Lawn Tennis Club* (London: HSBC, 2010), p. 45.

Chapter 10

1. Cas Fish, *British Tennis: The Scandal* (Caernarfon: R.A. Fish, 1996), pp. 102–3.

2. Ibid., p. 8.
3. Ibid., p. 70.
4. Interview with Raph Harvey (London, 13 March 2019).
5. Ibid.
6. *Pastime*, 20 August 1884 and *Lawn Tennis*, 30 August 1899, both quoted in Robert Lake, *A Social History of Lawn Tennis in Britain* (London: Routledge, 2015), p. 80.
7. Interview with Albert Lester (London, 20 March 2019).
8. The coloured community of South Africa comprises people who have ancestry from two of the various populations of the region such as Bantu, Afrikaner, Asian and white. In practice it usually refers to people from an Asian background or with one black and one Asian or white parent.
9. *Dundee Courier*, 9 November 1926.
10. *Gloucester Citizen*, 24 May 1949.
11. Davies, *Tennis Rebel*, pp. 100–1.
12. Alice Marble, editorial, *American Lawn Tennis*, July 1950.
13. Cecil Harris and Larryette Kyle, *Charging the Net* (Chicago: Ivan Dee, 2007), p. 57.
14. *The People*, 1 July 1956 and *Sunday Graphic*, 1 July 1956.
15. Quoted in Harris and Kyle, *Charging the Net*, p. 95.
16. Quoted in ibid., pp. 78–9.
17. Quoted in Caryl Phillps (ed.), *The Right Set* (London: Faber & Faber, 1999), p. 156.
18. *New York Times*, 28 August 2016.
19. See *Increasing BME Participation in Sport and Physical Activity* (Brentwood: Ploszajski Lynch Consulting, Ltd, 2005).
20. Interview with Yemisi and Boye Ifederu (London, 10 April 2019).
21. David Olusoga, *Black and British* (London: Macmillan, 2016), p. 525.
22. Interview with Raph Harvey.

Chapter 11

1. Interview with member of the club (Liverpool, July 2019).
2. *Jewish Chronicle*, 4 November 1898, quoted in David Dee, *Sport and British Jewry* (Manchester: Manchester University Press, 2014), p. 93.
3. *Jewish World*, 1 June 1906, quoted in Dee, *Sport and British Jewry*, p. 50.
4. See Dee, *Sport and British Jewry*, and also his unpublished PhD dissertation, *Jews and British Sport* (Leicester: De Montfort University, 2011).

5. See, respectively, *Yorkshire Post*, 10 September 1925; *Daily Mirror*, 7 May 1928; and John Testa, *Hazlewood Lawn Tennis and Squash Club* (London: Hazlewood LTC, 2009).

6. *Northern Whig*, 18 December 1925.

7. The same happened in Italy under Mussolini, as described lyrically in Giorgio Bassani, *The Garden of the Finzi-Continis* (London: Faber 1965).

8. Quoted in Bruce Schoenfeld, *The Match* (New York: HarperCollins, 2004), p. 131.

9. Cutler, *Inside Tennis*, p. 6.

10. Email correspondence with Norman Dale (Kent, April 2019).

11. Quoted in Schoenfeld, *The Match*, p. 38.

12. See Chapter 10.

13. *The Times*, 13 July 2019.

14. Interview with Albert Lester (London, 20 March 2019).

15. Ibid.

16. *Jewish Chronicle*, 29 November 1991.

Chapter 12

1. See Chapter 5.

2. René Kural, *Out! Om Dansk Tennis Club og tennisspilleren Leif Rovsing* (Copenhagen: Rhodes, 2012). Translated for me by Jeremy Crump who told me about Rovsing.

3. Nathan Titman, 'Making Work Out of Play', in Lake (ed.) *Routledge Handbook of Tennis*, pp. 203–10.

4. See ibid., pp. 203–10.

5. Tinling with Humphries, *Love and Faults*, p. 76.

6. Philip Hawk, *Off the Racket* (New York: American Lawn Tennis, 1937), p. 210.

7. See John Carvalho and Mike Milford, 'One Knows That This Condition Exists: An Analysis of Tennis Champion Bill Tilden's Apology for His Homosexuality', *Sport in History* 33(4), 2011, pp. 554–67.

8. Quoted in Duncan Macauley, *Behind the Scenes at Wimbledon* (London: Collins, 1965).

9. Tinling with Humphries, *Love and Faults*, p. 187.

10. Quoted in Susan Ware, *Game, Set, Match* (Chapel Hill: University of North Carolina Press, 2011), p. 4.

11. Billie Jean King with Cynthia Starr, *We Have Come a Long Way* (New York: McGraw Hill, 1988), p. 145.

12. Quoted in Rob Steen, *Floodlights and Touchlines* (London: Bloomsbury, 2014), p. 692.

13. *Sunday Times*, 9 December 2007.

14. Wilson, *Love Game*, p. 187.
15. Quoted in Susan Birrell and Cheryl L. Cole (eds), *Women, Sport, and Culture* (Champaign: Human Kinetics, 1994), p. 374.
16. *Slate*, 25 October 2012.
17. Wilson, *Love Game*, p. 299.
18. *Telegraph*, 23 August 2018.
19. Email correspondence with Stuart Hancock (Bedford, June 2019).
20. Ibid.
21. Email correspondence with Eric van der Palen (Amsterdam, June 2019).

Chapter 13

1. Forbes, *A Handful of Summers*, p. 201.
2. Email correspondence with Andrea Sanders-Reece (London, August 2019).
3. BBC Written Archives, 'Wimbledon Files 1964–1974'.
4. Hillyard, *Forty Years of First-Class Tennis*, p. 119.
5. Russell Davies (ed.), *The Kenneth Williams Diaries* (London: Harper Collins, 1993), p. 678.
6. *Evening Standard*, 20 June 1994, quoted in Stephen Wagg, 'The Wimbledon Effect', in Lake (ed.) *Routledge Handbook of Tennis*, pp. 372–81.
7. King with Starr, *We Have Come a Long Way*, p. 184.
8. Martin Amis, 'Tennis, the Women's Game', in *Visiting Mrs Nabokov* (London: Jonathan Cape 1993), pp. 60–8.
9. *Guardian*, 18 June 2010.
10. Andy Murray, *Coming of Age* (London: Arrow Books, 2009), pp. 222–48.
11. *Guardian*, 29 August 2012.
12. *File on Four*, BBC Radio 4, 10 February 2019.
13. Quoted in Wilson, *Love Game*, p. 211.
14. Quoted in Stephen Tignor, *High Strung* (New York: Harper, 2011), p. 71.
15. Ibid., p. 37.
16. Wagg, 'The Wimbledon Effect', pp. 372–81.
17. Evans, *Open Tennis*, p. 11.

Chapter 14

1. *Coventry Evening Telegraph*, 12 June 1972.
2. See Everitt and Hillway, *The Birth of Lawn Tennis*.
3. Interview with Anne Tyler (London, 10 May 2019).
4. *Bracknell News*, 15 July 1971.

5. *The Field*, 16 Jan 1875.
6. Donal Muir, 'Club Tennis: A Case Study in Taking Leisure Very Seriously', in *Sociology of Sport Journal* 8(1), 1991, pp. 70–8.
7. Interview with Paul Monaghan (London, 14 June 2019).
8. Interview with David Obodechina-Joseph (London, 10 April 2019).
9. Robert Lake, 'They Treat Me Like Scum', *International Review for the Sociology of Sport* 4(2), 2011, pp. 1–11.
10. Evans, *Open Tennis*, p. 7.
11. Email correspondence with Norman Dale (Kent, August 2019).
12. Email correspondence with Nigel Billen (London, August 2019).
13. Quoted in R.L. Fell, *Northern Lawn Tennis Club* (Manchester: Northern Lawn Tennis Club, 1936), p. 8.
14. Interview with Vivienne McNaughton (London, July 2019).

Conclusion

1. William Plumer Jacobs, *Tennis – Builder of Citizenship* (Clinton: Jacobs Press 1943), pp. 7–17.
2. Ibid.
3. Tinling with Humphries, *Love and Faults*, p. 304.
4. See Chapters 1 and 12.
5. See Chapter 2.
6. Wagg, 'The Wimbledon Effect', pp. 372–81.
7. See Chapters 5 and 6.
8. 'I regarded the place as merely an outdoor branch of the Young Conservatives.' Barnes, *The Only Story*, p. 5.
9. See Chapters 3, 5, 9 and 14.
10. Abraham Verghese, *The Tennis Partner* (London: Chatto & Windus, 1998), p. 60.
11. Interview with Vivienne McNaughton (London, July 2019).

Bibliography

Sources

This book was researched mainly in the British Library and the Kenneth Ritchie Memorial Library at the All England Club in Wimbledon. I am grateful to the British Library staff in Humanities 1 reading room and especially to Robert McNicol at Wimbledon. I am also grateful to the librarians in the Birmingham Reference Library and the London School of Economics, and Tom Hercock at the BBC Archives in Caversham.

For permission to quote from the diaries of Judy Haines I would like to thank Pamela Hendicott (and the help of David Kynaston) and to the BBC for allowing me to quote from their written archives. An earlier version of Chapter 6 appeared in *Prospect* in June 2017.

I was very pleased to find people prepared to be interviewed on the record about their tennis experiences. Thanks to Caroline Bhaguandas, Esther Bhaguandas, Nigel Billen, Norman Dale, Paul French, Boye Ifederu, Yemisi Ifederu, Albert Lester, Stuart Hancock, Leah Hartshorne, Raph Harvey, John Marcus, Vivienne McNaughton, Paul Monaghan, Jessica O Connell, David Obodechina-Joseph, Eric van der Palen, Nat Pithaida, Peter Saake and Anne Tyler. It was a pity I did not have the space to use more of their interviews, and in a few cases not use them at all. I trust I have represented them properly and I hope they think the experience was worth it.

Essential Books and Articles

Alexander, George, *Lawn Tennis* (Lynn, MA: H.O. Zimman, 1974).

Alexander, George, *Wingfield* (Lynn, MA: H.O. Zimman, 1988).

Baltzell, E. Digby, *Sporting Gentlemen* (New York: Free Press, 1995).

Cleather, Norah, *Wimbledon Story* (London: Sporting Handbooks, 1947).

Evans, Richard, *Open Tennis* (London: Bloomsbury, 1988).

Everitt, Robert and Richard Hillway, *The Birth of Lawn Tennis* (Kingston Upon Thames: Vision Sports Publishing Ltd, 2018).

Forbes, Gordon, *A Handful of Summers* (London: Heinemann, 1978).

Foster Wallace, David, *Consider the Lobster* (London: Abacus, 2005).

Gillmeister, Heiner, *Tennis: A Cultural History* (London: Leicester University Press, 1997).

Hargreaves, Jennifer, *Sporting Females* (London: Routledge, 1994).

Holt, Richard, *Sport and the British* (Oxford: Oxford University Press, 1989).

Holt, Richard and Tony Mason, *Sport in Britain 1945–2000* (Oxford: Blackwell, 2000).

Jeffreys, Kevin, 'The Triumph of Professionalism in Lawn Tennis', *International Journal of the History of Sport*, 26(15), 2009, pp. 2253–69.

Kay, Joyce, 'Grass Roots: The Development of Tennis in Britain 1918–1978', *International Journal of the History of Sport* 29(18), 2012, pp. 2532–50.

King, Billie Jean with Cynthia Starr, *We Have Come a Long Way* (New York: McGraw Hill, 1988).

Lake, Robert, *A Social History of Tennis in Britain* (London: Routledge 2015).

Lake, Robert (ed.), *Routledge Handbook of Tennis* (London: Routledge 2019).

Lowerson, John, *Sport and the English Middle Classes* (Manchester: Manchester University Press, 1995).

Lusis, Andy, *Tennis in Robin Hood's Country* (Nottingham: Andy Lusis, 1998).

McCauley, Joe, *A History of Professional Tennis* (Windsor: Short Run Books, 2000).

McKibbin, Ross, *Classes and Cultures: England 1918–1951* (Oxford: Oxford University Press, 1998).

McPhee, John, *Levels of the Game.* (New York: Farrar, Strauss & Giroux, 1969).

Robertson, Max, *Wimbledon 1877–1977* (Old Woking: Gresham Books 1977).

Robertson, Max (ed.), *Encyclopaedia of Tennis* (London: George Allen & Unwin, 1974).

Schoenfield, Bruce, *The Match* (New York: HarperCollins, 2004).

Sumner, Ann (ed.), *Court on Canvas* (London: Phillip Wilson, 2011), particularly the essays by Sumner and Susan Elks.

Tinling, Ted with Rod Humphries, *Love and Faults* (New York: Crown, 1979).

Todd, Tom, *The Tennis Players* (Guernsey: Vallency Press, 1979).

Tosh, John, *Manliness and Masculinities in 19th Century Britain* (London: Routledge, 2016).

Walker, Helen, 'Lawn Tennis', in Tony Mason (ed.) *Sport in Britain* (Cambridge: Cambridge University Press, 1989).

Wilson, Elizabeth, *Love Game* (London: Profile, 2014).

Additional Reading

Aberdare, Bruce, *The Story of Tennis* (London: Stanley Paul, 1959).

Adams, Tim, *On Being John McEnroe* (London: Yellow Jersey Press, 2003).

Agassi, Andre, *Open* (London: HarperCollins, 2008).

Aitken, A.J., *Lawn Tennis for Public Court Players* (London: Methuen 1924).

Allaby, David, *Wimbledon of the North* (Didsbury: E.J. Morton, 1981).

Amis, Martin, 'The Women's Game', in *Visiting Mrs. Nabokov* (London: Jonathan Cape, 1993).

Atkin, Ronald (ed.), *For the Love of Tennis* (London: Stanley Paul, 1985).

Austin, Bunny and Phyllis Konstam, *A Mixed Double* (London: Chatto & Windus, 1969).

Baddeley, Wilfred, *Lawn Tennis* (London: George Routledge 1903).

Barker, Paul, *The Freedoms of Suburbia* (London: Francis Wilkinson, 2009).

Barrett, John, *Wimbledon, the Official History* (London: Collins Willow, 2001).

Beamish, A.E. and W.G. Beamish, *Lawn Tennis for Ladies* (London: Mills & Boon, 1924).

Beauchampe, Steve and Simon Inglis, *Played in Birmingham* (Birmingham: English Heritage, 2006).

Birley, Derek, *Sport and the Making of Britain* (Manchester: Manchester University Press, 1993).

Brady, Sean, *Masculinity and Male Homosexuality in Britain 1861–1913* (Basingstoke: Palgrave, 2005).

Brenner, Michael and Gideon Reuveni (eds), *Emancipation Through Muscles* (Oxford: Oxford University Press 2008).

Brownlee, William, *Lawn Tennis its Rise and Progress* (Bristol: Arrowsmith, 1889).

Burrow, F.R., *Lawn Tennis* (London: Hodder & Stoughton, 1922).

Cavendish, *The Games of Lawn Tennis and Badminton* (London: Thos de la Rue, 1876).

Chipp, Herbert, *Lawn Tennis Recollection* (London: Merritt & Hatcher, 1898).

Clerici, Gianni, *Tennis* (London: Octopus, 1976).

Cutler, Norman, *Inside Tennis* (London: Evans Bros, 1954).

Davies, Mike, *Tennis Rebel* (London: Stanley Paul, 1962).

Dee, David, *Sport and British Jewry* (Manchester: Manchester University Press, 2014).

Doherty, R.F. and H.L. Doherty, *On Lawn Tennis* (London: Lawn Tennis Office, 1903).

Engelman, Larry, *The Goddess and the American Girl* (Oxford: Oxford University Press 1988).

Fish, Cas, *British Tennis, the Scandal* (Caernarfon: R.A. Fish, 1996).

Fisher, Marshall Jon, *A Terrible Splendour* (New York: Crown, 2007).

Gallwey, W. Timothy, *The Inner Game of Tennis* (New York: Random House, 1975).

Gibbons, W.G., *The Seeds of Lawn Tennis* (Coventry: Jones-Sands, 1986).

Harris, Cecil and Larryette Kyle DeBose, *Charging the Net* (Chicago: Ivan Dee, 2007).

Heathcote, J.M. and C.G. Heathcote, *Tennis, Lawn Tennis, Rackets, Fives* (London: Longmans Green, 1890).

Henderson, John, *The Last Champion* (London: Yellow Jersey Press, 2009).

Hillyard, George, *40 Years of 1st Class Lawn Tennis* (London: Williams & Norgate, 1924).

Huggins, Mike and Jack Williams, *Sport and the English 1918–1939* (London: Routledge, 2006).

Huizinga, Johan, *Homo Ludens* (London: Temple Smith, 1949).

Jeffreys, Kevin, *British Tennis* (Worthing: Pitch, 2019).

Jennings, Jay (ed.), *Tennis and the Meaning of Life* (New York: Harvest, 1995).

Jones, Stephen, *Workers at Play* (London: Routledge, 1986).

Lake, Robert, 'They Treat Me Like Scum', *International Review for the Sociology of Sport* 4(2), 2011, pp. 1–11.

Lambert Chambers, Dorothea, *Lawn Tennis for Ladies* (London: Methuen, 1910).

Lerry, Ronald, *Cradle of Lawn Tennis* (Birmingham: Stanford & Mann, 1949).

Little, Alan, *The Golden Days of Tennis on the French Riviera* (Wimbledon: Wimbledon Lawn Tennis Museum, 2014).

Little, Alan, *Lottie Dod* (Wimbledon: Wimbledon Lawn Tennis Museum, 2014).

Little, Alan, *Maud Watson* (Wimbledon: Wimbledon Lawn Tennis Museum, 2014).

Macauley, Duncan, *Behind the Scenes at Wimbledon* (London: Collins, 1965).

McCrone, Kathleen, *Sport and the Physical Emancipation of English Women, 1870–1914* (London: Routledge, 2014).

Marshall, Julian, *Annals of Tennis* (London: The Field, 1878).

Marshall, Julian, *Tennis Quips and Cuts* (London: Field & Tuer, 1884).

Maskell, Dan with John Barrett, *Oh I Say* (London: Willow Books 1988).

Mewshaw, Michael, *Ladies of the Court* (New York: Random House, 1992).

Millman, Ted, *A History of Professional Tennis* (London: Professional Coaches Association 1984).

Mills, Alan, *Lifting the Covers* (London: Headline, 2005).

Mitchell, Kevin, *Break Point* (London: John Murray, 2014).

Muir, Donal, 'Club Tennis: A Case Study in Taking Leisure Very Seriously', in *Sociology of Sport Journal* 8(1), 1991, pp. 70–8.

Murray, Andy, *Coming of Age* (London: Century, 2008).

Myers, A. Wallis, *Lawn Tennis at Home and Abroad* (London: George Newnes, 1903).

Osborn, Robert D., *Lawn Tennis, Its Players and How to Play* (London: Strahan & Co., 1881).

Oyler, Thomas, *50 Years of Lawn Tennis* (Maidstone: S.E. Gazette, 1925).

Payn, F.W., *Secrets of Lawn Tennis* (London: L. Upton Gill, 1906).

Pearson, Jeffrey, *Lottie Dod* (Birkenhead: Countrywise, 1988).

Perry, Fred, *Autobiography* (London: Stanley Paul, 1984).

Phillips, Caryl (ed.), *The Right Set* (London: Faber & Faber, 1999).

Phillips, Rowan Ricardo, *The Circuit* (New York: Farrar, Strauss & Giroux, 2018).

Piele, S.C.F., *Lawn tennis as a Game of Skill* (Edinburgh: William Blackwood, 1884).

Pronger, Brian, *The Arena of Masculinity* (London: GMP, 1990).

Revie, Alistair, *Wonderful Wimbledon* (London: Pelham, 1972).

Robertson, George, *Tennis in Scotland* (Edinburgh: Scottish LTA, 1995).

Seddon, Peter, *Tennis's Strangest Matches* (London: Robson, 2001).

Sexton, Adam (ed.), *Love Stories – A Literary Companion to Tennis* (New York: Citadel, 2003).

Shriver, Lionel, 'My Tennis Obsession', *Prospect*, May 2011.

Simpson, Brian, *Winners in Action* (Fakenham: JJG, 2005).

Smythe, Jasper, *Lawn Tennis* (London: George Routledge, 1878).

Steen, Rob, *Floodlights and Touchlines* (London: Bloomsbury 2014).

Tarran, Bruce, *George Hillyard* (Kipworth Beauchamp: Matador, 2013).

Tignor, Stephen, *High Strung* (New York: Harper, 2011).

Tilden, Bill, *Match Play and the Spin of the Ball* (London: Methuen, 1925).

Tingay, Lance, *100 Years of Wimbledon* (London: Guinness Superlatives, 1977).

Vaile, Percy, *Modern Lawn Tennis* (London: William Heinemann, 1904).

Verghese, Abraham, *The Tennis Partner* (New York: HarperCollins, 1998).

Wade, Virginia with Jean Rafferty, *Ladies of the Court* (London: Pavilion Books, 1984).

Ware, Susan, *Game, Set, Match* (Chapel Hill: University of North Carolina Press, 2011).

Wilberforce, H.W.W., *Lawn Tennis* (London: George Bell, 1889).

Wills, Helen, *Fifteen-Thirty* (London: Charles Scribner's Sons, 1937).

Acknowledgements

Four people have read this book in different drafts: Jeremy Crump, Andrea Sanders-Reece, Linda Tubby and Sophie Watson. I have valued their numerous thoughts, critical suggestions and unfailing support very much.

For comments on particular chapters I would like to thank John Ballard, June Barrow-Green, Carole Bellars, Trevor Blackwell, Lucy Bland, Emma Cameron, Philip Chandler, Sally Cox, Angela Dale, Brian Dineen, Jeremy Gray, Susan Greenberg, Rita Kilemade, Russel Levi, Alexandra Lewenstein, Sue McDougal, Tapiwa Mashingaidze, Walter Merricks, Andy Metcalf, Hywel Nelson, Rosemary Pringle, David Roylance, Mike Russum, Nigel Sands, Murray Selkirk, Roger Smith, Susan Tindale, Pam Walker, Jess Watson, Anne Williams and Kathleen Woodward.

At City University I would like to thank Julie Wheelwright and Peter Moore from the Creative Writing non-fiction MA course as well as fellow students Farrukh Akhtar and Eleanor Thomson. At the Society of Authors I would like to thank Kate Pool. And at Pluto Press, I would like to thank David Castle, Robert Webb, Dan Harding and Kieran O'Connor.

Finally, a special thank you to Rose Anne Varley and our daughter Sorcha Berry-Varley who have supported me over many of the years in which I have played tennis and tried to write about it.

Index

move from Church to Worple
Road 61, 215
post 1968 177–89
Renshaw rush 54, 94, 213
saved by Dohertys 56
saved by Lenglen 58–61, 98
today 5, 189–91, 201–5, 208,
218–20
Slazenger, Television
see also BBC, black tennis players,
GLBTQ, Jewish tennis
players

Wingfield, Walter 9–17, 19, 21,
23–4, 26–8, 30, 32, 50, 93, 96,
135, 193, 212
Winyard, Lionel 81, 88–9
Wintour, Anna 206
Wodehouse, P.G. 46, 164
Women's Tennis Association
(WTA) 171, 218
Workers' Wimbledon 78, 83–91,
216–17
working classes 70–1, 76, 82, 85, 87
workplace tennis 129–30